DATE DUE

BRODART, INC.

Cat. No. 23-221

POINT LOMA NAZARENE COLLEGE
Ryan Library
3900 Lomaland Drive, San Diego, CA 92106-2899

Social Norms and Economic Institutions

Social Norms and Economic Institutions

Edited by
Kenneth J. Koford and Jeffrey B. Miller

Ann Arbor
THE UNIVERSITY OF MICHIGAN PRESS

Copyright © by the University of Michigan 1991
All rights reserved
Published in the United States of America by
The University of Michigan Press
Manufactured in the United States of America

1994   1993   1992   1991   4   3   2   1

Distributed in the United Kingdom and Europe by
Manchester University Press, Oxford Road,
Manchester M13 9PL, UK

British Library Cataloguing in Publication Data

Social norms and economic institutions.
  I. Koford, Kenneth J.   II. Miller, Jeffrey B.
  306

ISBN 0-472-10242-7

Library of Congress Cataloging-in-Publication Data

Social norms and economic institutions / edited by Kenneth J. Koford
  and Jeffrey B. Miller.
      p.   cm.
  Includes bibliographical references and index.
  ISBN 0-472-10242-7 (cloth : alk. paper)
    1. Economics—Moral and ethical aspects.   I. Koford, Kenneth J.
  II. Miller, Jeffrey B.
  HB72.S59   1991
  330—dc20   91-21778
                                                           CIP

Contents

Introduction

Kenneth J. Koford and Jeffrey B. Miller

Why are wages "sticky"? How is it possible to sustain discriminatory practices in competitive markets? How does a caste system survive in India with
the support of lower castes? Why has it been so difficult to bring about
development in the Third World? Why has high unemployment continued for
so long in Europe? Why has it taken the U.S. balance of payments so long to
adjust to the shift in foreign exchange rates? These are difficult questions for
standard neoclassical economic models. In seeking explanations to such questions, some analysts have gone beyond the standard models and incorporated
the influences of social norms into their analyses.

Social norms and ethical values have a strong influence on the functioning of economic institutions, yet economic theory has not integrated either of
these concepts into its standard framework. This volume presents several
views on the advantages and difficulties of broadening the economist's behavioral model to include social norms and ethical values.

While ethical standards are not ordinarily included in economic theory,
economists do not ignore all "human feeling." Rather, when values beyond
self-interest seem appropriate, altruism, or sympathy for others' welfare, have
been included as preferences. This approach has developed rapidly and successfully, particularly in recent years, and it has been the basis for work in the
economics of the family. However, including ethical values, and in particular
social norms, presents problems different from those associated with altruism.
For example, altruism allows for smooth tradeoffs among alternatives, just as
standard utility maximization does. A person can choose to be a little bit more
or less altruistic, without any large consequences. But a person usually cannot be a little bit more or less honest, since the boundaries of honesty are
usually clear-cut. For example, a person who embezzles money from a firm is
not excused because the amount embezzled is small. We tend to make all-or-
none value judgments: a given action is either legitimate or it crosses the

We would like to thank Bill Griffith for helpful comments, and Jennifer Moore, Timur
Kuran, and Richard Weiss for helpful conversations.

line and is not. When an action is judged to be illegitimate, there is a finite penalty. Another difference is that people often conform to ethical standards without considering whether there will be a utility gain or not. They undertake an action because they believe it is "right" rather than because it will increase utility. While social norms guide behavior, they do not fit easily into the standard rational decision-making model used by economists. The social aspect of these norms is crucial. People care about how others will react to their actions. But this raises a number of questions: Why do people accept these norms? How does society impose or encourage certain norms? When society demands conformity to a norm, is it considered unethical to violate the norm? Social norms are not direct objects of choice: no one can do much to change a norm; yet they do change. An important question is how this change occurs.

Many social interactions are similar to a coordination game in which some defined kinds of consistency have a large benefit and the (Nash) equilibrium has very similar rules for all agents. While social coordination games have many Nash equilibria (following the "folk theorem" on repeated games; see, e.g., Rasmusen 1989, 92), there are reasons why agents might avoid the less desirable ones. Perhaps this is due to rational-foresight equilibrium notions (Riley 1979). Or, agents may exchange information to focus on some desirable equilibrium. Either way, people are seeking to coordinate their actions to achieve greater efficiency.

An alternative utilitarian route to social norms is through some form of reciprocity. Evolutionary theorists have found reciprocal altruism among many species; individuals do good for others, expecting some good in return. Something similar could develop as a Nash equilibrium as people adopt various reciprocity strategies. For these strategies to succeed, it must be easy for others to figure out what the strategies are, as Axelrod (1984) found with the success of tit-for-tat. So, strategies should be simple.[1] For example, people could adopt a clearly "nice" or "giving" approach to others under some circumstances, expecting correctly that others will respond in a similar fashion and both parties will benefit. Frank's models (1986, 1987, and 1988) of "visibly nice" behavior are of this sort. Then, the "yes-no" or "good-bad" dichotomies seen in norms make sense, for they are the result of having to send and interpret clear signals.[2]

---

1. Strategies could also be truly sneaky or subtle, as Badcock (1986) has argued, but their first-order effect should be clear. It should be emphasized that tit-for-tat's success came partly because Axelrod's environment seemed to encourage relatively simple rules. In reality, people may be more complex and subtle. Badcock (1986) and Trivers (1985) give examples of complex but evolutionarily stable strategies. See also Schofield 1985 for a formal analysis.

2. Rowe (1989) claims that a rule-utilitarian approach is sufficient to assure social equilibrium. Agents can choose to act according to fair rules of carrying out their promises, and they find that has higher utility than being free to renege upon promises.

However, social norms do not always have desirable properties. Changed circumstances may make specific social norms inappropriate, even though they were originally selected for efficiency reasons. Any look at history can come up with numerous examples where specific social norms have survived for a long time despite their inefficiency. Banfield (1958) for example, describes the norms in small towns in southern Italy as making sense in a past, traditional era, but as quite harmful in a rapidly growing, industrializing economy.

The volume begins with a general model that explicitly describes how customs and social norms constrain economic behavior and support economic institutions. The second part is concerned with the nature of people's ethical values. It examines the nature of ethical values and social norms in economics and philosophy. Its essays try to place ethical values in the formal structure of economic theory. In the third part, the nature of social norms in practice is examined through an experimental study in which people can choose to create and follow social norms. The experimental results find that norms are not consistent with either pure self-interest or with altruism; rather, it is a kind of social commitment similar to a social contract.

In the fourth part, the evolutionary equilibrium of social norms is examined. It turns out that a very likely equilibrium has some people committed to an ethical standard (such as a conscience), and others not committed to it. In the final part, social norms are applied to organizations, first to ethical rules for corporations and second to fair bargaining rules in the making of contracts.

The overall theme is the development of appropriate concepts of social norms that economists can use, and their application to the many organizations where these norms play a major role. We believe that developing successful applications is particularly important, for economists are unlikely to accept the concept into the general economic framework unless social norms provide a better explanation of some major economic realities than the more narrowly defined current model.

The first essay, by Koford and Miller, "Habit, Custom, and Norms in Economics," looks at social norms as a special case of the more general principles of habitual behavior and social custom. It gives a general framework within which the other papers can be placed. Koford and Miller first emphasize the importance of habitual behavior in daily life, and then the value of common patterns of habitual behavior, or custom. These common patterns, in turn, make individuals' habitual patterns much easier to carry out, as each person relies upon other people's mutually consistent habitual patterns.

This approach looks at the value of accepted institutional rules in providing a common structure or language that greatly assists common action. Some customary rules become social norms when people feel a moral obligation to conform. People also feel a moral obligation to punish those who violate social norms, providing additional reasons to conform to social norms. In a sense consistent with Hayek's evolutionary theory of social institutions (1953), following a common language or set of rules for making agreements is efficient in itself. However, while the stability of social customs helps people carry out their habitual actions, that stability makes change very difficult. The essay concludes with some examples of social norms that have remained static, even though conditions have changed enough that a different norm might now be more efficient.

If norms are important, how can one consistently incorporate both *individual* ethical values and *social* ethical norms into the standard economic model of individual choice? In their two companion pieces, "Amending the Economist's 'Rational Egoist' Model to Include Norms, Part I: The Problem," and "Part II: Alternative Solutions," William Griffith and Robert Goldfarb ask: How do ethical standards and social norms affect economic behavior? Can they be understood in the context of "rational agent" models of individual choice? If norms are just another element in a person's utility function, just another preference, the solution would be tidy and attractive. Standard economic tools, and the formal modeling of utility maximization, could be used to solve problems involving norms. However, Griffith and Goldfarb show that such an approach contradicts our intuitive sense of what utility means.[3] Many norms, like the Ten Commandments, seem more like constraints: "Thou shalt not. . . ." These norms create bright-line boundary constraints that prohibit people from doing some things. Such norms are not at all like utilities. It is not clear that people have "demands" for "acting honestly" or "not murdering," with smooth trade-offs and implicit prices. Furthermore, many people would say that they are not constrained to act honorably; rather, they choose to act honorably. Thus, for them, ethical values are matters of utility—of a special sort.

Ethical values that are social norms can be extremely powerful when they are tied to people's strong desire to be socially acceptable and successful. Marshall (1924, 73) approvingly quotes Nassau Senior on "the desire for distinction: a feeling which if we consider its universality, and its constancy, that it affects all men and at all times, that it comes with us from the cradle and never leaves us till we go into the grave, may be pronounced the most powerful of human passions." Thus, in contrast to the traditional approach of including in the utility function largely individual solipsistic desires for

---

3. The standard here is introspective, almost "Austrian": does this utility theory make sense to me? While both philosophers and Austrians favor introspection (see Mises 1963), Friedman argues that empirical success should dominate the intuitive feel of the assumptions. An intermediate position is that we know something about human motivations from introspection, and economists use that constantly in determining which variables to put into utility or demand functions.

goods, Marshall would have us include activities that show distinction. Distinction is shown relative to social values, and these, then, are likely to include the obedience of social norms.[4]

In Part 1, Goldfarb and Griffith examine the nature of norms in economics and in ethical theory, and look at some specific examples to show the general nature of the problem. They justify the need to examine moral issues by pointing out that many actions are directed by moral concerns as well as economic and legal pressures. Indeed it is the integration of these factors that determines outcomes. For instance, while long-term contracts have an obvious economic and legal component, without an ethical component many such contracts would not be viable ways to coordinate agents' activities, for legal sanctions alone would not be a sufficient enforcement mechanism. Ignoring the influence of social values on behavior can lead to an overemphasis upon self-interested behavior as the explanation of outcomes. On the other hand, a simplistic expansion of the concept of self-interested behavior to include social values, *must* account for the special way in which ethical standards influence decision making or it will also be misleading.

How, then, should ethical values and social norms be described in economic theory? In Part 2, Griffith and Goldfarb examine several ways that social values might be integrated into the "rational egoist" model. Three possibilities are described. The first incorporates norms as an influence on decision rules. In complex environments where strategic behavior determines outcomes, simple maximization rules can be difficult to discern. "Moral" decision rules may lead to higher payoffs. In a Prisoner's Dilemma game, for example, a strong norm never to confess can benefit all players. The difficulty with this approach is that it confuses social and individual maximization. The economist's decision-making model is one of individual maximization. The benefits from applying the norm as a part of a decision rule accrue to the group but do not necessarily maximize the rewards for each individual. Indeed, in the Prisoner's Dilemma game, a person gains by violating the norm and confessing.

A second alternative is to include norms in the "rational egoist" model as a constraint. Here norms are viewed as restrictions on the range of choices open to the individual. There are penalties associated with violating the constraints. If the norms are internalized by previous conditioning, it is a psychological penalty. Other norms may be enforced by social sanctions. The difficulty, here, is that sometimes norms are violated. But how can this happen in

---

4. Richard Weiss pointed out to us that only the middle class wishes to obey social norms. The upper class shows its high status by flouting norms, and the lower class has too little chance of acceptance to gain from obeying norms. The same principle should apply to people in an organization. Hechter (1987, 62–77) discusses childhood training versus genetics as sources of social norms.

a model where norms are a constraint? But then if norms are violated, aren't they more like preferences? This is the third alternative presented by Griffith and Goldfarb. Incorporating moral values as preferences also creates problems, however, for it is hard to see how smooth trade-offs will be made between purchases of ordinary goods and acting according to moral values. This problem has led Sen (1977) to suggest that there might be two scales—one for ordinary goods and one for moral values.

Goldfarb and Griffith conclude that none of these alternatives is adequate. They reason that there are important issues related to norms that are still unexplored in the economics literature. One fundamental philosophical issue that has long remained unresolved is whether acting morally is in an individual's self-interest. Such complexities may mean that these issues cannot be incorporated into economic models in a single, straightforward way.

While this conclusion may seem puzzling and difficult for economists, it *is* consistent with evidence on the nature of the mind, and with experimental studies of choice. The concept of maximizing units that can compare all possible choices and consistently choose the globally optimal outcome is not supported by the evidence (see, e.g., Hayek 1953, especially secs. 6.30 and 6.31; Pugh 1977).[5] An alternative model is one where there is a fairly wide range of "rational, utility-maximizing" choices, and then some basically "fixed" or "constrained" choices on some topics.

Timothy Brennan, in "The Trouble with Norms," argues that economists do not need to worry about the details of modeling norms. Economics is basically comparative-statics analysis: changes in exogenous variables cause adjustments to endogenous variables. There is a clear direction to these results, even when the details of individuals' utility maximizing are not clear. Those comparative-statics results will carry through whether norms are in the utility function or in the constraint—the job is to get that done, and go on to the observable implications.

In any case, Brennan argues, the distinctions among rule following, altruism, and constraints, do not capture the real issues of norms. Norms have to do with how people think about leading their lives. Such values develop and change. He suggests a process of discovery of personal values. At one time, personal or social norms would be constraints, but as one decided to commit oneself to them, they would be choices. So going from a static, one-time framework to a more evolutionary framework might make the sources of values, including social norms, clearer.

Some ethicists would say that we are not so radically individualistic that

---

5. Of course, if the decisions required have been repeated in a similar fashion for a long time, we would anticipate that individuals would eventually find approximately optimal responses to new examples of those same problems (Alchian 1950).

we "decide" whether or not to care for or help others. (Does a mother decide to leap into the river to save her child?) Brennan makes a related point: people gain utility when they choose to do right first but, as with other habitual actions, repetition reduces the utility gain (Margolis 1987, 47; Ornstein 1977, 55; Scitovsky 1976, chaps. 2 and 3). Somehow, our minds normalize our utility levels. As we move from *choosing* to do right to doing right habitually, the act moves from a utility to a constraint.

In "Norms versus Laws: Economic Theory and the Choice of Social Institutions," Mark A. Cohen describes society's choice of legal obligation versus social norms. While choice is a matter of individual decision making, it is society that chooses whether there will be laws or moral sanctions. The costs and benefits of legal obligations to be a "good samaritan" illustrate society's choice: laws have numerous undesirable side effects, which mean that they will often not be used. The natural alternative is a moral obligation; society (parents, relatives, friends, the community, community leaders) try to inculcate these values. Cohen goes on to describe the efficiency pressures that might lead a society to adopt the right legal and social rules. His analogy is to the argument that the common law is efficient because the incentives are greatest to change a particular rule when it is inefficient. A similar argument applies to other rules of social obligation.

In his "Comments," Dennis Mueller argues that the Griffith-Goldfarb problem of choosing a proper empirical model of norms is not as difficult as they claim. The economist's toolbox is really quite flexible, and the choice of the best specific model depends upon its empirical success. Depending on the specific conditions, ethical values should be utilities for others' outcomes, under other conditions utilities for others' utilities, and sometimes people could be considered to act selfishly subject to fairness constraints.[6] Mueller also emphasizes the importance of family-rearing and natural selection processes (of the Austrian trial-and-error variety) in determining preferences.

In their "Responses to our Commentators," Griffith and Goldfarb focus on two issues. First, they draw a distinction between the search for an appropriate paradigm and a "toolbox" approach where the model is adjusted—as little as possible—to treat specific problems. They argue that while toolbox adjustments will help provide tools to analyze specific problems, the standard results of welfare economics depend upon the narrow definition of utility, which excludes moral value concerns. So the toolbox approach can cause an unintended narrowing of concepts used in normative economics. Second, they

---

6. Mueller emphasizes the flexibility of the formal utility-maximizing approach, which is based on duality theory. In the theory of the firm, profit functions might be seen as basic. But, if the data are more appropriate, one can estimate production functions or cost functions; the basic relationship can be transformed (inverted) to one of these other functions using dual methods.

reemphasize the distinction between moral norms and moral values. "[M]oral norms suggest particular *standards* or *thresholds* below which action is immoral; above the threshold, the same action is not immoral, though it might be criticizable as weak." With this interpretation, to incorporate moral issues as simply either a preference or a constraint would mean the analysis was incomplete.

Other scholars have wrestled with the "utilities versus constraints" issue. Schwartz (1977) finds that people evaluate possible ethical situations in terms of emotional arousal (which seems like utility) or moral obligation (which seems like constraints). So there may be elements of both approaches present. An important aspect of a new situation may then be whether to frame a question in terms of emotional gains or moral obligation. Several economists have chosen the utility approach in modeling agent behavior. Becker (1974) includes others' welfare in people's utility functions, while Koford and Penno (1989) include values for truth telling in the utility function, and Jones (1984) describes values for conforming to others' expectations. Etzioni (1988), on the other hand, reviews a wide variety of models with interdependent preferences where actions often look like obligations. Utility would be lost by lying or by taking advantage of one's children, but these actions look more like constraints.[7]

A point highlighted by Mueller is that we should think about ethics less in abstract terms and more in empirical, sociological and historical terms. Such an approach is followed in Part 3.

John Orbell, Alphons van de Kragt, Robyn M. Dawes, and other colleagues have been carrying out a series of experimental studies of ethical norms in small groups; one such study, "Covenants without the Sword: The Role of Promises in Social Dilemma Circumstances," is reported here. Numerous studies have found that people act in an apparently ethical or altruistic manner.[8] However, there are a variety of alternative explanations for these apparently ethical actions. Orbell, van de Kragt, and Dawes first examine

---

7. They are often soft constraints, since one is physically able to violate them. But they can be hard if the marginal cost of violation is quite high. Just as being "a little bit pregnant" is a discrete jump, stealing or embezzling just a little amount is also a definite violation.

Etzioni (1988) criticizes this view, arguing that putting moral obligations in the utility function is not appropriate. The argument is similar to that in Sen 1987. Etzioni argues for a theory with two forms of preferences—utility and obligation. Thus, he appears to prefer moral obligations to be treated technically, rather like constraints.

8. For example, Moore (1978) describes some of the vast historical literature on cultural views of just and unjust actions, and links it to actions against injustice. Frolich, Oppenheimer, and Eavey (1987) experimentally tested people's views of fair rules similar to those proposed by Rawls (1971), and found that many people also followed those rules. See also Hegtvedt and Cook 1987 for a review of social psychology studies of fairness and justice in outcomes and procedural fairness.

these earlier explanations, and then run a series of experiments to test them. Following the lead of sociobiological models of altruism (e.g., Trivers 1985), economists have emphasized a pure altruistic motive (e.g., Becker 1981, chap. 8). But altruistic behavior in these circumstances is rejected by the data. A second possible explanation is that ethical responses depend upon the proportion of others that are expected to act ethically, but the evidence also fails to support this proposition. Rather, in these experiments people require a mutual commitment to action from all others in the group.[9] People look to others to make promises, and when everyone else makes mutual promises, they are far more likely to act ethically.

It must be emphasized that the Orbell, van de Kragt, and Dawes experiments reported here are for clear social dilemmas—that is, each agent is clearly better off acting selfishly. Formally, the experiments are similar to the Prisoner's Dilemma situation, in which a strategy of cooperation is strictly dominated by selfish behavior in the sense of a Nash equilibrium. Thus, there is a fundamental question of why most agents violate their self-interest. Since the experiments reject altruism and find that what others seem prepared to do is important, they reinforce the idea that ethical norms have a strong social component. It also suggests that a strong social rule for people is "keeping promises." That is why people expect others whom they have never met to make and keep promises.[10]

Richard Weiss, in "Alternative Social Science Perspectives on 'Social Dilemma' Laboratory Research," uses work on social norms in sociology, social psychology, and organization theory as a basis for discussing the Orbell, van de Kragt, and Dawes experiments. Weiss's first concern is that experiments can easily be biased in ways that could have created the results found by Orbell, van de Kragt, and Dawes. For example, the subjects could have been trying to convince the experimenters that they were good people, or they could simply have been conforming to the other subjects' behavior. The subjects' perceptions are crucial.

---

9. Extensive experiments investigating people's social values of fairness are reported by Frolich and Oppenheimer (n.d.). Their general conclusion is that most people favored a rule that maximized total economic gains subject to a rule establishing a floor for the worst off. Hoffman and Spitzer (1985) obtain similar, but more Lockean, views of fairness as viewed by college students. Palfrey and Rosenthal (1988) review the empirical literature, derive a formal model, and show that the data are consistent with an altruistic explanation, but they do not fully examine concepts of fairness. Hirshleifer (1983) describes models of social dilemmas in which mutual commitment is a sensible strategy.

10. That is, people may be "rule utilitarian": they are willing to adopt rules that seem to have long-term payoffs. Presumably socialization leads to the rule that, when people in a group all promise to act for the common good, everyone should abide by their promise (see also Rowe 1989). Conversations with David Haslett on rule utilitarianism were important in focusing our thoughts on this point.

Robert Inman, in his "Comment on 'Covenants without the Sword,'" first shows statistically that one can be confident that it really was "multi-lateral promises" that caused cooperation in the Orbell, van de Kragt, and Dawes experiments. He then discusses how striking these results are in the context of economic theory. The best strategy is clearly and obviously to promise to cooperate and then to cheat. So why doesn't that happen? Why don't people feel highly suspicious when others suggest multilateral prom-ises? Such behavior might be explained in terms of reputation in the repeated play of a game, but there is no repetition here. So some behavior has been found that is important, really occurs, and could teach economists something new about how people feel—perhaps about self-respect. Inman wonders, however, what would happen if the game were repeated, and people found that some others were cheating—would cooperation collapse?

In political science, experiments similar to those by Orbell, van de Kragt, and Dawes have been carried out to examine people's ethical values as well as their actual ethical behavior. Frolich, Oppenheimer, and Eavey (1987) and Frolich and Oppenheimer (n.d.) examined students' sense of distributive justice in experiments where the students could choose the fairness rule and then had to abide by it. Their results find that ". . . the chosen principle is maximizing the average income with a floor constraint." There is a trade-off between efficiency and equity. People consider what is "fair" as well as their self-interest. When the subjects discussed alternative ethical policies and then decided, as a group, which one they favored, they worked together willingly (for the common good). When the same policy was imposed, there was less cooperation (Frolich and Oppenheimer, n.d.). In a moderately different vein, Selten (1987) reports experiments where the majority fails to take advantage of the minority when it would be considered unfair. In experiments reported by Eavey and Miller (1984), subjects discuss fairness intensely; although they do not report any explicit promises, weaker parties "shamed" subjects into behaving "fairly." Thus, these experiments find, in a rather different experi-mental setting, the same pattern of promising and keeping promises shown in the Orbell, van de Kragt, and Dawes experiments.

Part 4 develops a theory in which social norms are equilibrium behavior in an evolutionary setting. These essays show how certain norms can survive in the real world, where people who do not follow those norms are competing for success. This work accepts the challenge of Part 1, "Can Norms Be Incorporated into Economics?" by showing how to incorporate such values.

In "Social Forces in the Workplace," Robert H. Frank uses evolutionary natural selection models to show how humans may have evolved basic physi-cal traits or moral values that determine their values of honesty, fairness, or conformity to ethical standards. He shows that organizations can (and do) use such values to develop effective ethical standards or norms. The natural selection approach shows that moral rules, social norms, or a common sense of fairness, might develop and flourish. Unlike values that must be intentionally chosen, these values can survive in a competitive social environment without people being aware of them. If these behaviors have had survival value for a long time in social interactions, humans could have evolved them. Frank shows that ethical norms of fairness and of general proper conduct are good candidates for such innate behavior. People have a strong propensity for certain specific types of behavior. Social training or childhood experiences teach how these general propensities should be applied in specific circumstances. These specific values are often reinforced by feelings of "a bad conscience" from unfair acts, or by physical responses such as blushing when (caught) lying. In a sense, people are committed to certain behaviors, even when it is not in their material self-interest. This is a fundamental challenge to the game-theoretic literature that has puzzled over assuring that people have commitments to certain behaviors. Often in that literature, the absence of even a tiny level of commitment leads to the unravelling of cooperative policies; Frank's argument suggests that that line of research is missing an important fact about human behavior.[11]

Frank then makes a second crucial point. Not everyone has the same ethical or moral values. Having a single value is not an equilibrium outcome. Rather, the equilibrium outcome is a distribution of different strengths of ethical norms. The argument goes essentially as follows: if everyone were equally ethical, there would be no reason for anyone to expend any effort to weed out less ethical types who would be more likely to take advantage. But in that case there would be a net advantage to being less ethical and taking advantage of others. As a result, people and organizations must have ways to distinguish among more and less ethical types, or they must find incentives that will attract the desired types. This leads to a situation where different ethical types can coexist. A selection process maintains an equilibrium distribution among different types. Heterogeneity exists in equilibrium. This differs from neoclassical models, which emphasize the survival of a single, most efficient type of firm. With interactions among economic agents, multiple types survive. (This point was made for somewhat different reasons by Austrians, such as Hayek).

In "Biological versus Cultural Indicators of Ability and Honesty," Kenneth Koford examines some problems with using evolutionary models to describe the equilibrium of biological and social norms. First, most indicators of ethical standards and honesty have both a genetic and a cultural component. Purely genetic responses with no cultural component are rare. Frank's ex-

---

11. Rowe (1989) has recently made similar points about the importance of commitment, but has attempted to show how it is an equilibrium strategy for self-interested players.

ample of blushing while lying has a clear genetic base, but people require a cultural indicator of what a lie is. Models of the coevolution of genes and culture have different properties than models of purely genetic evolution. Specific cultural values can evolve much more quickly than genetic changes. Because of this, it is hard for both a static cultural and genetic equilibrium to exist at once.

A second concern is whether multiple equilibria with simple traits are stable. In Frank's essay, the equilibrium has knife-edge properties. (In contrast, Frank's 1987 model has a stable equilibrium, but the model is more complex and converges slowly.) Some basic heterogeneity or randomness is needed to assure a stable equilibrium. In addition, there are important dynamic issues. In these models there is either a rapid movement to equilibrium, which will tend to overshoot, or a slow one, which may be too slow to reach the equilibrium before underlying conditions change. The disequilibrium properties of socially accepted norms therefore need to be examined. Disequilibrium norms may be common, and their properties could give more insight into actual social norms.

In the last part, the theoretical principles described above are applied to several specific institutions. "Corporate Crimes and Innovative Punishments," by Peter A. French, defines innovative standards of ethical behavior by corporations. Mark A. Cohen comments on the empirical applicability of French's ideas. The final essay, "Bargaining and Contract," by Jules L. Coleman, Steven Maser, and Douglas Heckathorn, describes how norms should be and are developed in the legal community.

French develops a new ethical principle, the "Principle of Responsive Adjustment," or PRA, which he describes, defends, and applies to agents in corporations. This principle follows on his previous work, where he considers whether corporate responsibility—holding collectives like corporations morally responsible—makes ethical sense.[12] While corporations in economic models are assumed to be single-minded profit maximizers, this objective may not—and probably should not—hold for executives and managers. Like most people (in their everyday lives), executives tend to believe in and uphold ethical standards. What are appropriate standards, given the needs of the corporation and the agents' incentives? French argues the standard should take into account the corporation's goal to maximize profits as well as managers' desire to act in a legal and proper manner.

French chooses a normative approach to find a desirable legal and ethical standard for corporate behavior. The basic problem is that it is hard to determine whether a corporation intended some harm. Corporate agents may have casually considered a wide variety of possible problems like pollution or

---

12. French 1984; see also May 1987.

worker safety. They may have corrected some problems, focused on others but failed to take corrective action, and completely failed to think about still others. If harm occurs, should the firm be liable for intentionally failing to deal with the problem? The standard chosen, PRA, must be consistent with general ethical values and accept practical limits on corporate ethical standards. PRA acknowledges that ethical standards have limited strength, so these standards provide social benefits only when they are obeyed, and they will be ignored if the individual gains are great enough. While people believe in normative rules because they are "right," French argues that society should choose rules that are effective or efficient.

French's Principle of Responsive Adjustment allows firms and their agents to make mistakes, but to make one particular mistake only *once*. If a firm is found to act illegally once in some "gray area," French argues that it is both unfair and inefficient to punish the firm and its agents, since they may not have known that the act was so harmful. But after the principle has been established that a particular act is illegal, a second action will be properly punished.

While French's argument might seem attractive to corporations in allowing them "one bite of the apple," it has a fundamental basis in the nature of corporations. Corporations are complex structures, and it is difficult to determine their intentions. Few top executives consciously intend to harm. To take a recent example, Exxon's CEO did not "intend" to pollute Alaskan waters with oil. Intentions and policies are inevitably different things. Broad intentions, which include profit maximization as one goal, must be described in terms of a variety of policies and trade-offs. Legal violations must be identified—as with pollution—and then solutions must be found and put into practice. So, an improper act may be committed without anyone really "intending" it.[13] PRA allows this *once*. But after the act is determined to be illegal, the firm is on notice that it must be on guard to prevent such acts in the future. PRA requires a firm to change its standard operating procedures to deal with a novel problem when the corporation has once committed a violation.

One can question French's argument in terms of its use of ethical theory.[14] First, *moral blame* cannot properly be assigned to individuals or corporations who do not intend harmful actions. Blame is, however, assigned if people see that a particular action will be harmful, and they nevertheless carry it out. But this is the standard view and does not need a PRA. Also, it is

---

13. While French does not discuss the matter explicitly, it is clear from his argument that, when there is specific intent to commit a clearly illegal act, PRA would not apply. Each corporation does not have the right (under PRA) to commit one homicide or one act of price fixing.

14. We are indebted to Jennifer Moore for these points.

questionable whether "shaming" corporations for their morally wrong actions would be successful. To be ashamed requires a social standard of proper conduct, and there is no established standard for corporations in our culture. Many business people believe that one can and should get away with what one can. In any case, corporations cannot feel "ashamed"; their employees can always feel "it was the other guy" who was responsible, or perhaps the "system." So in our individualistic culture, the "men and women of the corporation" are unlikely to feel shame.[15]

Mark Cohen examines several empirical issues regarding the PRA principle for corporate crime in his "Appropriate Sanctions for Corporate Offenders." The data on corporate crime suggest that the type of case that French is concerned with is relatively uncommon. While there is a fair amount of corporate crime, most cases involve small firms in which the manager is the owner and there are only a small number of other decision-making employees. Cohen also questions whether French should rule out fines as a proper penalty for corporate crime in favor of such "innovative" punishments as requiring polluters to install particularly effective, high-technology antipollution devices. While current fines may be ineffective, fines can act as an efficient deterrent in principle.

In "Bargaining and Contract," Coleman, Maser, and Heckathorn develop principles of fairness for professionals in bargaining and establishing legal contracts. Such standards are not imposed by a hierarchy, but by professional organizations and peer pressure—among lawyers and courts. Examining how fair standards are created and maintained in this profession shows how fair standards can be applied in professions in general.

Specifically, Coleman, Maser, and Heckathorn examine the fair principles of bargaining to reach contractual agreement. In bargaining, the parties must keep in mind that any contract is incomplete, and that the contract may not be adhered to by one party or another. In either of these cases, civil courts may impose common law remedies, or parties may impose purely private sanctions. Coleman, Maser, and Heckathorn develop their analysis using a Prisoner's Dilemma framework with a continuously divisible distribution of rewards, and work out a "fair" bargaining equilibrium.[16] There are several phases to the bargaining game: search for an appropriate partner, division of the mutual gains, and possible defection after the agreement has been made.

---

15. French's *moral* argument works best, therefore, for organizations that have some overall "sense of mission," in James Q. Wilson's (1989) terms. There are numerous relatively communitarian organizations in which agents *may* feel such shame—say, those involved in a military fiasco like the Iran rescue operation, or a bungled policy like the Iran-Contra affair. In such cases, there may be a feeling of guilt by association from failures, or a feeling of pride from being a member of a well-functioning organization.

16. An interesting related discussion of bargaining equilibrium based upon repeated interactions and reputation is in Rowe 1989.

The fair equilibrium turns out to be efficient and, for informed players, is a genuine equilibrium strategy. This equilibrium also depends upon a number of factors that help determine the relative strengths of the players' positions. Transaction and bargaining costs, however, might limit the applicability of an efficient Coase theorem–type contract. These include elements of uncertainty, specifically player heterogeneity, spatial dispersion, levels of risk, and other factors similar to those in industrial organization models of contracting problems. Coleman, Maser, and Heckathorn describe these factors and show how they lead to specific biases. They then analyze third-party intervention, such as a court or arbitrator. Efficient intervention by a third party affects all of the previous results. The result is an analysis that combines formal game-theoretic analysis with application to real-world bargaining.

Overall, this volume examines social norms and ethical values in economic institutions from a theoretical, an experimental, and an applied perspective. The different essays bring a varied overview to the problem of understanding individual values and choices in a social or organizational setting. The essays emphasize the importance of social norms in determining outcomes in human institutions (a claim often denied by economists) and examines their specific nature in a number of situations. Several points might be emphasized.

First, the traditional view of social behavior that economists have used is inadequate. Social norms are not just utilities *or* constraints. Rather, they combine some elements of each and have some unique properties that have not been included in any economic model to date. Individual social values and social norms are quite varied, and considerable study and exploration will be needed to determine how individual norms should be modeled.

Second, there are numerous empirical cases where people act according to clear moral values that are not self-regarding. And these values are not strictly altruistic, either. Rather, they seem to be moral "rules." Sometimes these rules have efficiency justifications, as Frank points out, but the efficiency arguments are not the reasons people choose them. It would be extremely valuable to understand how and why people accept such moral values. The evolutionary-biological approach that Frank has pursued may give us insight into this matter.

Third, economic theory without social norms may not be rich enough to explain some economic institutions, particularly those involving mutual trust and cooperation. The internal workings of firms and other organizations are examples. Adding social norms and values to the standard economic behavioral model could provide the extra dimension needed to explain behavior in these settings.

Fourth, economists present a worldview in their teaching and in their policy advice. Critics often claim that this view is excessively narrow, even inhuman. If social ethical values and social norms were included as a part of the economist's worldview, it would enrich the analysis in significant ways and, perhaps, make it possible to explain more adequately the variety of experience that is observed in non-Western countries.

REFERENCES

Alchian, Armen A. 1950. "Uncertainty, Evolution, and Economic Theory." *Journal of Political Economy* 58:211–21.
Arrow, Kenneth J. 1963. *Social Choice and Individual Values.* New Haven: Yale University Press.
Axelrod, Robert. 1984. *The Evolution of Cooperation.* New York: Basic Books.
Axelrod, Robert. 1986. "An Evolutionary Approach to Norms." *American Political Science Review* 80:1095–1112.
Badcock, C. R. 1986. *The Problem of Altruism: Freudian-Darwinian Solutions.* Oxford: Blackwell.
Banfield, Edward C. 1958. *The Moral Basis of a Backward Society.* New York: Free Press.
Becker, Gary S. 1974. "A Theory of Social Interactions." *Journal of Political Economy* 82:1063–91.
Becker, Gary S. 1981. *A Treatise on the Family.* Cambridge, Mass.: Harvard University Press.
Eavey, Cheryl L., and Gary J. Miller. 1984. "Fairness in Majority Rule Games with a Core." *American Journal of Political Science* 28:570–86.
Etzioni, Amitai. 1988. *The Moral Dimension: Toward a New Economics.* New York: Free Press.
Frank, Robert H. 1986. "The Nature of the Utility Function." In *Economic Psychology: Intersections in Theory and Application,* ed. Alan J. MacFadyen and Heather W. MacFadyen. Amsterdam: Elsevier.
Frank, Robert H. 1987. "If *Homo Economicus* Could Choose His Own Utility Function, Would He Want One with a Conscience?" *American Economic Review* 77:593–604.
French, Peter. 1984. *Collective and Corporate Responsibility.* New York: Columbia University Press.
Frolich, Norman, and Joe A. Oppenheimer. N.d. *Choosing Justice: An Experimental Approach to Ethical Theory.* Berkeley: University of California Press. Forthcoming.
Frolich, Norman, Joe A. Oppenheimer, and Cheryl L. Eavey. 1987. "Choices of Principles of Distributive Justice in Experimental Groups." *American Journal of Political Science* 31.
Hayek, Friedrich A. 1953. *The Sensory Order: An Inquiry into the Foundations of Theoretical Psychology.* Chicago: University of Chicago Press.
Hechter, Michael. 1987. *Principles of Group Solidarity.* Berkeley: University of California Press.
Hegtvedt, Karen A., and Karen S. Cook. 1987. "The Role of Justice in Conflict Situations." In *Advances in Group Processes,* ed. Edward J. Lawler and Barry Markovsky. Greenwich, Conn.: JAI Press.

Hirshleifer, Jack. 1983. "From Weakest-Link to Best-Shot: The Voluntary Provision of Public Goods." *Public Choice* 41:371–89.

Hoffman, Elizabeth, and Matthew Spitzer. 1985. "Entitlements, Rights, and Fairness: An Experimental Examination of Subjects' Concepts of Distributive Justice." *Journal of Legal Studies* 14:259–97.

Isaac, R. Mark, and James M. Walker. 1988. "Communication and Free-Riding Behavior: The Voluntary Contribution Mechanism." *Economic Inquiry* 26:585–608.

Jones, Stephen R. G. 1984. *The Economics of Conformism.* Oxford: Blackwell.

Koford, Kenneth, and Mark Penno. 1989. "Equilibrium in Markets and Organizations When Some Agents Are Ethical." Presented at the annual meeting of the American Political Science Association, Washington, D.C., 1988. Revised July 1989.

Margolis, Howard. 1987. *Patterns, Thinking, and Cognition.* Chicago: University of Chicago Press.

Marshall, Alfred. 1924. *Principles of Economics.* 8th ed. London: Macmillan.

May, Larry. 1987. *The Morality of Groups: Collective Responsibility, Group-Based Harms, and Corporate Rights.* Notre Dame, Ind.: University of Notre Dame Press.

Mises, Ludwig von. 1963. *Human Action.* New Haven, Conn.: Yale University Press.

Moore, Barrington. 1978. *Injustice: The Social Bases of Obedience and Revolt.* Armonk, N.Y.: M. E. Sharpe.

Ornstein, Robert E. 1977. *The Psychology of Consciousness.* New York: Harcourt Brace Jovanovich.

Palfrey, Thomas R., and Howard Rosenthal. 1988. "Private Incentives in Social Dilemmas: The Effects of Incomplete Information and Altruism." *Journal of Public Economics* 35:309–32.

Pugh, George E. 1977. *The Biological Origin of Human Values.* New York: Basic Books.

Rasmusen, Eric. 1989. *Games and Information.* London: Blackwell.

Rawls, John. 1971. *A Theory of Justice.* Cambridge, Mass.: Harvard University Press.

Riley, John. 1979. "Informational Equilibrium." *Econometrica* 47:331–59.

Rowe, Nicholas. 1989. *Rules and Institutions.* Ann Arbor: University of Michigan Press.

Schofield, Norman. 1985. "Anarchy, Altruism, and Cooperation." *Social Choice and Welfare* 2:207–19.

Schwartz, Shalom H. 1977. "Normative Influences on Altruism." In *Advances in Social Psychology,* vol. 10, ed. Leonard Berkowitz. New York: Academic Press.

Scitovsky, Tibor. 1976. *The Joyless Economy: An Inquiry into Human Satisfaction and Consumer Dissatisfaction.* London: Oxford University Press.

Selten, Reinhard. 1987. "Equity and Coalition Bargaining in Experimental Three-Person Games." In *Laboratory Experimentation in Economics,* ed. Alvin E. Roth. Cambridge: Cambridge University Press.

Sen, Amartya. 1977. "Rational Fools: A Critique of the Behavioral Foundations of Economic Theory." *Philosophy and Public Affairs* 6:317–44.

Sen, Amartya. 1987. *On Ethics and Economics.* Oxford: Blackwell.

Trivers, Robert. 1985. *Social Evolution.* Menlo Park, Calif.: Benjamin/Cummings.

Wilson, James Q. 1989. *Bureaucracy.* New York: Free Press.

Part 1
A Theory of the Function
of Norms in Economic
Organizations

What role do norms play in the effective functioning of economic organizations? This introductory chapter shows how habitual behavior leads to stable customary practices and social norms in the workplace. In turn, customs and norms provide an anchor for economic institutions that rely on customary practices and stable expectations. In a complex society, consistent and stable expectations of others' behaviors are highly valuable, so that social customs and norms are highly functional to the firm.

The chapter also provides a framework for thinking about the overall subject of this volume. Understanding how norms influence social institutions is important background when considering how norms may be incorporated into a model of individual behavior, as is done in Part 2. For the experimental studies of norms of mutual commitment described in Part 3, these norms are best understood initially in the general social context where common action can be mutually beneficial. Finally, to analyze the actual rules of fairness in business and law described in Part 5, an understanding of how norms of fairness are created and socially enforced is important.

Habit, Custom, and Norms in Economics

Kenneth J. Koford and Jeffrey B. Miller

Sociologists and organization theorists have studied how habit, custom, and norms determine social outcomes. Although economic systems are really just a type of social organization, economists have neglected these factors. There is a good reason why: they generally lie outside the realm of the rational maximization model that economists use. Furthermore, habit, custom, and norms tend to inhibit change, while economic analysis shows how economic systems change in response to external events. However, these factors play an important role in many contexts by constraining human action. Ignoring these constraints can lead to predictions that overstate people's response to changes in their environment.

This chapter analyzes how habit, custom, and norms can be integrated into a economic model. We argue that they have important efficiency properties. Due to the complexity of economic life, people establish habitual patterns that determine much of what they do. This lets people focus their decision-making energies on a narrow set of problems. These patterns, supported by institutional arrangements, also make decision making easier, since the behavior of others becomes more predictable.

Since rational decision making is applied to only a subset of actions, outcomes will not be optimal (for individuals or groups). In this sense, our argument has much in common with Simon's theory of bounded rationality (1972). An important distinction, however, is that we are concerned with the selection of problems to be decided, whereas Simon is concerned with how decisions are made.

If economic behavior is influenced by habit, custom, and norms as well as rational optimization processes, focusing exclusively on the latter can lead

The authors would like to thank Timur Kuran, Tom Hammond, David Ermann, and Richard Weiss for helpful comments on earlier drafts of this chapter. Remaining errors are the responsibility of the authors. An earlier version was presented at the 1989 annual meeting of the Eastern Economic Association, Baltimore, Md.

to a misunderstanding of economic events. We argue that all these factors play a role in most institutional settings. While habit, custom, and norms may be most important in "traditional" settings like households, they also influence behavior in markets and hierarchies. Likewise, rational choice, while most closely associated with market decisions, also plays a role in households.

In a few cases, the impact of habit, custom, or norms on behavior has been included in economic analysis. Along with laws, they are seen as part of the social framework within which economic activity takes place. In several cases, explicit recognition of this framework has improved our understanding of economic observations. Other observations could be explained better if these factors were included in the analysis, especially those where current explanations provided by rational decision-making models are very complex and unsatisfactory.

The next section distinguishes the concepts of habit, custom, and norms. We then describe why these social behaviors are important in complex economic environments. The second section relates these forces and rational decision making in different institutional settings. The third section uses habit, custom, or norms to provide better explanations of economic behavior and suggests some additional areas where these factors might usefully be brought into the analysis.

Habit, Custom, and Norms

> As Alfred Whitehead has said in another connection, "It is a profoundly erroneous truism . . . that we should cultivate the habit of thinking what we are doing. The precise opposite is the case. Civilization advances by extending the number of important operations which we can perform without thinking about them." This is of profound significance. . . . We have developed these practices and institutions by building upon habits and institutions which have proved successful in their own sphere and which in turn become the foundation of civilization we have built up. (Hayek 1945, 528)

> Modern thought explains things either scientifically or historically, chiefly the former in natural phenomena, the latter in human. . . . Human society must always be largely of the original institutional character; custom and habit must rule most of what people feel, think, and do. Institutions, I repeat, are more or less explained historically rather than scientifically and are little subject to control. (Knight 1957, 20).

Incorporating habit, custom, and norms into economic analysis explicitly recognizes important factors that limit "rational" action. By providing continuity to action, they support existing institutional arrangements, and, in turn, they are reinforced by these institutional arrangements. On the other hand, if they change, the constraints shift and create a new environment where different outcomes are possible.

Habitual behavior is repetitive behavior that is undertaken without forethought. It is unreflective behavior in the sense that a person carries out the action without explicitly reflecting on how it might be done differently.[1] Sometimes such actions do not affect other people, but are simply a matter of individual routine (e.g., putting on socks in the morning). Custom, on the other hand, implies a social structure. Following Weber, custom is defined as "activity which is kept on the beaten track simply because men are 'accustomed' to it and persist in it by unreflective imitation" (1968, 319).[2] Custom dictates that individuals in a particular group, faced with identical circumstances, respond the same way. When others' actions are predictable, people can form reliable expectations about those actions and respond accordingly. Habitual behavior of others is predictable only if the people know each other well. Customary behavior is predictable among strangers as long as the group's customs are known.

Explicit recognition of habit and custom leads to a different behavioral model than economists are accustomed to analyzing, for many actions are not rational (i.e., are not the outcome of some utility calculus); rather they depend on previously constructed patterns of behavior.

But integration of habit and custom into the behavioral model does not rule out rational behavior. Indeed, routine behavior will determine most individual action even among supposedly rational agents. As Simon (1972) emphasizes, agents have a limited capacity to calculate (i.e. "bounded rationality"). They cannot attend to many matters at once.[3] Because it is impossible to consider every action consciously, the enormous repertory of habitual and customary actions serve an important function. By predetermining most actions, agents can focus their attention on the few conscious analytical or optimizing choices they must make.[4]

The establishment of common patterns can generate large gains. This is

---

1. Camic (1986) traces the study of habit in sociology. He argues that it disappeared from sociology when sociologists tried to distinguish their field from psychology, and that sociologists should return to a study of this important aspect of human behavior.

2. Max Weber's (1968) theory of society develops the concepts of our typology using somewhat different terminology. He defines custom roughly as we do (1968, 319). Our habitual behavior is his *traditional behavior* (chap. 1:2, 25). Our "social norms" are his *conventional behavior:* there is no legal enforcement, but rather "general disapproval" of violators. He notes that "standards of respectability" are enforced this way. Weber defines *norms* to include legally sanctioned behavior, and concentrates on legally enforced norms (e.g., 1968, 312).

3. Psychologists have studied this much more than economists. *Most* individual actions are carried out habitually.

4. Heiner (1983) describes why stable behavior would develop and offers an explanation that is at variance with the concept that only optimal behavior will survive.

illustrated by something as simple as establishing the normal hour for having lunch. As long as there is a normal lunch hour, little time is wasted bargaining about when a group should get together to eat. Consistent expectations are all that is required. The actual time is not important. Indeed, lunchtime in the United States and in Spain are quite different.

While this behavioral model is based on Simon's notion of bounded rationality, it is not quite the same as Simon's (1972) model of decision making. Simon considers the decision-making problem to be complex because the future is uncertain and there are so many possible paths events can take. Optimization is impossible. In contrast, satisficing occurs here, not because the decisions themselves are complex (although they could be), but rather because life would be too complex if agents had to carefully consider each daily action from an optimizing point of view.[5] If, at any given time, people consciously make decisions about only a small fraction of their actions, then it is unlikely that their actions taken together will be optimal. In this environment, satisfactory actions rather than optimal actions are likely to prevail.[6]

Social norms also constrain behavioral patterns. Norms can be distinguished from customs in that individuals who violate the norm can expect to be punished.[7] Often norms do not define a precise set of proper actions but, rather, rule out a whole range of actions. Norms do not necessarily lead to repeated behavior, although they can do so by limiting choices.[8] General adherence to social norms does not fall neatly under either unreflective behavior or rational decision-making behavior. Depending on the circumstances, either might occur. In this regard Coleman's (1987) distinction between "internalized norms" and "externally sanctioned norms" is useful. There is a large overlap between internalized norms and customs. Once learned, these norms become part of customary practice and individuals rarely reflect on them when they act. On the other hand, externally sanctioned norms are often obeyed because people calculate that being punished would be too

---

5. Imagine, for example, the difficulty associated with getting out the front door in the morning if each action from the time one awoke to the time of departure was the result of a "rational decision."

6. Abreu and Rubinstein (1988) and Banks and Sundaram (1989) have formalized some notions of complexity and have analyzed what kind of outcomes would result if information processing is limited.

7. Trivers (1985) shows that many species engage in moralistic aggression when "cheating" is observed in others. A sense of justice and fairness seems to be an important trait in primates.

8. Ullman-Margalit (1977) provided a typology of norms. Elster (1989) gives some examples of different types of norms. See Akerlof 1980 for a formal model that incorporates norms and Axelrod 1986 for a description of how different types of sanctions can be used to enforce norms. North (1981, 1988) develops a theory in which the occurrence of social norms is due to high market transaction costs.

costly. If individuals carefully weigh the cost of violating a norm before taking an action, this behavior can be incorporated into the rational decision-making calculus. In either case, when norms are followed, the individual's behavior is restricted.[9]

Habit, custom, and norms reduce the complexity of social and economic life. Since satisficers analyze and change only a small fraction of their actions, there must be great regularity in daily life. Norms, because they rule out certain behavior by others, also make actions by others more predictable. This reduces the uncertainty that decision makers face. While the environment can still be complex, it will be easier to reach satisfactory decisions. This can be seen in the context of Simon's (1972, 160ff.) example of the chess game. Simon points out there are about 10^{120} possible games of chess. Deciding which game to play cannot be determined using presently known optimization techniques. But this may overstate the difficulty of the decision. If the two players are familiar with chess, certain reasonably predictable patterns of play will evolve. If the two players play each other often, there is even more predictability. Decision making is not nearly as complex as it would be if all possibilities had similar probabilities of occurrence.[10]

Thus, incorporating habit, custom, and norms into the behavioral models modifies them in two ways. First, these factors constrain agent action by creating spheres dominated by repetitive behavior and by limiting actions to those areas which are in compliance with social norms. Second, the behavior of other agents is more predictable. This reduces the complexity that a decision maker faces when outcomes depend on the actions of others.[11]

Habit, custom, and norms are like two different forms of capital. Repetitive behavior that determines most actions is a type of human capital. It frees up time so that the person can attend to a narrow set of problems. The costs of recreating this human capital are experienced when a person takes a new job or moves to a new neighborhood. Considerable time and effort must be exerted in performing common everyday tasks until new satisfactory patterns are established.

Behavior that satisfies social norms and establishes predictable patterns creates a positive externality that lowers decision-making costs for others. It is

---

9. See Griffith and Goldfarb (in this volume) for a discussion of the difficulties of integrating norms into a rational decision-making model.

10. Chess masters have learned a finite set of strategies that have historically generated winning combinations. When masters play against each other, a viewer can often describe the early action as moving from one known formation to another.

11. This model of behavior is still very restrictive. Granovetter (1985) argues that economic behavior must be seen as embedded in social institutions. He would characterize the model presented here as being both under- and oversocialized. We would argue that there is still much to be gained by expanding the model, even in this limited way.

a kind of *social capital*. This social capital is not costless to produce. Some norms are taught in school. Other norms or codes of professional conduct must be enforced.[12] Likewise, habitual or customary behavior, while repetitive now, originally had to be learned. The investment in social capital does not always benefit the individual directly, but it may be an essential factor in the community's production function.[13]

This capital investment does not mean that existing habits and norms represent economically efficient structures. Arthur (1989) has shown that, even where decision makers seek efficient outcomes, increasing returns can lead to a sequence of adoption that locks production into an inferior technology. So while investments in norms make decision making easier, norms do not necessarily make the economy more efficient.[14]

When circumstances change, the value of existing habits and norms can depreciate quickly. Previously established patterns are no longer as efficient as they were, but agents will be hesitant to abandon old routines and norms. Abandoning established routines is like fully depreciating old capital while making a new investment. Establishing new customs and norms is like making a new public investment, except there is no organized mechanism for bringing about the change. Thus, habits, customs, and norms create rigidities not only because they are based on very structured behavior, but also because the cost of creating new patterns and norms is often perceived to be very high.[15]

Different Modes of Organizing Economic Activity

When economists discuss modes of organizing economic activity, they normally limit the discussion to markets, hierarchy, and tradition.[16] Markets are usually seen as organizing economic activity by exchange relations between self-interested agents. Hierarchies are characterized by their procedures and the authority relationship between superiors and subordinates. Traditional

---

12. See Coleman 1987 for an elaboration of this point and his discussion of the term *social capital*.

13. Akerlof (1983) describes cases where upholding a norm does yield individual benefits although violation of the norm would appear to be advantageous.

14. Sudgen (1989) sees norms changing as a result of an evolutionary process. Elster (1989) is more sanguine. He sees how pressures to improve welfare may bring changes in norms but argues that a strong random element is perhaps the most important force.

15. The inefficiency of a norm may not be known simply because no one is prepared to challenge it. For this reason, many customs and norms remain long after their initial usefulness is past. See Kuran 1988 for a general discussion of these issues.

16. This terminology is used by Heilbroner (1980), but it parallels discussions of these issues by Polanyi, Arenberg, and Pearson (1957) and Ouchi (1980). Schelling (1978, 127) describes social organization as structured around markets, government, and moral forces.

organizations are described as guided by customary practice. These three modes are sometimes described as being separate means of organizing activity. For example, there are discussions of market economies, command economies, and primitive economies.

The rational decision-making model has recently been extended to analyze hierarchy and tradition-based organizations.[17] This section describes how habit, custom, and norms play an important role in directing economic activity in all three institutional settings. We also argue that laws in society and procedural rules within an organization play a role similar to norms. Both constrain action and punish deviation, although they use different mechanisms for determining compliance and meting out punishments.[18]

Markets

The importance of habitual behavior and social constraints in markets can be seen in the example of the local fish market (discussed by Marshall). Self-interested buyers and sellers come to the market because they expect to gain from the exchanges that take place there. But the structure of the market can be more accurately explained by reference to habit, custom, norms, and laws. For instance, the location and many actions of the seller are a matter of routine. Sales start at the same time each day and the way customers are treated becomes routine. Many of the same customers frequent the same stall each day. Customers and sellers are also constrained by the rules of the market. These rules may be determined by government authorities (such as health regulators) or by the market organization or they may be informal rules enforced by norms. The rules allow for the partially free play of price in response to supply and demand.

How customary behavior structures a market can have important economic implications. Okun (1981) explains macroeconomic instabilities by distinguishing between two types of markets—auction markets and customer markets. In auction markets, prices fluctuate with supply and demand, but in customer markets prices are sticky. In these customer markets, "products are sold with price tags set by the seller" (Okun 1981, 138) and repeat business is important. Customers return if their experience has been positive, and there is considerable continuity over time. If customers cannot rely on their past experience to inform them about the future, they will not return. Price stability, at least in a relative sense, becomes important.

---

17. Williamson's (1985) analysis of markets and hierarchies finds that the distinction between hierarchical relationships and market relationships can become blurred at the boundaries of firms.

18. See Cohen's comments on Griffith and Goldfarb for a comparison between laws and norms.

This argument can be rephrased in terms of our model. Customers who frequent particular stores become accustomed to shopping there. It becomes habitual behavior. Certain needs are consistently satisfied by buying from particular sellers. There are efficiencies on both sides of the market. Customers gain by limiting their search and following established routines; sellers gain because they can predict the needs of their repeat customers. If sellers maintain reasonably stable prices, customers do not reflect on the possibility of going elsewhere, and these patterns are maintained.

Norms can also affect the nature of the market. The notion of "buyer beware" implies that, in some markets, it is presumed that buyers may be misled by sellers. In such a fish market, buyers must be knowledgeable about fish. This will limit the breadth of the market. Sometimes, acquiring sufficient information before the exchange occurs is not possible; the market will fail unless norms are established that protect the buyer (i.e., the market for lemons). Roadside automobile service is an interesting example. Because of the situation, consumers feel they might be exploited, yet Kahneman, Knetsch, and Thaler (1986) have found that motorists are reasonably satisfied. Another example is the wholesale diamond trade in New York. Theft would be very easy as gems are inspected by various individuals, so the market is founded upon strong norms of trust. Ostracism is quick for those who deviate (Granovetter 1985).[19]

Thus, a broader analysis of how markets operate recognizes the influence of routine behavior as well as norms and laws. Acquiring goods through markets is costly. Establishing routine methods of search reduces buyer costs. Sellers (or groups of sellers) can further lower buyer search costs by establishing norms that assure buyers that they will be treated fairly. Where norms are hard to enforce, markets can still function if laws can provide sufficient guarantees that the buyer will be protected.

Hierarchies

Hierarchical environments have a similar interplay among rational decision making; habit, custom, and norms; and legal and procedural constraints. Consider the work environment within a hierarchy. Most individuals take many actions as part of the "normal routine"—arrival time, work location, a cup of coffee in the morning. Interactions with other workers are normally defined by customary practices that new workers must learn before they can really contribute. Workers are expected to carry out assignments in accordance with accepted procedures. These procedures are sometimes docu-

---

19. In another context, Frank (1987) argues that there are advantages to having a reputation for being honest when others are seeking partners.

mented but are rarely so detailed that they do not leave the worker considerable discretion. Workers are then rewarded on the basis of their performance.

The rational behavior model has been used to describe important aspects of individual behavior in a hierarchy using principal-agent models, where bargaining occurs between superiors and better informed subordinates. In these models, new definitions of self-interested behavior have arisen. For example, Williamson (1975) defines the term *opportunism* as "self-seeking with guile" and suggests economic agents will pursue their self-interest even if it means being less than totally truthful. This characterization of individual behavior is not entirely satisfactory, however. While some people will seek an economic advantage by being dishonest, others will not because they consider such behavior unethical.[20] Furthermore, behavior will vary depending on existing norms. In a different environment, a person is likely to behave differently.[21]

These norms, along with customs and procedures, make up *corporate culture*. Local environments can benefit if specialized practices, culture, are established to reduce the cost of more specific tasks.[22] In some instances this extends even to the development of a specialized language. Such a language can be quite efficient, as it greatly condenses expressions and increases precision, although chance and history play a role.[23]

Specialization can extend across technical dimensions as well. For instance, even in areas such as engineering design, the safety level that is built into equipment is not universally defined. It is through internal practice that firms work out tolerances that are considered acceptable for their products.[24]

---

20. Williamson has qualified his earlier statements about the pervasiveness of opportunism. See Williamson 1985, especially the appendix to chap. 2. In contrast, Badcock (1986) describes subtle deceit in many important interpersonal contexts and develops evolutionary arguments for its pervasiveness. Finally, Koford and Penno (1989) show how organizations will create incentives to obtain more ethical agents as employees.

21. At Naval Supply Centers, employees do inventories of warehouses, and reports are then filed with headquarters. The expectation is that the reports will find that a high percentage of the items warehoused will be in the correct location. If employees know that a warehouse will fail the test, they inventory a good warehouse along with the poor one. They then average the two together and report that inventory accuracy is satisfactory. Such behavior is tolerated. Apparently total fabrication of the report is not.

22. Kreps (1984) sees corporate culture as simple principles that are communicated to all concerned. He argues that a firm's existence depends on its reputation. Its reputation, in turn, depends on how consistently it acts. But "reputations are assets fairly specialized and immutable once created." Like norms, then, social sanctions are applied when behavior is not consistent with previous practice.

23. Abrams (1983) studies language as used by economists. He notes that notation in economics textbooks varies considerably for identical concepts, and points out that, in a similar way, there are more different human languages than seem necessary for efficiency.

24. The different level of tolerances can cause serious problems when firms are working jointly to make components of a large project. Pate-Cornell (1989) discusses these problems as

If customs and norms in an organization differ from those of the larger society, how do such specialized customs and norms arise? How can the organization control their development? That organizations are concerned about such questions is apparent from the literature on corporate culture. Examples also exist where businesses have manipulated their corporate cultures. The decision by Japanese automobile manufacturers to set up plants in the United States provides a case in point. When the Japanese arrived, they not only tried to locate in areas where the work force might have appropriate work habits but also tried to influence the atmosphere of the plants.

The ability to determine corporate culture has its limits, however. The internal work ethic, an important aspect of corporate culture, varies greatly among firms and often does not support the goals of the organization (Leibenstein 1987). In some organizations, rewards are based on relative performance. In this "rat race," workers compete to succeed, and success is defined in very individualistic terms. Teamwork frequently suffers. Other organizations consist of many workgroups where rewards are group related. In these environments, informal norms or quotas for work often evolve. Working too much or accomplishing too much can lead to social sanctions.[25]

Many difficulties also have to be surmounted when attempting to change ongoing practices. Different corporate cultures are often cited as a source of difficulty when two organizations attempt to merge. Such events can be very threatening to people working in these organizations, since it is not possible to discern the full implications of the changes. Customs and norms are, by their nature, long-standing and rarely subject to challenge. With a merger, actions that have long gone unquestioned will be evaluated. Activity that was previously in the unreflective sphere is suddenly thrust into the reflective sphere. This inspection and evaluation of previously routine operations greatly increases the initial cost of a merger. Still, the customs and norms of the other organization provide a focal point when a search is undertaken to determine how arrangements should be restructured, reducing the cost of new social capital.[26]

Resistance to change occurs partly because individuals have become accustomed to certain practices and partly because these practices represent an investment for these individuals. Abandoning these practices is a devaluation

---

they relate to the space shuttle, and Pate-Cornell and Seawell (1988) address these issues in the context of general safety concerns.

25. Sometimes even a "rat race" environment can be subverted by strong group norms not to excel.

26. The concept of zero-based budgeting is similar in its intent. By reviewing all operations, not just those that are likely to change, it attempts to increase efficiency. This is a very costly procedure, since the scope of the review is so broad. It is likely to succeed only if more efficient methods are found or new objectives are determined. However, zero-based budgeting itself does not provide direction in finding these new methods or directions.

of the capital that they have built up over time. Furthermore, not everyone affected by the change will necessarily see it as beneficial. Since customs and norms represent the foundation upon which other actions are taken, changing them means entering a realm that is very uncertain. This increases people's resistance.[27]

Tradition

Just as tradition was the principal organizing force in primitive societies, it can also be a dominant organizational force in modern society. The family is an important production unit that is organized largely along traditional lines. As elsewhere in the economy, specialization can increase productivity. Family members take on different roles. Some roles have traditionally been identified as male or female responsibilities. A particular family may follow tradition, or bargaining may be used to assign responsibilities. Other duties are assigned to children who are told what to do.

Yet, dramatic social changes have occurred in recent years. These changes have created enormous pressures for families to move away from traditional roles. These adjustments have been a paradox to economists. The cultural norm was that men worked and women kept house—a division of labor. As women have increased the number of hours they work outside the home in recent years, it would make sense for the time they spend on housework to fall and for men's hours to rise. The hours women spend has fallen, but men's hours have risen very little. The difference has been made up by purchasing more services on the market. As telling as the number of hours is the glacial change in the specific tasks men and women do in the household. There is a strong tendency to follow traditional patterns (Bergmann 1986; Gronau 1976; Juster 1985).

These observations are consistent with a theory that customary practice is an important element in organizing households, and that such customs and norms will change slowly.[28] Furthermore, while the pressures to change are significant, an operational focal point for a new set of standards has not developed. So while change is occurring, there is uneasiness about the new arrangements.[29]

---

27. *Bureaucratic resistance* has some of the same properties. When changes are proposed for an organization, individuals, not wishing to devalue the capital they have acquired in doing things "the old way," will try to incorporate them into presently existing patterns of behavior. This can greatly distort the original intent of the change.

28. See Bergmann 1986 (267) for a critique of the neoclassical approach to this problem. Hochschild (1989) presents several case studies and surveys other work in the area. She notes that even when women earn more than men, women still do relatively more of the housework.

29. There is an argument that a more equal division of housekeeping tasks is a reasonable focal point. Even husbands who subscribe to the egalitarian ethic do little more housework than the others (Hochschild 1989). For a discussion of alternative ethics, see Bergmann 1986 (271).

Explicit recognition of the importance of habit, custom, and norms provides a straightforward explanation of many economic puzzles. In a variety of institutional settings, we observe more stability and more resistance to change than can be easily explained by models that omit these factors.

Habit, Custom, and Norms in Economic Analysis

Thus far we have argued that descriptions of economic behavior should recognize the persistent social patterns associated with habit, custom, and norms. Good analysis, however, tries to simplify reality; cutting through the complexity of observed events to concentrate on those aspects that are the principal determinants of outcomes. This section provides some additional examples that show how explicit recognition of these persistent patterns in the analysis can improve our understanding of important economic problems.

In a few cases the effect of these additional factors have been included in economic analysis. Thus, in the literature on the principal-agent problem, which deals with the problem of asymmetric information, incentives are devised to encourage agents to reveal information honestly or to perform a task where the principal has insufficient knowledge to proceed without assistance. Many complicated schemes can be devised to generate optimal incentives, but most are second best in the sense that not all the multiple objectives can be reached. In addition, many of the incentive schemes are very complex and would be difficult to implement in the real world.

Most of these models assume that agents will act opportunistically. Another solution to these incentive problems is for agents to develop codes of ethical conduct. Arrow (1973) argues that many professional organizations attempt to establish such codes because they recognize that the informational asymmetry in the principal-agent relationship can lead to abuse. If an ethical code is not established, the profession will suffer.

In labor markets, Akerlof (1980) argues that more than one equilibrium is possible with different social norms.[30] If the norm is discrimination, the social cost of hiring a black person may be very great. In another regime where people are less discriminatory, a different equilibrium can result.[31]

This notion that there can be several equilibria that depend on others' behavior also underlies the recent work on hysteresis. These theories have been used to explain European unemployment experience (e.g., Blanchard and Summers 1988). *Hysteresis* is a term derived from physics that refers to the failure of an object to return to its previous position after a disturbance

---

30. Our social norms are similar to Akerlof's term *custom.*

31. Kuran (1987) points out that in some instances the disadvantaged group will support the existing norm. He provides a rationale for the support that lower castes give to the Indian social system.

ends. One possible explanation for such behavior in economics is the adjustment of behavior constrained by custom. While there is resistance to change because of customary behavior, once change occurs, new patterns will be maintained as the new customary practice. It becomes difficult to dislodge these new practices; the removal of the original disturbance may not be enough to move economic behavior back to its original position, as standard economic theory would predict.[32]

Customary behavior may also explain regularities that otherwise seem paradoxical. For example, price markups are remarkably constant over long periods of time (Cyert and March 1963). But why do these markups differ from one country to another? Similarly, we know that shares in sharecropping societies are inexplicably constant.[33]

Such examples show that habit, custom, and norms play a role in a very broad range of economic issues. Still, direct reference to these factors in the economics literature is quite limited. Yet, along with laws, these factors help define the framework within which economic activity takes place. The recognition that laws influence the economic environment has led to extensive analysis of the effect of legal changes in property rights. Going beyond this, economists have also asked how and why laws are changed.

Just as models recognizing the importance of laws on economic behavior have also been used to examine why laws change, a more complete model of the influence of habits, customs, and norms needs to explain how they change. If we understood how customs and norms came into being, the theory could be applied more generally and would have more predictive content.[34] Beyond the fact that there is resistance to changing these features of the economic landscape, we know very little about the process. We do know that attempts are sometimes made to control change. When management attempts to control corporate culture or a profession establishes a code of ethical conduct, efforts are being made to influence norms of behavior. We know less about the reasons for success and failure in these situations.

Sometimes technology drives change.[35] The medical profession has always seen its principal duty as keeping people alive as long as possible. Recent advances in medical knowledge have made it possible to extend life by

---

32. Recent advanced theoretical models in which there are large fixed costs that constrain adjustment may be able to explain these patterns. However, they are complex explanations for a simple, well-established phenomenon.

33. See Ransom and Sutch 1977 (89–91). Shaban (1987) finds that share rules in India are consistently applied within small local areas, but the rules will differ between communities only a few miles apart.

34. Jones (1984) makes a similar point. He presents a theory that explains the development of custom by expanding the behavior model of economic man to include the need to conform.

35. Institutionalists see technological change as the driving force for change and "ceremonial" behavior as a constraint. See Bush 1987 for a survey of this area.

novel techniques, but the expense in keeping people alive and the characteristics of that "life" have raised doubts about whether this is the right thing to do—whether the old norm still makes sense. The debate over "the right to die" has been couched in strongly emotional and moral terms—what should the norms be?—not in terms of costs and benefits.

This example shows that the interaction between norms and the economy is not necessarily driven by efficiency, as Griffith and Goldfarb's discussion of norms makes clear. The relationship is not well understood. Sometimes norms change and the economy responds. In other situations, economic pressures will cause norms to change.

The women's movement is a case where changes in customs and norms have had widespread economic consequences. When women entered the labor force in large numbers, women had less time to devote to various nonpaid activities both inside and outside the household. As a result, traditional social patterns have been under pressure to adjust. New demands have been placed on the market to provide additional services, such as child-care. Business is being asked to provide new forms of maternity leave. Nonprofit organizations are attempting to survive with less volunteer labor. In many of these areas there has been resistance to change. Society still seems to be groping for appropriate "new" customs.

Concluding Remarks

Habit, custom, and norms are an important influence on economic behavior. Because of the complexity of the economic environment we rely on habit, custom, and norms to determine most of our actions. As a consequence, we are closer to being satisficers than maximizers.

Along with laws, these factors provide a structure within which economic activity takes place. Because they are an important part of the social capital that lets the economic system function more smoothly, people resist changing them. This adds to the stability of the economic climate. Ignoring these factors can lead to complex explanations of simple phenomena and, in other instances, can lead to faulty predictions about how the economic system will change.

When changes in habits, customs, and norms do occur, the impact can be large. Understanding how and why these factors change can, therefore, improve our knowledge of how economic systems change.

REFERENCES

Abrams, B. 1983. "An Economic Analysis of the Language Market." *Journal of Economic Education* 14 (Summer): 40–47.

Abreu, D., and A. Rubinstein. 1988. "Structure of Nash Equilibrium in Repeated Games with Finite Automata." *Econometrica* 56:1259–82.

Akerlof, G. 1980. "A Theory of Social Custom, of Which Unemployment May Be a Consequence." *Quarterly Journal of Economics* 44:749–76.

Akerlof, G. 1983. "Loyalty Filters." *American Economic Review* 73:54–63.

Arthur, B. 1989. "Competing Technologies, Increasing Returns, and Lock-in by Historical Events." *Economic Journal* 99:116–31.

Arrow, K. 1973. "Social Responsibility and Economic Efficiency." *Public Policy* 21:303–18.

Axelrod, R. 1986. "An Evolutionary Approach to Norms." *American Political Science Review* 80:1095–1112.

Badcock, C. R. 1986. *The Problem of Altruism: Freudian-Darwinian Solutions.* Oxford: Blackwell.

Banks, J. S., and R. K. Sundaram. 1989. "Repeated Games, Finite Automata, and Complexity." Working Paper, University of Rochester.

Bergmann, B. 1986. *The Economic Emergence of Women.* New York: Basic Books.

Blanchard, O., and L. Summers. 1988. "Beyond the Natural Rate Hypothesis." *American Economic Review* 78:182–87.

Bush, P. 1987. "The Theory of Institutional Change." *Journal of Economic Issues* 21:1075–1116.

Camic, C. 1986. "The Matter of Habit." *American Journal of Sociology* 91:1039–87.

Coleman, J. 1987. "Norms as Social Capital." In *Economic Imperialism: The Economic Method Applied Outside the Field of Economics,* ed. G. Radnitzky and P. Bernhoz. New York: Paragon House.

Cyert, R., and J. March. 1963. *A Behavioral Theory of the Firm.* Englewood Cliffs, N.J.: Prentice-Hall.

Elster, J. 1989. "Social Norms and Economic Theory." *Journal of Economic Perspectives* 4:99–117.

Frank, R. 1987. "If *Homo Economicus* Could Choose His Own Utility Function, Would He Want One with a Conscience?" *American Economic Review* 77:593–604.

Granovetter, M. 1985. "Economic Action and Social Structure: The Problem of Embeddedness." *American Journal of Sociology* 90:481–510.

Gronau, R. 1976. "The Allocation of Time of Israeli Women." *Journal of Political Economy* 84:S201–20.

Hayek, F. 1945. "The Use of Knowledge in Society." *American Economic Review* 35:519–30.

Heilbroner, R. 1980. *The Making of Economic Society.* 6th ed. Englewood Cliffs, N.J.: Prentice-Hall.

Heiner, R. 1983. "The Origin of Predictable Behavior." *American Economic Review* 73:560–95.

Hochschild, A. 1989. *The Second Shift: Working Parents and the Revolution at Home.* New York: Viking.

Jones, Stephen R. G. 1984. *The Economics of Conformism.* London: Blackwell.

Juster, F. 1985. "A Note on Recent Changes in Time Use." In *Time, Goods, and Well-Being,* ed. F. T. Juster and F. P. Stafford. Ann Arbor, Mich.: Survey Research Center, Institute of Social Research, University of Michigan.

Kahneman, D., J. Knetsch, and R. Thaler. 1986. "Fairness as a Constraint on Profit Seeking: Entitlements in the Market." *American Economic Review* 76:728–41.

Knight, F. 1957. "Comment on Boulding." *American Economic Review* 47:18–21.

Koford, K., and M. Penno. 1989. Equilibrium in Markets and Organizations When Some Agents Are Ethical." Presented at the annual meeting of the American Political Science Association, Washington, D.C., 1988. Revised July 1989.

Kreps, D. 1984. "Corporate Culture and Economic Theory." Paper prepared for the Second Mitsubishi Bank Foundation Conference on Technology and Business Strategy, Stanford University.

Kuran, T. 1987. "Preference Falsification, Policy Continuity, and Collective Conservatism." *Economic Journal* 97:642–65.

Kuran, T. 1988. "The Tenacious Past: Theories of Personal and Collective Conservatism." *Journal of Economic Behavior and Organization* 10:143–71.

Leibenstein, H. 1987. *Inside the Firm*. Cambridge, Mass.: Harvard University Press.

North, D. 1981. *Structure and Change in Economic History*. New York: Norton.

North, D. 1988. "Institutions and a Transaction Cost Theory of Exchange." Political Economy Working Paper no. 130, Washington University.

Okun, A. 1981. *Prices and Quantities: A Macroeconomic Analysis*. Washington, D.C.: Brookings.

Ouchi, W. 1980. "Markets, Bureaucracies, and Clans." *Administrative Science Quarterly* 25:120–42.

Pate-Cornell, M. 1989. "Organizational Extensions of PRA Models and NASA Application." In *Proceedings of PSA 89 International Topical Meetings on Probability, Reliability, and Safety Assessment*. La Grange Park, Ill.: American Nuclear Society.

Pate-Cornell, M., and J. Seawell. 1988. "Engineering Reliability: The Organizational Link." In *Proceedings of the Fifth ASCE Specialty Conference on Probabilistic Methods in Civil Engineering*. New York: American Society of Civil Engineers.

Polanyi, K., C. Arenberg, and H. Pearson, eds. 1957. *Trade and Market in the Early Empires*. New York: Free Press.

Ransom, R. L., and R. Sutch. 1977. *One Kind of Freedom: The Economic Consequences of Emancipation*. New York: Cambridge University Press.

Schelling, T. 1978. *Micromotives and Macrobehavior*. New York: Norton.

Shaban, R. A. 1987. "Testing between Competing Models of Sharecropping." *Journal of Political Economy* 95:893–920.

Simon, H. 1972. "Theories of Bounded Rationality." In *Decision and Organization: A Volume in Honor of Jacob Marschak*, ed. C. B. McGuire and R. Radner. London: North-Holland.

Sudgen, R. 1989. "Spontaneous Order." *Journal of Economic Perspectives* 4:85–97.

Trivers, R. 1985. *Social Evolution*. Menlo Park, Calif.: Benjamin/Cummings.

Ullman-Margalit, E. 1977. *The Emergence of Norms*. Oxford: Oxford University Press.

Weber, M. 1968. *Economy and Society*. New York: Bedminster Press.

Williamson, O. 1975. *Markets and Hierarchies: Analysis and Antitrust Implications*. New York: Free Press.

Williamson, O. 1985. *The Economic Institutions of Capitalism*. New York: Free Press.

Part 2
Can the "Rational Egoist" Model Be Expanded to Include Norms?

The standard economic model of preferences includes a rational egoist. This individual can be both self-interested and altruistic, but so far does *not* pay any attention to norms. In two essays, William Griffith and Robert Goldfarb describe the nature of norms and examine how they might be included in economists' models of rational choice. Their first essay examines the way norms are described in ethics and philosophy, emphasizing the close connection between personal norms and social norms, and they show that "maximizing utility" appears to describe normative choices poorly. Their second essay examines specific ways in which norms could be included in the "rational egoist" models of economics and other social sciences. Norms could be considered as elements of people's utilities or as constraints on behavior, but both of these approaches have disadvantages. Griffith and Goldfarb consider it more attractive to view norms as preferences, but find that no current approach seems fully satisfactory.

The remaining chapters in Part 2 comment on the Griffith and Goldfarb arguments. In "The Trouble with Norms," Timothy Brennan argues that the comparative statics approach to empirical work allows economists to obtain clear and useful predictions without requiring a detailed understanding of peoples' utility functions or of their internal norms. In any case, Brennan argues, the relatively static framework chosen by Griffith and Goldfarb neglects the way we learn about our values—by experience, which gradually modifies and enriches our understanding of our preferences. In "Norms versus Laws: Economic Theory and the Choice of Social Institutions," Mark A. Cohen discusses the social benefits of norms enforced by law. He notes, however, that laws sometimes have serious disadvantages. In these circumstances society may encourage the development of feelings of moral obligation to do what is right. Neither law nor moral obligations are likely to be efficient in the economic sense.

Dennis Mueller's "Comments" argues that the practical use of economic theory does not really require an analysis of what norms "really" are to people. Norms can be treated as constraints or values or in various other ways that are mathematically tractable. All of these can lead to predictions that are empirically testable. The ability to test and falsify the theory is far more important than how norms are incorporated into the formal model. Mueller also points out the merits of a social development approach to preferences: people obtain many of their preferences from their families and through their personal experience.

Griffith and Goldfarb's "Response to our Commentators" argues that norms are important as a paradigm rather than just an element in the economist's toolbox. Norms are a part of one's view of the world and should be analyzed in those terms.

Amending the Economist's "Rational Egoist" Model to Include Moral Values and Norms, Part 1: The Problem

William B. Griffith and Robert S. Goldfarb

. . . the moral order established by general norms of behavior and abstract rules of conduct is decisively important. Such rules have to guide behavior. . . . They lower uncertainty among members of society concerning the probable range of each other's behavior. They contribute in this way to the coordination of social life in complex societies. Norms and rules thus act as constraints which are advantageously respected. No society without a moral order can function and survive in competition with other societies with more moral order. (Brunner 1987, 317)

What does it mean for society to "enforce its values by personal ethical standards or social norms," and what has that topic got to do with the economist's "rational egoist" model of individual choice? In this chapter, we set out some issues associated with this topic, and explain why analyzing the economic paradigm may have some bearing on them.

Moral Guidance and "Economic Man"

We substitute the terms *guidance* or *coordination* for *enforcement* because the force with which moral values and norms guide behavior is a point of debate.

Coordination by Moral Values/Norms

The following brief stories, which we think would be widely accepted in our culture, portray some ways in which our society might guide individual choice to produce outcomes deemed socially desirable.

The authors are grateful for support from a Dilthey Fellowship during the summer of 1987, and for helpful comments from Ken Koford, Michael McPherson, Stephen Smith, and partici-

Consider how our society might picture an adult individual going about the activities of daily life. Imagine this person seeking employment: one might think of this individual as considering job offers reflecting the value employers would place on his services, and choosing the offer which gives him the most favorable combination of whatever he values: pay, status, power, vacation time, etc. He may not choose the activity he would most prefer to be engaged in, just in itself. Instead, his choice reflects the intersection of what he prefers and what others value; his choice can be described as guided by a structured labor market. Similarly, we think of how he spends his pay, how much and where he saves or invests (e.g., for some combination of income, growth, and safety) as guided by markets for goods and investments. In all of these cases, however, the individual may also be factoring into his decisions social evaluations not necessarily reflected in the prices he faces, e.g., if he chooses the life of a poorly paid social worker or an impoverished artist over better-paying opportunities.

In a quite parallel way, we may suppose the same individual to be refraining from some activities (e.g., from driving away in a car he does not own but finds with a key in the ignition) and undertaking some others he quite dislikes (e.g., filling out a complicated report on his income and paying taxes on it, taking time off from work to serve on a jury, etc.). In these areas, he is guided by explicit requirements of the law, backed up by sanctions for failure to comply, although again, in accepting guidance here he may well also be considering how nonofficial members of the society (e.g., his relatives, neighbors, co-workers) might react to learning of his failure to comply.

Consider another type of decision this same individual might face, and what guidance society might offer about his actions. Suppose his college education has been paid for in part by an older sibling, and he is now asked by family members to divert a major part of his discretionary income toward a younger sibling's college tuition bills. There is probably no legally enforceable contract here, even if, at the time of accepting help, he had more or less explicitly promised to help in return. Nonetheless, if he is reluctant to help, there is likely to be significant pressure on him to accede: argument, personal criticism, perhaps insistently repeated "reminders," ultimately even ostracism within the family.

To a lesser degree, the same individual would probably be "guided" by society toward stopping to help an elderly person whose car had run off the

pants in presentations at the George Washington University Socioeconomics Seminar, the Conference on Enforcement of Social Values at the University of Delaware, the University of Maryland Baltimore County Economics Department, the National Economists' Club in Washington, D.C., the Society of Government Economists in Washington, D.C., and the Conference on Socioeconomics at the Harvard Business School.

road in an isolated area. To a still lesser degree, contributing some funds to a citywide charity campaign or participating in a neighborhood or building committee might be seen to be a socially defined and (if necessary) "enforced" obligation, even though in this country (at least with rare exceptions) there would not be any legal liability for failing to be a "good samaritan" (Kaplan 1978, 291ff.).

We offer four remarks about these sketches, admitting that these interpretations may be more controversial than the sketches themselves. First, even in the case of market guidance, we have suggested that most people would take it as common sense that nonmarket incentives that reflect moral evaluations may hover in the neighborhood, though economic analysis often ignores such supplementary incentives.

Second, in the case of legal rules, one typically supposes that it is not always the threat of sanctions alone that induces people to do what the law demands. Again, however, economic analysis typically pays little attention to this aspect of law-abidingness, except for special cases such as reporting income for tax purposes.

Third, it seems reasonable to suppose that in the college tuition scenario, the individual's decision may well be responsive to the social guidance he is getting, despite the absence of either clear market incentives or legal liability for nonperformance. Of course, any given individual might well defy social pressure to contribute, and go his own way. True enough, but individuals also refuse to let market incentives dictate all decisions (e.g., in accepting a lower return to invest in a "socially responsible" corporation's stock) and, clearly, many disobey the law despite its coercive inducement to obey. By itself, this "failure of influence" does not distinguish the three forms of guidance.

Fourth, we note some apparent advantages to social guidance by moral norms and values. It is by now well understood that market incentives can and do sometimes produce socially undesirable results, as, for example, in cases of pollution, or when rapidly advancing technology in a situation of intense competition leads firms to rush into a technologically complex new process of production or offer a new, high-tech product without reasonably effective testing for a socially desirable level of safety protection for workers and consumers. But it is also well known that regulation by statute or administrative rule making often lags seriously behind inventive evasion and is, moreover, often unreasonably restrictive and inflexible (cf. Bardach and Kagan 1982). In such situations there might be advantages to relying on individual judgments, "conscientiously" applying general moral rules to complex new situations in ways that do not require the cumbersome process involved in establishing and applying legislative or regulatory restraints or, alternatively, in the after-the-harm-is-done, grotesquely expensive tort liability system.

Of course there might very well be disadvantages to relying on moral norms and values as well. For example, moral judgments by firms and individuals should be more flexible, contextual, and unrestricted by complicated procedures than legal decisions. But if we presume that effective moral codes require some social pressures analogous to legal sanctions to be effective, we must recognize that such social sanctions will similarly be applied without benefit of detailed factual inquiry or evenhanded procedural protections. Thus, innocent persons may suffer while skillfully deceptive or powerful offenders may escape. On more purely economic criteria, other disadvantages may also be present.

A major question raised by these alternatives is the following: Why is it, as Kenneth Arrow has remarked (1967, 9), that our society has "tended to minimize noncoercive obligations relative to the predominant role they have played elsewhere"? Why do we generally treat, with scoffing cynicism, suggestions that we as a society might more often systematically attempt to appeal to individuals' sense of moral obligation?[1] And why do we generally seem so oblivious to the role (noticed above) played by moral values and norms in complementing market and legal guidance of individual choice?

Our Starting Point

We suggest as our analytical starting point one particular factor contributing to our society's limited reliance on moral obligation: the increasing dominance, in our public discourse about public policies and institutional structures, of the classical economic model of the rational individual decision maker. This model has traditionally provided no conceptual room for explicit consideration of these noncoercive obligations in many choices.

Rather than defending this claim of the influence of "economic man" models, we accept it to develop a derivative topic. Our focus will be on some recent literature in economics and philosophy containing interesting suggestions about the possibility and desirability of integrating moral values and norms into the basic microeconomic model of the economic agent. We offer some brief remarks justifying attention to this topic before proceeding to develop it.

First, in the nineteenth century, economists (e.g., Mill 1877) defended the model of economic man as a double abstraction, that is, as applying to individuals only in those activities in which "wealth getting" was the dominant purpose, and even then applying only when corrected for the extent that other motives entered in a particular case. But in recent years, economists

---

1. The literature on professionals and their codes is full of such cynicism. For a useful compilation of studies, many of which manifest this point of view, see Blair and Rubin 1980.

have vigorously applied this economic model to a variety of behaviors not normally recognized as directed toward "wealth getting," such as voting behavior, lobbying of legislators and regulators, choice of family size, etc. (Hirshleifer 1985). Moreover, this movement, sometimes referred to as "economic imperialism," has been powerfully influential and probably will become more so (Radnitzky and Bernholz 1987). To the extent that the economic model of man retains its traditional features, it will continue to crowd out attention to the role of moral values and norms. But if the economic model, with its explicit attention to the interdependence of individual choices, is susceptible of modification to include moral values and norms, it might provide an improved framework for analysis. In particular, it might allow more systematic consideration of the interaction of moral values and norms with other incentives and social structures, issues that have not so far been satisfactorily addressed by philosophers, political scientists, or sociologists. As has recently been pointed out, there are difficult but important questions about the consistency of an admixture of altruism and egoism with attainment of a Pareto-optimal equilibrium (Kolm 1983), and serious questions about the "costs of creating and maintaining a social norm" (Bergsten 1985, 115). Economists might well provide a useful conceptual framework for answering these questions. After all, as Arrow and Hahn noted in an oft-quoted passage, it is one of the great intellectual triumphs of economics to have shown the theoretical coherence of the disposition of economic resources in a "decentralized economy motivated by self-interest and guided by price signals" (1971, vii) and it would seem worthwhile to try to build on this foundation to answer somewhat broader questions.

Second, and on the other side of the coin, there would seem to be some danger in placing too much reliance on the economic model of man as currently understood. Two dangers stand out in particular. The first is a tendency of economists, when pressed about the narrowness of the concept of "self-interested" man to which they appeal, to defend the claim of universal self-interested behavior by simply taking any behavior as ipso facto "self-interested" when chosen by some self, which reduces the hypothesis to a nontestable tautology (see McPherson 1984, 77; Stigler 1981, 189). The second danger is that of the postulate of universal self-interested action taking on the status of what Robert Merton called a "self-fulfilling prophecy"; that is, a statement which is false to the facts at the time asserted but which becomes subsequently true because it is believed to be true (cf. Grofman 1974). This would appear to be an especial danger resulting from the thriving application of the economic model to the understanding of issues of public choice (Oppenheimer 1985).

In the remainder of this section, we sketch what we take to be a traditional, "standard" model of the economic decision maker, and note briefly the stimulus provided by recent well-noticed efforts by prominent economists to provide constructive suggestions for how this standard model might be modified to take into account moral values and/or norms.[2]

In the second section of this chapter, we organize and analyze the various reasons offered in the economics literature for attempting to integrate moral values or norms into the economic model of man. Finally, the third section develops some of the formidable problems this project engenders.

The "Standard Model" of Economic Choice

To be more explicit we briefly sketch what we take to be the traditional, "standard" economic model of economic decision making or choice, the target model for adding moral elements.

The Rational Self-Interested Maximizer

From the early 1870s until around 1960, when economists began to give sustained consideration to models incorporating substantial imperfections of knowledge and foresight, there gradually developed what we will call the traditional or "standard" model of the economic decision maker. This model still has enormous importance because economists usually try to minimize departures from it, whatever the complications in decision making being considered. This instinct itself is attributable to the usefulness and analytic power that results from embedding the model in the competitive market equilibrium framework, as Arrow has pointed out (Arrow 1987, 203). It should be noted that this model constitutes a paradigm rather than a specific theory (Hogarth and Reder 1987, 2); its application in particular contexts usually requires specific "supplementary assumptions" (Arrow 1987, 205–6). A key issue turns out to be just which supplementary assumptions consistently cohere with it.

Features of the model central to our purpose are summarized below; recognizing that there may be some disagreement in the details, we nonetheless offer this as a useful compilation from diverse sources.[3]

Self-Interested, or "Egoistic"

This property seems to have emerged as part of the historical attempt to construct an idealized theory of "perfect market exchange" for a private

---

2. In a companion paper (Goldfarb and Griffith n.d.), we have developed at some length our reasons for believing that the central core of assumptions in economics remains typically impervious to criticism, no matter how cogent, unless accompanied by explicit suggestions about how the paradigm might be modified to respond to the criticisms and still retain most of its former uses.

3. A fuller account of the historical development of this model will be available in our companion paper (Goldfarb and Griffith n.d.). Probably the single most helpful historical source to be noted is Stigler 1957; a useful contemporary source is Hogarth and Reder 1987.

ownership economy. For markets to function perfectly and arrive at a determinate price, it was thought necessary to posit the individual agent as "exchanging from a pure regard to his own requirements or private interests . . . anyone will exchange with anyone else for the slightest apparent advantage. There must be no conspiracies . . . " (Jevons 1871, 133). In the context of a private ownership economy, the naturally postulated goal of transactions is increased individual control over resources for want-satisfaction. "Each controls his own actions with a view to results that accrue to him individually" (Knight 1921, 77). *Wants* are taken as given and independent of what others want or possess, for reasons that appear to have their historical roots in the hedonistic psychology of the early marginalists. That some good or service satisfies a want of an agent, hence gives pleasure, is taken as a matter of fact (this differs from many ethical theories, such as Stoicism, which suppose that one can alter or renounce a want, or cease to accept its fulfillment as pleasurable). Thus, it is on the facts about "just perceivable increments of pleasure" that the science of economics might be built (Edgeworth 1881, 99).

Rational Maximizer
To appreciate the traditional meaning of rational maximization, one needs to see clearly the gradually emerging picture of the decision-making context as developed by economists in the later nineteenth and early twentieth centuries. Agents are stipulated to have *perfect knowledge* of the (real) current stage of affairs (offers, demands, their own and others' production technology, etc.); they also possess an ability to discern the *entire set of feasible actions* in the situation; further, because equipped with *unlimited capability* to calculate the outcomes of actions (as in Newtonian mechanics), economic agents, as Frank Knight said, "are supposed to know absolutely the consequences of their acts and to perform them in the light of their consequences" (1921, 77). The latter clause means that agents act on the basis of a deliberate (later interpreted as complete and consistent) ranking of the outcomes, given their preferences. Constraints are also taken as simply given: "There must be no way of acquiring goods except through production and exchange in the free market" (Knight 1921, 78). *Rationality* here simply means picking the most highly ranked alternative.

For future purposes we add some brief interpretative remarks to this sketchy summary. First, this is a theory of what Jon Elster (1985) calls "thin rationality," in that reason's only activity is the selection of the best means to ends, and no process of reflecting on (and thereby changing) tastes is envisioned, nor presumably is there any difficulty in the ranking of outcomes, given those tastes. Nor does rationality have any reference to the well-foundedness of the beliefs on which action is based, given the assumption of perfect knowledge and foresight.

Second, the enduring attraction of maximization as an interpretation of rationality for economists may be partly explainable in terms of mathematical tractability. That is, economists may be so wedded to a model of rational choice as maximizing nonlinear utility functions subject to linear constraints because they have convenient techniques from calculus to deal with such formulations. Is the special convenience of this calculus-driven version of thin rationality a major determinant of economists' preferences for this particular rational choice framework?

Third, the theory describes the agent as being affected not at all by whether others do well, poorly, better, or worse than the agent, etc. This represents a point between malevolence, which is usually worse, and benevolence, which might be thought to be better. In any case, as Boulding once remarked (1969, 6), "Anything less descriptive of the human condition could hardly be imagined."

Fourth, given the embedding of this economic decision maker in the context of perfectly competitive markets, with no agent able to exercise market power and all economic factors on which decisions are based taken as given parameters, it apparently was presumed that all that one needs to know about others' interests and choices would be reflected in the market. Of course, this assumes an absence of externalities and an "acceptable" distribution of resources so that all have something to offer and can make effective demands in the market, but this again was not taken as something the individual economic agent needed to be concerned about.

Some Stimulating Suggestions

In contrast to this "standard" model of the economic decision maker, there have recently appeared a number of sophisticated criticisms articulated by well-known economists. Many have focused mainly on the rationality assumption, but three economists in particular caught our attention because of their focus on the "egoism" property and stimulated this inquiry. The first was Amartya Sen's "Rational Fools" (1977); the second, Albert Hirschman's "Against Parsimony" (1985); and the third, Jack Hirshleifer's "Expanding Domain of Economics" (1985). What struck us was that these criticisms were offered by very prominent figures in the mainstream of contemporary work; they combined far-reaching criticisms of what one referred to as economists' "tunnel vision about the nature of man and social interaction" with constructive suggestions about how the paradigm might be modified to incorporate some elements of moral values or norms. All appeared to suggest that economics had reached a new stage in its development as a discipline that made problems, earlier pushed to one side, no longer avoidable.

As we began to investigate this literature, we found it lacked the integration and intellectual connections among contributors needed to make further analytic progress; the conversation or debate needed to advance the discussion was missing. This made it extraordinarily difficult to evaluate and appraise. In general, this body of work seemed disconnected, yet considerable conceptual overlap exists. The use of moral terminology was often confusingly nonstandard or loose, and alternative possibilities were seldom systematically explored. So we took as our first task analyzing and organizing the literature in a systematic way. It is this first project, trying to get an overview in order to begin to appraise promising directions, that is reported in this and the following chapter.

We now turn, therefore, to an analysis of the various kinds of justifications offered in the economics literature for considering the modification of the microeconomic paradigm by the incorporation of moral values or norms.

Reasons Given in the Economics Literature for Introducing Moral Values or Norms

There are both positive and normative economics arguments for incorporating moral values and norms. These are not always easy to keep perfectly separate, but the rough division helps to reveal the diverse nature of the justifications offered.

Positive Economics

Positive economics embodies economics-as-social-science description, theory, and explanation. For those economists who adopt Milton Friedman's views about methodology, the only sound motivation for considering change in the core of the microeconomic paradigm is predictive failure. Other economists find justification for considering such changes in experimental and introspective evidence of increasingly severe conceptual problems. These problems make the standard defenses for excluding moral considerations less and less compelling. We have tried to focus on those justificatory arguments that seem to carry more weight or typify an important class of concerns.

Possible Help with Predictive Problems
We start with a sample of problems encountered in more traditional economic fields that have led some critics to suggest incorporating moral concepts: (*a*) the "stickiness" of prices and, especially, wages, which some see as suggesting the potential explanatory role of loyalty between buyers and sellers in preventing (i) maximum feasible markups when demand sharply exceeds supply, and (ii) wage cutting when excess labor supply exists (Akerlof 1980 and 1984; Okun 1983); (*b*) difficulties in explaining the structure of wages, which some critics have attributed to the linkage of relative wage expectations, and the importance of concern among both employers and employees

for something like fairness (Solow 1980; Stiglitz 1986, 182ff; Thurow 1975 and 1985); (c) the private provision of public goods, which some observers claim to be greatly in excess of what would be predicted in a society made up only of self-interested agents. Explaining this last phenomenon may require assuming a certain amount of altruism (that is, concern for others' welfare as well as one's own) or, at least, a willingness to cooperate beyond one's narrowly defined self-interest (see Margolis 1982 for a summary of the literature).

There are also a number of newer subfields only recently seen as within the scope of application of the economic conception of man. Predictive failures here are less disturbing to many economists, being more on the periphery of economics as traditionally understood, but nonetheless appear to cast doubt on the range of applicability of the standard model. Perhaps most notable here is the economic analysis of voting behavior, which suggests that upon making an "economic" calculation of the cost in effort versus the likelihood of one's vote influencing a political outcome, no one would choose to vote. As Dennis Mueller remarked in his presidential address to the Public Choice Society (1986), this prediction has the embarrassing consequence of being off by eighty million voters or so in the last presidential election. Similarly, Hirshleifer (1985, 53) notes that there are a number of areas in which early predictive successes have been followed by puzzling failures. For example, he points out that the received theory sheds some light on criminal behavior but is unable to offer needed predictions, such as which of two persons from equally impoverished backgrounds will decide that a career of crime will be the selfishly maximizing choice.

Experimental and Introspective Evidence of
Conceptual Difficulties
There have long been worries about the adequacy of the standard economic model of man based on its dissonance with introspective experience about how people actually make decisions. Starting from almost the same time that Jevons and Edgeworth were locking into place the "perfect knowledge" assumption, T. Cliffe Leslie (1879) led the questioning of whether economic decision makers could plausibly be assumed to have such knowledge, even approximately. Similarly, in the 1930s, it was hard for many economists to reconcile their models, showing how perfect market coordination of individual decisions achieved equilibrium, with massive unemployment and many economies in disarray.

Once models of economic decision making incorporating both informational and market structure imperfections began to be admissible within mainstream economics, some additional factors began to emerge that made the old defense against paying attention to moral constraints somewhat outmoded.

For instance, if imperfectly informed agents enter transactions with different amounts of information, the possibility of such previously inconceivable (literally, in the standard model) activities as deliberate deception, shifting of risks, and discrimination against certain classes of agents became not only possible but, in the self-interested model, even uniformly predictable. Moreover, if market competition were admitted to be sometimes imperfect, then some agents might have market power, raising possibilities of coercion or collusion to gain market power.

These developments produce significant conceptual problems for the standard model, and the emergence of experimental evidence about what appears to go on in such imperfect decision-making contexts make the problems seem less and less avoidable (Kahneman, Slovic, and Tversky 1982). For example, even under mere *event uncertainty* (i.e., ignoring uncertainty about the reactions of other agents), it has been recognized (at least since the 1940s) that a rule more complicated than maximizing expected values of outcomes is needed (Marschak 1949; Tintner 1941). When one adds the necessity of taking other agents' reactions into account in modeling many "small numbers" market situations, it is clear that the requirement is for a *strategic* rule that represents the "best the agent can do," given what others may do in response to his or her actions. But this begins to resemble a situation in which there is a search for something that may turn out to be not too different from a *moral* rule of behavior. Resolutely ignoring this similarity and, hence, the rich literature available in ethical theory appears increasingly ostrichlike, as Amartya Sen has repeatedly suggested.

Further, experimental evidence (recently summarized in Kahneman, Knetsch, and Thaler 1986) appears to confirm introspective and anecdotal experience that many agents appear not to exploit every possible advantage in ways rigorously self-interested maximizers would. But then the question arises for the economic modeler of what factors, previously overlooked because apparently not needed under the stronger structural assumptions of competitive markets and perfect information, may actually be constraining the decision makers in this fashion. An example of the discovery of a role for moral norms, once any of these imperfections is admitted, is Arrow's unearthing of an economic role for professional ethics in the presence of information asymmetries creating "moral hazard" (Arrow 1963 and 1974).

Normative Economics

Historically, from Adam Smith through Pareto to Arrow, an important claim of optimality has been made for perfectly competitive markets (Arrow 1963 and 1983). The (relatively weak) sense of optimality involved, basically due to Pareto, is that, at a competitive equilibrium, no individual can improve his or her level of satisfaction without worsening the satisfaction level of someone else. The "self-interested maximization" assumption and very strong assumptions about the absence of any real uncertainty contribute to this result, because if there are advantageous trades to be made, the agents will identify and make them in the process of achieving equilibrium.

But the positive economics literature has relaxed a number of these very strong conditions. This has led some economists to wonder what other factors should get credit for allowing markets to function as well as they seem to do in the absence of perfect information and perfect competition. Phelps (1975) and McKean (1975) along with Reder (1979) and Leibenstein (1982) have suggested that, perhaps, adherence to moral values or norms actually lessens deception or coercion in real markets, but that such behavior does not receive appropriate acknowledgement by economists. Reder argues, for example, that economists fail to notice the resources wasted in attempts at self-protection and government protection from deception and shirking of obligations; an implication is that willing adherence to moral norms should lessen these resource costs. Similarly, Koford and Penno (1988) note inefficiencies arising in principal-agent relations if trustworthiness cannot be assumed and monitoring devices are expensive.

A second set of concerns about the normative contribution of moral values can be found in the literature. McPherson (1984) and Bergsten (1985) (among others) have noted the important but mostly unnoticed role of moral values or norms in supplementing legal instruments such as statutes, regulations, and detailed contractual agreements. As McPherson put it, "there are too many subtle opportunities to cheat, and too few police officers, to make it plausible that the *only* effective motives supporting moral behavior are the prospects of financial or criminal penalties for immorality" (1984, 77).[4]

A final consideration on which several writers have laid great stress is the following. Suppose that adherence to moral norms or values really does contribute significantly to Paretian social welfare, but economists fail to recognize this contribution. If this is true, then ignoring the role of moral norms will lead to a failure to see and be concerned that this important social capital may be eroding over time (Brunner 1987; Hirsch 1976). Brunner argues that this erosion of social capital implies a destruction of that moral order without which "no society . . . can function and survive in competition with other societies . . ." (Brunner 1987, 377). As Bergsten (1985, 115) puts it, "For

---

4. At a somewhat deeper conceptual level, Winch (1971, 166) has noticed a certain inconsistency in the proposal that a society made up of self-interested maximizers would adopt the Pareto optimality criterion, i.e., that a change of social states is an improvement if and only if the welfare of at least one individual is increased and none decreased. Why would solely self-interested economic agents be conceived as caring about how others fare in defining an "improved" state of affairs? Presumably, *any* self-advancing state of affairs that can somehow be imposed would count as an improvement for such agents.

social norms to work, they must be brought into being, maintained, and enforced. These activities involve costs . . ." and economists should apply their analytical apparatus to studying the generation and maintenance of norms rather than simply ignoring the whole set of questions.

Having briefly surveyed some justifications in the economic literature for incorporating moral norms into the microeconomic paradigm of the individual decision maker, we now turn to a short discussion of some of the serious difficulties with such a project.

Reasons for Caution about Attempts to Incorporate Moral Values and Norms

In our review of the wide variety of literature in this area, we have encountered numerous conceptual roadblocks that also appeared to obstruct the progress of writers in this field without their being aware of it. We present several of the most prominent under three headings: lack of clarity about the terminology being brought into economics; (perhaps as a consequence) a lack of full appreciation of how far apart the concepts of "moral man" and "economic man," as traditionally understood, should initially be seen to be; and hence, some seriously misleading "warping" of both sets of concepts to make them fit.

Lack of Clarity about Borrowed Concepts

In considering the possible linkage of moral concepts with concepts of economics, most writers seem to start with what they take to be a commonsense understanding of "everyday morality," that is, a conception of morality that they presume to be widely accepted and noncontroversial in form, at least, if not in content. They then try to see how this commonsense morality may be made to fit, to some degree, with the economic model of decision making.

What they fail to consider, however, is that ethics, or the philosophical theory of morality as developed over the generations, has by now produced a reasonable degree of consensus about what constitutes morality or "the moral viewpoint" (Baier 1958), at least within Western culture. Unless one pays some attention to more or less standard meanings of moral terms, just as one does for economic terms, there is a good chance of serious miscommunication.

Consider, for example, the concept of a *moral norm* or rule of behavior as distinguished from other sorts of norms or rules.[5] At least the following would seem ordinarily to be implied in calling a norm or rule "moral." First,

---

5. Although for some purposes the differences between *norms*, or standards against which behavior is to be judged, and *rules*, thought of as explicit enough actually to guide behavior, are important, we shall treat them as roughly equivalent here. We also leave aside questions of

the rule takes into account more than simply the immediate, narrow self-interest of the agent (as Gauthier [1986, 1] puts it succinctly, "Were duty no more than interest, morals would be superfluous"). In fact, most theoretical accounts of morality adopt a perspective as highly idealized as the classical economic model of decision making, assessing the rule from the standpoint of a completely impartial, empathetic, and fully informed observer, who considers the entire set of consequences. Second, some degree of internalization of the rule is normally presupposed, so that following the rule is not conceptually tied to the immediate risk of adverse consequences or sanctions. Third, acceptance of the rule implies, in general, a willingness to impose the rule both on oneself and on others similarly situated; that is, the rule has built in a certain generalizability or social dimension. Fourth, while to use or apply a rule "rationally" in the context of economics usually means to calculate consequences in a certain way, in moral theory *rational* often refers to a process of identifying the key features of proposed actions to determine which of several competing rules should apply. It also denotes the process of determining whether an action that apparently falls under the scope of a given rule should or should not be taken as falling within understood exceptions to that scope.

Similarly, when economists discuss the concept of *altruistic behavior,* they often fail to note that this term, as ordinarily used, means something more than "a person's utility function includes attention to other persons' welfare" (Brunner 1987, 373). Even a dictionary definition includes reference to "unselfish" concern with others' welfare (*Random House Unabridged*), or "uncalculated" consideration of others' interests (*Webster's Third International*). Certainly, in ethical theory altruism is normally taken to mean something more than mere self-constraint in the interests of self-protection from retaliation ("strategic prudence"). The term in its moral connotation includes, as does a moral rule, an element of conceptual generality, that is, a concern for others not based only on some limited factual relationship such as kinship but on general conceptual features that put the "other" on a similar footing with the agent and allows the other's interests to be weighted similarly to the agent's.

These assertions suggest considerable difficulties in coherently tying these conceptions to the economic model of decision making.

Built-in Conflict with the Economic Model

Suppose one contrasts the traditional starting position of a moral agent versus an economic agent facing a decision. Although the economic agent, as em-

---

whether *adherence* to a moral norm involves more than mere *conformity* to the rule (i.e., also doing the right things for the right reasons, as Aristotle said), since our primary interest is in characterizing observable behavior.

phasized above, is very considerably idealized (in the sense that limitations of knowledge, calculational ability etc. may be assumed away), nonetheless in important respects the agent is taken as factually determined. His or her preferences, "tastes," or wants are simply given; however unjustifiable or perverse they might be by some standards, if "chosen" or included in the most preferred state, all want satisfaction counts toward the achievement of optimality. In contrast, preferences are conceived as criticizable and rejectable in moral theory (Nagel 1967) and some preferences (e.g., sadistic satisfaction from watching torture) would not count positively in morally ranking a state of affairs. The view in moral theory that preferences are criticizable and rejectable has the additional implication that moral values are not likely to be physiologically given "tastes," but may instead be chosen through interaction and reflection. Such moral "taste-building" learning processes are not a part of the standard economic model of the individual agent.

Similarly, in those parts of moral theory to which economists are likely to appeal, the theory contains a built-in concern for others, or concern for justifiability to others, which contrasts starkly with the self-interested economic agent. The self-interested agent presumably chooses without caring what preferences others have except as those are reflected in prices, nor what resources others have or do not have so long as there are buyers and sellers with whom to exchange.

Likewise, with economic versus moral "decision rules," the models start out far apart. The economic agent's only problem is establishing his rank ordering of preferred outcomes by a "black box" process that presumably involves weighing the projected states of affairs against given tastes. In contrast, even utilitarian approaches, close though they are in many ways to the economic model, conceive of the moral agent as weighing outcomes ideally, in terms of effects on others just as much as effects on himself or herself. This requires some "stepping outside oneself" to project how those effects would be evaluated from the other's standpoint.

On nonutilitarian conceptions of moral rules, the contrast is even sharper. Although the economic agent weighs the set of all *feasible* actions for purposes of choice (presumably meaning within the budget constraint and not otherwise illegal), the moral agent in any kind of "natural law," deontological, or Kantian conception typically does not even consider the full set of feasible actions but simply eliminates and does not weigh those involving impermissible actions. If someone is considering killing his spouse and refrains because he considers the risk of prison too great, his choice not to murder may conform to the moral prohibition against taking human life but, on this set of moral conceptions, he has nonetheless not "acted morally."

Another contrast might be put in this way. In moral theory one is nearly always building outward from a conception of persons interacting, involving at least a minimal capacity to see things from another's point of view. This is one reason why moral codes or systems are most readily identifiable in a small-group context, even if we suppose them to have the conceptual generality noted above. In the economic context, however, there is no built-in concern for what the decision represents to the (usually anonymous) other party, who is assumed to be looking after his or her own interests in the same way (Buchanan 1965; McKenzie 1976; cf. Braybrooke 1983 on "neighbors' vs. traders' morality").

Caution: "Sharp Bends" in Language to be Expected

We wish to issue the following warning on the basis of the contrasts we have just noted. We tend to agree with those economists such as Hirshleifer (1985) and Brunner (1987) who have argued that there is no turning back to earlier lines of defense, such as John Stuart Mill's. There is a strong need for a greater coherence in the overall approach to explanation in the social sciences, and economics should not now back away from the challenge. The hope of gaining understanding of large social structures by grounding explanations on choices by the individual agent is too compelling to give up. But as we have seen, the economic model is not likely to easily accommodate the incorporation of the moral agent's perspective.

Hence, what we must expect is that there will be efforts to bend and trim conceptions to make them fit into a new, synthesized model, with attendant dangers of misunderstanding and inconsistency. When economists begin discussing preferences or norms, for example, they naturally assume that what they mean by these words cannot be very different from what others mean, and they believe that, with a little concept stretching, a new scheme can be achieved. This turns out to be especially dangerous where economists pick up terms used in several different disciplines, such as *internalization* or *altruism*. These are used in psychology and sociobiology as well as in philosophy, but with somewhat different meanings, not necessarily all immediately compatible or coherent. In reading this literature, it is often a major task to sort out what meaning(s) the author had in mind in attempting to adapt a term used outside economics. Often the effort to bring to bear some explanatory theory from another discipline may depend, in crucial ways, on specific connotations not clearly perceived or at least set out by the author, and this makes the usefulness of the adaptation very hard to assess. This is a problem in all interdisciplinary work, of course, but we have found it especially bothersome in this particular multidisciplinary context.

With these warnings in mind about the difficulties of incorporating moral concerns into the economist's rational egoist model of the individual, we turn in the next chapter to a consideration of alternative ways of modifying the standard model to include moral values and norms.

REFERENCES

Akerlof, George. 1980. "A Theory of Social Custom, of Which Unemployment May Be One Consequence." *Quarterly Journal of Economics* 94:749–75.

Akerlof, George. 1984. "Gift Exchange and Efficiency Wage Theory." *American Economic Review* 74:79–83.

Arrow, Kenneth. 1963. "Uncertainty and the Welfare Economics of Medical Care." *American Economic Review* 53:941–73.

Arrow, Kenneth. 1967. "Public and Private Values." In *Human Values and Economic Policy,* ed. S. Hook. New York: NYU Press.

Arrow, Kenneth. 1974. *The Limits of Organization.* New York: W. W. Norton.

Arrow, Kenneth. 1983. "General Economic Equilibrium: Purpose, Analytic Technique, Collective Choice." In *Collected Papers of K. J. Arrow.* Vol. 2. Cambridge, Mass.: Harvard University Press.

Arrow, Kenneth. 1987. "Rationality of Self and Others in an Economic System." In *Rational Choice: The Contrast between Economics and Philosophy,* ed. Robin Hogarth and Melvin Rader. Chicago: University of Chicago Press.

Arrow, Kenneth, and Frank Hahn. 1971. *General Competitive Analysis.* San Francisco: Holden Day.

Baier, Kurt. 1958. *The Moral Point of View: A Rational Basis of Ethics.* Ithaca: Cornell University Press.

Bardach, Eugene, and Robert Kagan. 1982. *Going By The Book: The Problem of Regulatory Unreasonableness.* Philadelphia: Temple University Press.

Bergsten, Gordon. 1985. "On the Role of Social Norms in a Market Economy." *Public Choice* 45(2):113–37.

Blair, R., and S. Rubin, eds. 1980. *Regulating the Professions: A Public Policy Symposium.* Lexington, Mass.: Heath/Lexington.

Boulding, Kenneth. 1969. "Economics as a Moral Science." *American Economic Review* 59:1–12.

Braybrooke, David. 1983. *Ethics in the World of Business.* Totowa, N.J.: Rowman and Allenheld.

Brunner, Karl. 1987. "The Perception of Man and the Conception of Society: Two Approaches to Understanding Society." *Economic Inquiry* 25(3):367–89.

Buchanan, James. 1965. "Ethical Rules, Expected Values and Large Numbers." *Ethics* 76:1–13.

Edgeworth, Francis. 1881. *Mathematical Psychics.* London: Kegan Paul.

Elster, Jon. 1985. *Sour Grapes: Studies in the Subversion of Rationality.* Cambridge: Cambridge University Press.

Gauthier, David. 1986. *Morals by Agreement.* Oxford: Oxford University Press.

Goldfarb, Robert, and William Griffith. N.d. "The Theory-as-Map Analogy and Changes in Assumption Sets in Economics." In *Socioeconomics: Toward a New Synthesis,* ed. A. Etzioni and P. Lawrence. Armonk, N.Y.: M. E. Sharpe. In press.

Grofman, Bernard. 1974. "Rational Choice Models and Self-Fulfilling and Self-Defeating Prophecies." In *Developments in the Methodology of Social Science,* ed. W. Leinfellner and E. Kohler. Dordrecht: D. Reidel.

Hirsch, Fred. 1976. *Social Limits to Growth.* Cambridge, Mass.: Harvard University Press.

Hirschman, Albert. 1985. "Against Parsimony." *Economics and Philosophy* 1:7–21.

Hirshleifer, Jack. 1985. "The Expanding Domain of Economics." *American Economic Review Directory* (December): 53–68.

Hogarth, Robin, and Melvin Reder. 1987. "Introduction: Perspectives from Economics and Psychology." In *Choice: The Contrast between Economics and Psychology,* ed. Robin Hogarth and Melvin Reder. Chicago: University of Chicago Press.

Jevons, W. S. 1871. *Theory of Political Economy.* London: Macmillan.

Kahneman, Daniel, Jack Knetsch, and Richard Thaler. 1986. "Fairness as a Constraint on Profit Seeking: Entitlements in the Market." *American Economic Review* 76:728–41.

Kahneman, Daniel, Paul Slovic, and Amos Tversky. 1982. *Judgement under Uncertainty: Heuristics and Biases.* Cambridge: Cambridge University Press.

Kaplan, John. 1978. "A Legal Look at Prosocial Behavior: What Can Happen If One Tries to Help or Fails to Help Another." In *Altruism, Sympathy, and Helping,* ed. L. Wispe. New York: Academic Press.

Knight, Frank. 1921. *Risk, Uncertainty, and Profit.* New York: Houghton Mifflin.

Koford, Kenneth, and Mark Penno. 1988. "Accounting, Principal-Agent Theory, and Self-Interested Behavior." In *Implications of Agency Theory for Business Ethics,* ed. R. E. Freeman. In press.

Kolm, Serge-Christophe. 1983. "Altruism and Efficiency." *Ethics* 94:18–65.

Leibenstein, Harvey. 1982. "The Prisoner's Dilemma in the Invisible Hand: An Analysis of Intrafirm Productivity." *American Economic Review* 72:92–97.

Leslie, T. Cliffe. 1879. "The Known and the Unknown in the Economic World." In *Essays in Political and Moral Philosophy.* London.

McKean, Roland. 1985. "The Economics of Trust, Altruism, and Corporate Responsibility." In *Altruism, Morality and Economic Theory,* ed. Edmund Phelps. New York: Russell Sage Foundation.

McKenzie, Richard. 1976. "The Economic Dimensions of Ethical Behavior." *Ethics* 87:208–21.

McPherson, Michael. 1984. "Limits on Self-Seeking: The Role of Morality in Economic Life." In *Neoclassical Political Economy,* ed. D. Colander. Cambridge: Ballinger.

Margolis, Howard. 1982. *Selfishness, Altruism, and Morality.* Chicago: University of Chicago Press.

Marschak, Jacob. 1949. "The Role of Liquidity under Complete and Incomplete Information." *American Economic Review* 39:182–93.

Mill, John Stuart. 1877. *Essays in Some Unsettled Questions of Political Economy.* 3d ed. London: Longmann Green.

Mueller, Dennis. 1986. "Rational Egoism Versus Adaptive Egoism as a Fundamental Postulate for a Descriptive Theory of Human Behavior." *Public Choice* 51(1):3–23.

Nagel, Ernest. 1967. "Preference, Evaluation, and Reflective Choice." In *Human Values and Economic Policy,* ed. S. Hook. New York: NYU Press.

Okun, Arthur. 1983. "The Invisible Handshake and the Inflationary Process." In *Economics for Policy-making: Selected Essays of Arthur M. Okun.* Cambridge, Mass.: MIT Press.

Oppenheimer, Joe. 1985. "Public Choice and Three Ethical Properties of Politics." *Public Choice* 45:241–55.

Phelps, Edmund. 1975. "Introduction." In *Altruism, Morality, and Economic Theory,* ed. Edmund Phelps. New York: Russell Sage Foundation.

Radnitzky, Gerard, and Peter Bernholz, eds. 1987. *Economic Imperialism.* New York: Paragon Press.

Reder, Melvin. 1979. "The Place of Ethics in the Theory of Production." In *Economics and Human Welfare: Essays in Honor of Tibor Scitovsky,* ed. M. Boskin. New York: Academic Press.

Sen, Amartya. 1977. "Rational Fools: A Critique of the Behavioral Foundations of Economic Theory." *Philosophy and Public Affairs* 6:317–44.

Solow, Robert. 1980. "On Theories of Unemployment." *American Economic Review* 70:1–11.

Stigler, George. 1957. "Perfect Competition, Historically Contemplated." *Journal of Political Economy* 65:1–17.

Stigler, George. 1981. "Economics or Ethics?" In *The Tanner Lectures on Human Values II.* Salt Lake City: University of Utah Press.

Stiglitz, Joseph. 1986. "Theories of Wage Rigidity." In *Keynes' Economic Legacy,* ed. J. Butkiewicz, K. Koford, and J. Miller. New York: Praeger.

Thurow, Lester. 1975. *Generating Inequality.* New York: Basic Books.

Thurow, Lester. 1985. *The Zero Sum Solution.* New York: Simon and Schuster.

Tintner, Gerhard. 1941. "The Theory of Choice under Subjective Risk and Uncertainty." *Econometrica* 9:298–304.

Winch, D. M. 1971. *Analytical Welfare Economics.* London: Penguin Books.

Amending the Economist's "Rational Egoist" Model to Include Moral Values and Norms, Part 2: Alternative Solutions

Robert S. Goldfarb and William B. Griffith

A number of attractions and difficulties of incorporating moral norms and/or altruistic preferences into the economist's model of the individual were identified in the previous chapter. Among the attractions are the possibility that incorporating moral considerations might aid in overcoming predictive problems, that it might help resolve introspective difficulties with current versions of economic theory, and that it might give a more satisfactory view of factors affecting how well markets function. Difficulties include the very different conceptual bases underlying the ideas of "moral man" and "economic man," and the danger that each view will be misleadingly warped in trying to combine their features. In the face of these attractions and difficulties, a number of analysts have proposed alternative modifications of the standard model; in this chapter our aim is to provide a systematic account of these different attempts, in the process developing an appreciation for the issues involved.

In considering alternative approaches to incorporating moral values and norms, two kinds of classifying questions arise. First, suppose we describe standard versions of the microeconomic model of the individual as a "rational egoist" model. Then a useful question is whether a particular way of incorporating moral considerations modifies the economist's notion of "rational" or modifies narrow self-interest or "egoism."[1]

A second classifying question arises from considering three important ingredients of the standard framework: the individual's preferences, the constraints he or she faces, and a decision procedure or decision rule by which he or she tries to pick the best available alternative. In this context, the question is whether a particular way of incorporating moral concerns modifies prefer-

---

1. Our use of the term *rational egoism* is borrowed from Mueller (1986). The resulting classificatory division is not new; it is used effectively, for example, in Hirshleifer 1985.

ences, modifies constraints, or modifies the individual's decision rule. Many of the proposed revisions are usefully confronted by these two classification schemes.

Using this latter question as an organizing device for this chapter, we will consider four alternative perspectives about moral values and norms that appear in the literature: (1) norms as decision rules or decision procedures, (2) norms as constraints, (3) moral values as preferences, and (4) attempts to explain the generation and maintenance of moral values and norms.

Norms as Decision Rules or Decision Procedures

The Notion of Norms

As we indicated in the previous chapter, a number of scholars (Bergsten 1985; Brunner 1987; Hirshman 1985; Phelps 1975; Sen 1977) have focused on the apparent existence of "normlike behavior" such as truthfulness. But to analyze how this behavior might modify the economic model we need to understand what various writers seem to mean by norms. A broad conception, seemingly consistent with many writers' usages, is the following. Norms are rules of behavior that constrain the individual's interactions with others; in particular, these rules often operate to constrain the full-blown pursuit of "narrow self-interest." Bergsten (1985) states that "Social norms are those (extra-legal) rules or standards of behavior that act as constraints on economic self-interest" (133, n. 1). Ullman-Margalit (1977) provides as a "first rough characterization" that "a social norm is a prescribed guide for conduct or action which is generally complied with by the members of society" (1977, 12). She describes "a subclass of social norms," called "norms of obligation," with the following characteristics. There is "a significant social pressure for conformity to them . . . ; the belief by the people concerned in their indispensability for the proper functioning of society; and the expected clashes between their dictates on the one hand and personal interests and desires on the other" (1977, 13).

Norms as Decision Rules

A familiar analysis using the standard microeconomic model involves maximizing the individual's utility subject to a budget constraint. The individual with well-defined preferences uses a decision rule to "maximize," to pick his or her best or "optimal" point on the budget constraint. One thing that makes the meaning of maximization or "doing the best one can" quite clear in this setting is the absence of strategic interaction; the budget constraint is invariant to the behavior of small numbers of other individuals.

Now, suppose instead that the individual faces a situation involving strategic interaction. A widely used illustrative example is the so-called Prisoner's Dilemma. In such gaming or strategic interaction situations, what it means to "do the best one can" is not at all straightforward.[2] In this setting, norms may serve as plausible analogs to the optimization rules adopted in the less complex budget constraint case. Several writers view normlike rules as being chosen precisely because they serve to ensure relatively attractive outcomes for the individual in Prisoner's Dilemma situations.

At the beginning of this chapter we asked what aspect of "rational egoism" each approach proposed to modify. The "norms-as-decision-rule" view is quite consistent with both the rational and the egoist component of rational egoism. In particular, if the norm chosen typically provides an advantageous outcome in strategic interaction settings, it is consistent with the economist's "instrumental" or "thin" meaning of rationality.[3]

Illustrations from a Range of Writers and Disciplines
A number of writers (Axelrod 1984; Coleman 1987; Gauthier 1986; Schotter 1981; Ullman-Margalit 1977) express opinions that are, at least in part, consistent with viewing norms as decision rules. That these researchers come from a wide range of disciplines—economics, philosophy, political science, sociology—indicates a widespread concern with strategic interaction problems, a fertile foundation for considering norms.

It is useful to point out some analytical issues raised and points of view espoused by specific writers. An especially interesting feature of the work of the philosopher David Gauthier is his tying of the need for moral rules or norms to the existence of externalities or market failures; he quite explicitly characterizes the ideal market as a "moral free-zone" in which "the divergent and seemingly opposed interests of different individuals fully harmonize." The problem is that the (ideal) market "is not always to be had. . . . Morality arises from market failure" (1986, 83–84).

Thus, it is the presence of strategic interactions not ideally harmonized

---

2. For example, if both players adopt a so-called dominant strategy in a Prisoner's Dilemma game, they both worse off than if they both do not. Yet a dominant strategy, which is a strategy insuring that the individual does as well as he or she can *whichever strategy the other player picks,* resembles a kind of maximization. Sen (1974) puts the point as follows: "one of the interests in games like the Prisoner's Dilemma lies in the fact that the usual postulates of rational behavior (even after taking into account the preferences of others) yields a situation that is inferior for all. Thus the concept of individual rationality becomes very difficult to define" (1974, 55). Another useful discussion is in Radner 1986 (398).

3. Elster (1985) distinguishes "the thin theory of rationality" from the "broad theory." Thin rationality is described as leaving "unexamined the beliefs and the desires that form the reasons for the action whose rationality we are assessing, with the exception that they are stipulated not to be logically inconsistent. Consistency, in fact, is what rationality in the thin sense is all about: . . . consistency within the system of desires; and consistency between beliefs and desires on the one hand and the action for which they are reasons on the other hand" (1985, 1). Broad rationality requires, in addition, that "beliefs and desires be rational in a more substantive sense."

by a perfectly-functioning market that create a place for moral norms. Gauthier argues that an individual "reasoning from nonmoral premises, would accept the constraints of morality on his choices" (1986, 5). Such principles of morality are contractarian, "introduced as the objects of fully voluntary *ex ante* agreement among rational persons. . . . As rational persons understanding the structure of their interaction, they recognize a place for mutual constraint, and so for a moral dimension to their affairs" (1986, 9). In our language, these moral norms provide decision rules allowing jointly desirable results; that is why they are adopted by "social contract."[4]

Axelrod studies the tendency of desirable joint outcomes to emerge in repeated Prisoner's Dilemma games. He runs a series of computer "contests" in which various strategies submitted by knowledgeable contestants were played off against each other. A quite simple strategy (called Tit-for-Tat) embodying considerable willingness to give one's opponent the benefit of the doubt does better, on average, than all other submitted strategies (some of which were very untrusting and "nasty"). Axelrod uses this striking result about the power of a strategy that encourages jointly beneficial solutions to argue that, in repeated Prisoner's Dilemma situations, there can be a strong tendency for unenforced cooperation to develop, yielding desirable outcomes for both players. Axelrod illustrates this tendency with examples as diverse as the behavior of Congress and trench warfare in World War I.

Axelrod's approach, while not directly concerned with norms, also seems to suggest that rules or norms might develop in gaming situations precisely in order to bring about desirable joint outcomes. Note that repeated experience in playing the game produces the rule.

Difficulties with the "Norms-as-Decision-Rule" View

We will discuss two of many potential difficulties. First, there are analytical problems with treating norms as Prisoner's Dilemma solutions. Knowledge that other players have adopted such norms may make it attractive for a particular player to fail to obey the norm ("cheat"). This is particularly likely in games involving many players, where individual cheating may be harder to detect (note that Axelrod's computer contest results involved two-person, rather than multiperson, games). In such a situation, the norm solution is likely to break down. Moreover, the association between the adoption of the norm and its status as a decision rule for achieving a desirable outcome is attenuated, since sometimes the maximizing thing to do is not to obey the rule.

---

4. In an intriguing discussion of what he calls the "calculus of morality," Viktor Vanberg (1988) considers the individual's choice of moral rules as a constitutional choice rather than a situational choice. As he puts it, "Can it be rational to be *always moral* if it is *not always rational* to be moral?" (1988, 19). He provides a very revealing comparison of the strong similarities and subtle distinctions between his "constitutional position" and Gauthier's (1986, 25–28).

The notion that cheating might be hard to detect is just one example of an imperfect information problem. The more imperfect the information about payoffs, reactions of other players, and so forth, the more problematical it becomes that a normlike solution could arise. Indeed, one criticism of Gauthier's derivation of morality (in the form of rules) arising to solve strategic interaction problems is the huge informational requirements seemingly involved in Gauthier's scheme (see Braybrooke 1987; Foreman 1988). Conversely, as Phelps (1975) notes, norms may sometimes arise precisely because of the existence of imperfect (especially asymmetric) information; but if imperfect information spawns them, then analyses based on Prisoner's Dilemma games with "very good" information is unlikely to adequately explain these norm-generating processes.

Second, note that, in this approach, the norm must be chosen by the individual because it represents a way of achieving a materially advantageous result.[5] For example, suppose that people were to fail to cheat because of deeply held feelings that it is "right" to obey a "noncheating" norm. This would not fit the "norms-as-decision-rules" type of explanation, despite the achievement of the desirable Prisoner's Dilemma solution.

Sociologist James Coleman provides an especially useful general insight consistent with this example. Coleman distinguishes between norms "enforced primarily through external sanctions exercised at the time the action takes place" and those based on "internalized sanctions to be exercised by the actor himself as future occasions of action arise" (1987, 138). Norms enforced through external sanctions might fit our category of "norms-as-decision-rules," while "norms-as-internalized-sanctions" in many (though not all) interpretations would not; as the previous noncheating example suggests, these internalized sanctions may not be chosen by the individual as solutions to Prisoner's Dilemma–type situations. In fact, they may not be "chosen" at all. Thus, Coleman's insight suggests that "norms-as-decision-rules" may not provide a complete analysis of how norms might enter the economic model of the individual.[6]

An intriguing sidelight on the "norms-as-decision-rule" view versus the view that norms are internalized sanctions that exist prior to the game is

---

5. Some might object to identifying (as a "moral norm") any decision rule accepted *because* it is thought to produce materially advantageous results for the choosing agent. In this view, one's motivation must involve the intent to be moral, or to "do one's duty." But this is a fundamental conceptual issue on which defensible positions differ, and, for the analytical issues this chapter considers, we recommend eschewing this particular linguistic limitation.

6. Coleman views externally sanctioned norms as rules the individual chooses to adopt and obey in order to obtain desirable results. An individual "may accept the legitimacy of others' rights to partially control his action" because it gives him a "legitimate right to control other's similar actions. Rejecting that legitimacy constitutes an action against the legitimacy of his right on those other occasions" (1987, 142).

provided in Sen 1974. He briefly reviews elements of various moral systems or principles (associated with Kant, Rawls, Hare, Suppes, and Harsanyi) in order to ask whether the moral principles involved are consistent with attaining desirable solutions in Prisoner's Dilemma situations. The answer is "yes" in every case, but there is certainly no suggestion that an individual's moral system is adapted because it provides a Prisoner's Dilemma solution.

Norms as Constraints

Instead of norms arising as decision rules, it is at least logically possible that norm-rules might enter the individual's decision problem as constraints. That is, rather than *choosing* the norm because it allows him or her to reach a desirable solution, the individual might see these norm-rules as *constraining* his or her available choices.

The analogy here is with budget constraints, which the economic agent presumably ordinarily sees as externally imposed and accepts without question. However, moral norms are often thought of as internalized, as part of one's subjective "conscience," rather than externally enforced. Thus, some account is needed of how such internal constraints emerge and function without necessarily being consciously chosen or even consciously accepted.

Some Illustrative Views

Coleman (1987) and economist Dennis Mueller (1986) both suggest that such internalized constraints are imposed by behavioral conditioning. Coleman puts it as follows: "[A]s soon as we take the perspective of the parent of a small child or a person who must cope with a psychopath, we immediately see the rationality of attempting to create an internal sanctioning system, a 'conscience' or 'superego' that would make unnecessary the continuous external policing of action. . . . Elementary knowledge of psychology, or even experience in social life, indicates that internalization of norms can and does take place" (1987, 149).

Mueller sounds a similar theme. "Behaviorist psychology teaches us that individual acts that are followed by positive reinforcers (rewards) increase in frequency. . . . Through this type of operant conditioning we first learn to behave cooperatively in prisoner's dilemma contexts. . . . The child who is rewarded for helping carry the groceries in volunteers to help put the garden tools away. . . . These principles of psychology should be familiar to every parent and teacher, to anyone who has ever trained a dog" (1986, 5–6).

We raise again our question about whether a particular approach to incorporating norms modifies "rational" or "egoist." We leave the question of whether egoism has been modified for the reader to ponder, and focus on rational. Treating rules as constraints still seems consistent with the economist's "thin" notion of rationality in the following sense: the individual is still optimizing subject to (presumably) given constraints. Norm-constraints may differ from the more usual budget constraints in that the norm-constraint is somehow "internal," but it is still presumably predetermined rather than, for example, being part of a chosen decision rule.

Mueller disagrees with our assessment that this behaviorally conditioned individual is rational. He questions the rationality, from the individual's point of view, of having an internal psychological makeup that predisposes him to cooperate. In fact, a major theme of Mueller's article is that the cooperative behavior many of us learned as children through behavioral conditioning is strong evidence that we need to abandon the rational component of the "rational egoist" model common to economics.

Some Concerns about Norms-as-Constraints

We mention three of the many questions about this approach. A first concern is that norms somehow do not fit the economic category of constraints very well. Vanberg (1988) suggests that, in common economic terminology, "preferences are the subjective, intrapersonal determinants of choice, and constraints are the objective, external determinants. . . . [T]his . . . would seem to require us either to classify morality as a subjective, intrapersonal preference variable, or as an objective, external constraint variable" (1988, 7). But since moral norms are in some ways external yet imply some internalization, they do not, from this point of view, seem to fit the constraint category perfectly. Another version of this "fit" problem is put forth by Elster (1986), who refers explicitly to norms as constraintlike, but goes on to claim that they "differ from ordinary constraints in that they can also be violated" (1986, 23). While this claim seems of questionable merit, since ordinary budget constraints can also be violated (for example, by stealing), it is illustrative of the nervousness analysts feel in classifying norms as constraints.

A second concern focuses on the blurring of the line between norms-as-constraints and norms-as-preferences. Supposedly the cost of violating a norm is psychological discomfort. But if it hurts psychologically to violate the norm-as-constraint, that seems to some observers like saying "I obey the norm because it feels better when I do," which sounds very much like a preference. Put differently, it feels better when I indulge in eating an apple, and also when I indulge in obeying a norm, so a norm is like an apple, an argument in my preference function. Thus, the line between norms-as-preferences and norms-as-constraints is blurred.

A third concern refers to difficulties in getting analytical/predictive results from a norms-as-constraints framework. A satisfactory theory encompassing norms-as-constraints seems to require an explanation of and predictions about what kinds of norm-constraints arise under what conditions. Economists have not typically focused on these kinds of questions and do not seem to have an absolute or comparative advantage in trying to answer them.

Moral Values as Preferences

Our discussion of norms-as-constraints raised the issue of the difficulty of definitively classifying internalized norms as constraints or preferences. Thinking of moral values as norms or rules may lead to a constraint interpretation, while the perception that the "cost" of violating a norm is psychological discomfort may lead one to think of disutility and, therefore, preferences. There are, in fact, a number of perceptive writers in economics and related fields who explicitly or implicitly treat moral concerns as part of preferences.[7]

If moral concerns are to be treated as part of preferences, do they enter directly as rules/norms, or in some other form? Using the broader concept of an ethical or moral *value* rather than a norm or rule possesses a prima facie appealing feature: it does not prejudge the trade-offs available to the individual between moral and other kinds of arguments in the utility function. In contrast, if moral rules enter the utility function, then presumably disobeying a rule subjects the individual to a discontinuously large decrease in utility, and trade-offs at the margin between the moral value underlying the rule and other arguments of the utility function are not possible.[8] One might well prefer to avoid initially assuming such discontinuities, allowing exploration of the possibility of smoother trade-offs at the margin.

Rationality and the Form of Preferences

Viewed from one perspective, there does not seem to be a serious problem of consistency of moral values with the economist's "thin view" of rationality. Just as the individual's taste for oranges or distaste for playing bridge is treated as given and not subject to dispute, his or her taste for honesty or aversion to cruelty might be treated analogously.[9] The individual simply ra-

---

7. See, for example, Etzioni 1986; Hirschman 1985; Sen 1974. A useful skeptical review of so-called multiple utility frameworks, which often include moral values in utility functions in complex ways, is Brennan 1989.

8. To illustrate the distinction between a moral value and a norm or rule based on that moral value, consider an individual who values honesty. Here the moral value is honesty, while a norm or rule based on this value might be "never tell a lie, except in the following unusual situations . . ."

9. Robert Frank (1987) turns the typical economics treatment of tastes as given and exogenous on its head by suggesting that one might model tastes as endogenous, choosing them in a way consistent with "selfish" maximization. "Instead of treating tastes as a datum, I retreat a step

tionally satisfies his or her tastes within his or her given constraints.[10]

While treating moral values as given is consistent with the thin theory of rationality's treatment of commodities, it may also be true that taking moral values as given is less plausible and has less intellectual appeal than taking the taste for oranges as given. While the source of the individual's tastes for oranges presumably involves physiological mechanisms of little interest to economists, the source(s) of predilections for honesty and fairness might very well turn out to be endogenous to one's economic experiences. Hence, changes in this taste might itself affect (and be affected by) a market's ability to function well. We shall return to a discussion of the sources of moral values within a society in section 4.

An interesting and complex view of the nature of moral values has been suggested by Hirschman (influenced in turn by Sen 1977), and it is useful to explore the consistency of this kind of view with the standard, thin notion of rationality in economics. Hirschman (1985) distinguishes between ordinary tastes and values according to the sustained reflection associated with changing them. Economists, he says, have focused on "impulsive, uncomplicated . . . and generally minor (apples vs. pears) changes in tastes." This kind of taste "is almost defined as a preference about which you do not argue—*de gustibus non est disputandum.*" These unreflective tastes are to be contrasted with values: "A taste about which you argue, with others *or yourself*, ceases ipso facto being a taste—it turns into a value" (1985, 9). This distinction between "unreflective" tastes and values suggests a more complex

---

and ask 'What kind of tastes would maximize the attainment of selfish objectives?' This is essentially the behavioral biologist's approach. . . . It treats tastes not as ends in themselves, but as means for attaining important material objectives" (1987, 593). Frank adds in a footnote, "In the biologist's view, tastes are no different from other characteristics. All are selected for their capacity to promote survival and reproduction" (1987, 593). The "selfish" taste to be chosen in Frank's major example is honesty, because that trait (combined with the right signaling device displaying the signaler's honesty) allows a more desirable outcome in nonrepeated Prisoner's Dilemma games.

10. One sometimes hears sloppy talk among economists alleging that "if behavior is not narrowly self-interested, it is not economically rational." Such talk is incorrect. If tastes are a datum about the individual and not disputable, then a taste for honesty (or widespread "altruistic" tastes for the well-being of one's children) can no more be labeled *irrational* than can a taste for oranges. Economist Charles Plott has usefully stated the underlying consistency of "norms (or altruism) as preferences" and the economist's view of rationality. "[T]here has been no way of separating theories of altruistically based behavior and moralistic behavior from preference theory or rational choice theory. . . . [P]reference theory requires no theory about the source of preferences. . . . The fact that preferences might include or reflect moral considerations does not, on the surface, contradict a theory of rational choice or maximizing behavior. Moral considerations might influence the shape and form of preferences, but that does not contradict the existence of preferences or choices based upon them" (Plott 1987, 140–41). For a general attack on the claim that rational must mean "narrowly self-interested," see Sen 1987 (15–16).

view of rationality. If values (unlike preferences as economists usually model them) are changeable through rational persuasion, then they are also more likely to be endogenous to the economic model; the behavior and events the individual experiences and observes may lead him or her, upon reflection, to modify his or her existing values. A simple view of rationality as based on unchanging tastes that are not "chosen" is simply not adequate in this framework.

The possible endogeneity of values can have important societywide implications. For example, values like honesty, which McPherson (1984), Phelps (1975), and Bergsten (1985) argue may make the market operate "better," may be destroyed or enhanced by the very operation of the market. Hirschman argues that the endogeneity of values-as-preferences has been ignored by economists when they proclaim the superiority of fines over prohibitions and standards. A function of prohibitions and standards may be to "stigmatize antisocial behavior and thereby to influence citizens' values and behavior codes" (1985, 10).

These interpretive problems about the nature of rationality suggest that incorporating moral values as preferences raises serious analytical issues. Indeed, complex problems about the appropriate form of the utility function arise even before the issue of rationality is joined. For example, both Sen (1974 and 1977) and Etzioni (1986) have proposed that the incorporation of moral values into preference functions requires complicated modifications of the way in which utility functions are written. Sen (1974 and 1977) has argued that capturing the notion of values existing at a deeper reflective level than ordinary tastes may necessitate that they enter preference functions in a very mathematically complex way: "[W]e need to consider *rankings of preference rankings* to express our moral judgements" (1977, 337; see n. 11 below and the mathematical description in Sen 1974, 62–63 for a more explicit description of such ranking). These rankings of preference rankings are often referred to as "metapreferences" or "second-order preferences."

Sen has several arguments for a metapreference type approach. One claim is that one preference function cannot adequately represent all the phenomena we might want to capture: "a person is given *one* preference ordering, and when the need arises this is supposed to reflect his interests, represent his welfare, summarize his idea of what should be done, and describe his actual choices and behavior" (1977, 335). A more concrete justification (Sen 1974) applies in a world of strategic interdependence involving, for example, Prisoner's Dilemma situations. Here, the agent's own preferences among outcomes may depend on the preferences he or she assumes others have. If each agent assumes others act only on narrowly self-interested preferences, the usual less-than-optimal solution is assured. But any agent might "rationally" prefer that his or her own and the other agents' preferences might be less narrowly self-interested, since this would allow the achievement of a more desirable collective outcome. This ranking of his or her own alternative possible preferences by the agent might then be said to represent his or her "moral preferences." He or she might even try to act on the basis of such moral preferences in situations where such behavior might be likely to elicit similar "less narrowly self-interested behavior" by others.[11]

Another proposal about the form the utility function needs to take to incorporate moral values comes from Etzioni (1986). He has argued that correctly incorporating moral values requires giving up what he refers to as the economist's "monoutility" conception of preferences in favor of a "multiple utility" conception. Under this view, moral acts have an "imperative" quality and other distinctive characteristics such that they are not subject to simple trade-offs between moral concerns and other arguments of the utility function. For Etzioni, "moral and pleasure 'preferences' are qualitatively different," so that "items or means of satisfying them cannot simply be 'traded off' or substituted for one another" (1986, 178). Both the Sen and Etzioni analyses illustrate that the nature of the trade-off between moral values and ordinary goods is a crucial issue in modeling these values as preferences. Concerns about how to specify these trade-offs reflect fundamental considerations of moral theory.

Egoism and Moral Values as Preferences

Including moral values in preferences clearly modifies the "egoism" part of the "rational egoist" model in at least two senses. First, moral values like honesty suggest an unwillingness to always pursue personal advantage by any and every available means. Second, some writers include altruism as part of what current authors mean by moral values, and altruism is by definition not egoism. Indeed, thinking of moral values as preferences analogous to tastes

---

11. The mathematical structure of a metapreference ranking has been described by Sen (1977, 337) as follows. "A particular morality can be viewed, not just in terms of the 'most moral' ranking of the set of alternative actions, but as a moral ranking of the rankings of actions (going well beyond the identification merely of the 'most moral' ranking of actions). Let X be the set of alternative and mutually exclusive combinations of actions under consideration, and Y the set of rankings of the elements of X. A ranking of the set Y (consisting of action-rankings) will be called a meta-ranking of the action set X. It is my claim that a particular ranking of the action-set X is not articulate enough to express much about a given morality, and a more robust format is provided by choosing a meta-ranking of actions (that is, a ranking of Y rather than of X)."

We indicate the existence of a metapreference analysis not because we are convinced it is the correct modeling technique for moral values—indeed, one of the authors believes it introduces excessive mathematical complications—but because its existence indicates the complex issues that arise when modeling moral values as preferences.

for commodities leads to some difficult conceptual problems in dealing with indisputably moral notions such as altruism.

Hirshleifer identifies the following problem about the meaning of *self-interest* in this context:

> Suppose a person's ends in life include the well-being of others. If so, do *their* interests become his "self-interest"? . . . [A]nswers in the affirmative rob the concept of self-interest of any distinguishable content. But it is not easy to separate "self-interested" satisfactions from the psychic sensations generated by the experiences of others. (1985, 55)

As an example of the problem of drawing appropriate distinctions, Hirshleifer presents Sen's (1977) effort to distinguish between sympathy and commitment. "If you are tortured, it makes me ill" represents what Sen calls sympathy, which Sen views as a kind of self-interest. "It does not make me feel worse, but I think it is wrong" represents, for Sen, a commitment beyond self-interest. Hirshleifer finds this categorization unappealing and presumably not analytically robust enough for economic modeling purposes.[12]

Preferences versus Constraints

There remains the issue of the difficulty of definitively classifying internalized norms as constraints versus preferences. This issue is not addressed directly by the "morals-as-preferences" authors, who seem to start from the proposition that moral values *are* part of preferences. However, a somewhat different preference framework may allow clarification of the relation between moral concerns as preferences and as constraints, and the relation between values and rules or norms. In Lancaster's (1966) "characteristics" framework and in Becker's (1965) work on the allocation of time, the arguments of preference

---

12. A related difficulty involves the relationship of moral values to altruism. Phelps (1975) lists behavior such as honesty and trustworthiness as examples of altruism. We have treated these same behaviors as representing moral values rather than altruism, and believe it is not analytically fruitful to use the terms interchangeably. We would argue against interchangeability as follows. First, moral values in the form of rules or norms can be considered decision rules in gaming situations; such an interpretation of norms does not warrant the term *altruism*. Second, altruism is usually (and usefully) taken to mean "concern for others"; moral values (ethical codes) may be based on quite different underlying concerns (what is "required"), and only indirectly (if at all) on a concern about the welfare of other persons. (The use of the term *altruism* in the sociobiology literature also suggests distinguishing the term from *moral value*. "Sociobiologists define an altruistic act as one which decreases the chances of survival and reproduction of the actor while increasing the chances of survival and reproduction of another member of the species" [Schenk 1987, 191].) In any case, the fact that the term *altruism* can be subject to such different interpretations suggests the conceptual difficulties in putting moral values into preferences.

functions are fundamental characteristics or properties of goods (Lancaster) or activities (Becker). In Becker's version, goods and time inputs produce outputs of utility-generating "commodities"; the produced "commodities" are what provide utility. Thus, Becker's framework for analyzing preferences includes both a utility or preference function (whose arguments are activities), and a set of production functions indicating how these activities are produced using goods and time.

Applying a Beckerlike framework to moral concerns, suppose some basic moral concerns appear in the utility function, along with other "commodities." However, to raise the level of these "moral concern" variables—that is, to produce morally desirable outcomes that contribute to utility—requires specific types of behaviors describable by a "production function" whose entries might include rulelike behaviors and activities. Notice that, in this framework, there are production function entries that look like "rules-as-constraints," but (unlike the earlier "norms-as-constraints" category, in which the source of the constraints qua constraints was a puzzle) their very existence is tied to the presence of moral concerns in the utility function. This tie-in also seems to resolve the apparent paradox of constraints generating psychological costs that look like utility items.[13]

Whether this modeling strategy will turn out to be fruitful remains to be seen. This uncertainty illustrates, yet again, the conceptual complexity associated with moral-values-as-preferences.

Some Additional Issues in Treating Moral Values as Preferences

Several additional issues deserve to be mentioned. First, if we ignore the alternative inspired by Becker, treating moral values as preferences still leaves the problem of how to get from these preferential values to the moral norms or rules that seem to exist. How does one model the generation of rules from values?

Second, the empirical usefulness of a preference-based approach would seem to depend on identifying how these moral-values-as-preferences are generated, differences in such preferences across groups, or shifts over time. These appear to be daunting empirical tasks for which economists do not seem to have an absolute or comparative advantage.

Third, one might respond to the preference-constraint debate with the

---

13. Our thinking about a Lancaster-Becker approach was generated by a discussion in Vanberg (1988) and comments by our colleagues, Professors Joseph Cordes and Anthony Yezer. Our treatment diverges from Vanberg's, who wants to develop Becker's framework to avoid putting moral concerns in the preference function, and focuses instead on "what affects people's explicit and implicit theories about the payoffs from morality" (1988, 16). Although he does not use a category like our "norms-as-decision-rules," his suggested treatment, involving what he calls "the calculus of morality," is analogous to reasoning about "sensible" decision rules.

reaction that, for many issues, it only matters that moral concerns are internalized, *not* the exact manner or "location" in which they are internalized. Specifically, the predictive or positive economics results associated with internalized moral concerns would be largely the same, whether they showed up as constraints or as preferences. In this sense, arguing over whether it is a constraint or a preference may be unproductive. The counterargument might be based on an assertion about normative economics. It is not at all clear that the welfare implications of "norm-as-constraint" and "norm-as-preference" are identical. If a norm is a preference, it directly affects the individual's achieved utility level. If a norm is a constraint, the effect on the individual's welfare of violating it is indirect and requires considerable additional definition.

Fourth, the general analytical superiority of this approach versus a norms-as-decision-rules or a norms-as-constraints approach is by no means clear. Moreover, if some norms function as decision rules, while others are internalized, this would, at the very least, require a combined use of the categories "norms-as-decision-rules" and "moral-values-as-preferences."

Processes of Generation and Maintenance of Moral Values and Norms

Whether moral concerns enter as decision rules, constraints, or preferences, how they are generated or emerge is of considerable importance for both positive and normative questions. On positive grounds, if moral elements affect behavior, the theory's predictive abilities depend on being able to model the emergence and maintenance of these moral elements. On normative grounds, if certain moral elements may make markets work "better"—as Phelps (1975), Bergsten (1985), Brunner (1987), Gauthier (1986), and Coleman (1987) among others all argue or imply—then one needs to be concerned with the emergence and maintenance of these "desirable" moral elements.

Economists who have attempted to explain the emergence and maintenance of norms have seemingly tended to assume that explanations could fairly readily be borrowed or manufactured from concepts available in biological evolution or cultural development theories. Such efforts appear to be far more problematical than one might have expected. We limit our discussion to the following issues in this tentative and developing literature: (1) disagreements about the "optimality" of the process of generation and maintenance, and (2) identification of cross-generational transmission mechanisms for moral values and norms. We touch upon the following aspects of transmission mechanisms: behavioral conditioning as a single generation transmission mechanism, cultural versus biological evolution as multigenerational mechanisms, and "invisible hand" versus "group selection" mechanisms in cultural evolution.

Disagreements about the Optimality of the Process

A striking feature of this literature is the apparent difference of opinion among commentators about the optimality of the norm-generating process and the surprisingly tenuous bases on which these opinions seem to rest. Mueller and Coleman provide an intriguing juxtaposition in this regard. As indicated earlier, both argue that behavioral conditioning by parents are a source of internalization of norms in children. Yet this shared view does not seem to lead to a consensus about the longer-run optimality of the process. Mueller seems to suggest that "group optimal" norms will result: "Over time, those social institutions for conditioning cooperative behavior will survive that maximize group survival chances" (1986, 18–19). "Competition for survival selects gene structures *as if* the evolution of the species were maximizing the probability of survival. Where cooperation has significant advantages for all members of a group, the group will adopt mores and laws which condition people to behave *as if* they were maximizing" a utility function reflecting the welfare of others (1986, 18). The model Mueller has in mind is "based on *as if* maximization of a socially conditioned or an evolutionarily molded objective function," and is "a model of *adaptive* behavior" (1986, 19).

While Mueller's view seems to suggest a "group optimal" evolutionary process, Coleman analyzes the parent's incentives to undertake the effort to internalize norms in their children. There is a social externality in the process, since the parents do not gain all the benefits of appropriately socializing the children. This seems to imply that the process need not be socially optimal, and Coleman discusses factors leading to a decrease in "parental effort to internalize" over time. A similar concern about "the attrition in this social capital" of social norms and rules is expressed by Brunner, who considers its source a puzzle demanding investigation (1987, 388).[14]

This divergence of opinion is of interest in itself, as an indication of how limited our knowledge is in this area. But Mueller's citing of an evolutionary process with apparent optimality properties suggests a more fundamental question which may have important implications for the evolution of norms. What grounds are there, in the evolutionary biology literature itself, for expecting achievement of global optimality in evolutionary processes? Surely, if that literature is skeptical about achievement of optimality, we would need to

---

14. Yet another concern about the possible nonoptimality of the process is stated in Schotter 1981: there may be a problem that social norms will, in fact, be maintained beyond their useful lives. Schotter sees normlike phenomena, which he calls "social institutions," arising in response to particular "evolutionary economic problems," but the process has the potential flaw that these norms then develop lives of their own, and may linger long after the reason for their existence (the problem they were designed to ameliorate) disappears. "The distressing fact is that what is functional to meet today's problem may be totally inadequate in meeting the tests our society faces tomorrow" (1981, 2).

be very wary about strong optimality assertions in norm generation. A distinguished sociobiologist argues that global optima are extremely unlikely in biological evolution.

> [E]volutionary trajectories seldom if ever lead directly toward global optima. . . . Conceivably there is an ideal ant—with a huge brain and steel jaws, perhaps—but it is not within reach of the ten thousand contemporary species of *Formicidae* during the remaining time allotted to them or to any other form of life on earth. A great variety of other only slightly inferior designs can be imagined, but they too represent virtually unattainable adaptive peaks. For this reason long-range evolution is excessively difficult if not impossible to predict, and extremum principles have proved to have limited utility in evolutionary biology. (Lumsden and Wilson 1981, 195)[15]

Thus, if a strong optimality argument is to be made about norm generation, it must rest on a foundation quite different from a simple analogy with biological evolution. No such strong foundation currently exists, to the best of our knowledge.[16]

Building a Theory of the Generation and Maintenance of Moral Values and Norms

Current discussions contain ingredients that are candidates for a yet-to-be-developed comprehensive analysis of the generation and maintenance of

---

15. Biologist and noted essayist Stephen Jay Gould presents a view of historical evolution of species that also discounts the usefulness of a "global optimum" approach. "Thus, the paradox. . . . Our textbooks like to illustrate evolution with examples of optimal design—nearly perfect mimicry of a dead leaf by a butterfly. . . . But ideal design is a lousy argument for evolution, for it mimics the postulated action of an omnipotent creator. Odd arrangements and funny solutions are the proof of evolution—paths that a sensible God would never tread but that a natural process, constrained by history, follows perforce. . . . Which brings me to the giant panda and its 'thumb'" (1982, 20–21). "The panda's 'thumb' is not, anatomically, a finger at all . . . (but represents) familiar bits of anatomy remodeled for a new function" (1982, 22). "So the panda must . . . settle for . . . a somewhat clumsy, but quite workable, solution. The sesamoid thumb wins no prize in an engineer's derby. It is . . . a contraption, not a lovely contrivance. But it does its job and excites our imagination all the more because it builds on such improbable foundations" (1982, 24).

16. Hirshleifer refers to a natural selection literature in anthropology, and points out that this "is an instance of a more general (and somewhat controversial) quasi-economic evolutionary modeling principle known as the *adaptationist hypothesis* or *the optimization theory:* that morphology and behavior, on both the individual and social levels, can be explained 'as if' chosen to maximize the chances of evolutionary success. Especially on the social level, a number of difficulties have been encountered owing mainly to the fact that what is best for the individual may not be best for the group" (1985, 62).

moral values and norms. Coleman and Mueller provide one seemingly important element with their stress on behavioral conditioning as a transmission mechanism from parent to child for moral values and norms. An attractive side benefit of focusing on behavioral conditioning is that it links the research interests of psychologists to those of economists.

Vanberg (1988) has suggested a possible way of enriching this behavioral conditioning approach. Even if moral attitudes or norms are initially internalized via behavioral conditioning, the maintenance or persistence of these attitudes is likely to depend on their "generating sufficient advantages or rewards" (1988, 29). The individual can evaluate how well the moral values and rules he or she was taught seem to work. This viewpoint creates a nice link between initial attitudes not "chosen" by the individual and the Gauthier-like idea that one can bring rational choice processes to bear on moral attitudes.[17]

Turning to longer-run or multigenerational transmission mechanisms, existing discussions suggest a number of potential and sometimes competing modes of explanation not yet incorporated into a comprehensive explanatory scheme.

Cultural versus Biological Evolution

As Hirshleifer puts it, "no one can seriously deny that morphology and biochemistry play *some* role in social behavior, just as no 'sociobiologist' of repute has ever ruled out the influence of cultural determinants" (1985, 64–65). But our reading of social science–oriented discussions of the biological evolution literature (see especially Campbell 1983; Hirshleifer 1985, 64–66) indicates that no one has yet drawn from that literature strong and revealing connecting paths between "nature" and "nurture" in the generation and maintenance of moral attitudes or behavior. Particularly telling is Campbell's list of six possible evolutionary routes to modeling collaboration versus "competition with one's fellows." Only one item on the list is explicitly biological, and the commentary suggests that explanations appropriately integrating these routes remain to be produced.[18]

---

17. Bergsten (1985) raises the issue of whether those norms that make the market function "better" are likely to be destroyed or enhanced by the very functioning of the market. For example, does operating a market induce a "main chance" mentality that devalues market-beneficial traits like honesty? Notice that this is a version, at a much more aggregate systemwide level, of the view that one's moral views may be endogenous to one's social and economic experiences.

18. A major focus of Campbell's article is to show that so-called kin-selection models in evolutionary biology cannot readily explain the "ultrasociality" found in the social insects (termites, ants, bees, and some wasps). Campbell suggests that this phenomenon is of interest to social scientists because an analogous level of ultrasociality is found in "urban humankind" (though not in other vertebrates). Campbell produces an explanation of the development of

Another reason why cultural rather than biological explanations of norm generation and maintenance may be a first line of attack is presented by Vanberg (1986) in his interpretation of Hayek. While both "*innate, genetically inherited* universal rules of human behavior" and "*learned, culturally transmitted* rules of human conduct" can be expected to have an effect, the process of genetic evolution is likely to be a much slower process, so that "for the purposes of social theory, innate behavioral rules can be assumed to be essentially uniform over time and space. . . . The cultural rules, on the other hand, appear to be exceptionally variable" (1986, 77).

Even if biological evolutionary explanations of norm generation do not turn out to be directly important, there is a more indirect methodological route by which they might make major contributions. Concepts such as kin selection, biological altruism, and moralistic aggression used in evolutionary biology may be useful for generating analogous cultural evolutionary concepts, just as the whole notion of evolutionary selection in biology already informs discussions of cultural evolution (see Vanberg 1986, 81) and natural selection models in economics (see Alchian 1950; Langlois 1986, 243–47).

Invisible Hand versus Group Selection Explanations
of Cultural Evolution
As has been widely noted (see, for example, Langlois 1986, 241–47; Vanberg 1986; and the authors cited in both studies), one type of explanation for the development of normlike rules is the so-called invisible hand explanation. Such explanations trace to the actions of large numbers of individuals pursuing their own self-interest outcomes that they did not consciously intend to produce. While the typical economist's association of invisible hand explanations with Adam Smith may lead to the impression that these explanations imply optimality, there is no guarantee that optimality need result. Vanberg argues rather convincingly that, while invisible hand stories might generate solutions to so-called coordination problems (for example, everyone benefits from general acquiescence to agreeing to drive on the same side of the street), solutions to Prisoner's Dilemma situations are only likely to emerge in re-

---

ultrasociality in these insects that shows that "the human route" to ultrasociality "had to be entirely different" (1983, 17). An implication of the example would seem to be that the biological evolutionary models are not currently developed in a way that produces compelling human social evolutionary explanations.

With respect to his list of six more general evolutionary routes, Campbell points out that "Analysis at any one of these levels may contribute to the general theory of what is optimal, the possible routes to getting there, and modes of retaining such a solution." He urges attention "to the question of the proper explanation of . . . behavior, in terms of the rational-irrational, individual-group, biological-social alternatives" (1983, 23). In short, integration of biological explanations of social phenomena with other explanations is in its infancy.

stricted cases, but not in general. Moreover, even in the coordination problem case, solutions need not be optimal.

If not an invisible hand, then what? One alternative is what Vanberg, following Hayek, calls *group selection*. Such explanations look for mechanisms by which rules that are advantageous to a group come to be selected by that group. Vanberg argues that the group selection mechanisms he identifies tend to be incompatible with invisible hand explanations, and to have their own difficulties as explanations of how desirable rules or norms might arise to deal with Prisoner's Dilemmas. A cultural rule that is advantageous for the group need not be obeyed unless it is also advantageous for the individual; thus, a demonstration that it is group-advantageous alone does not ensure its adoption, given the likelihood of free riding. Vanberg concludes that "systematic analysis of the idea of cultural evolution does not provide any reason to assume that there is some general spontaneous process at work on which we could rely for the generation of appropriate rules" (1986, 97).

If the invisible hand and the Hayek-Vanberg type of group selection explanations seem inadequate, what other explanations might be offered? The claim that moral values such as honesty may, in fact, enter preferences suggests another line of explanation. If moral concerns are sometimes in preferences, how did they get there, and what maintains them? One line of inquiry would be to investigate whether principles embodied in laws might come to be internalized as moral values (see Hirschman 1985, 43–44). A related question is the existence of mechanisms by which religious principles, as "chosen" by the religious "group," come to be internalized as moral values by new generations of members. This general question of whether public institutions—churches, schools, levels of government, which are themselves sometimes subject to a kind of group selection—can affect the establishment and transmission of moral preferences seems worth pursuing.

Conclusions

Several questions provoked by the discussion in this chapter and the previous one call for concluding comments. First, in view of the distinctive difficulties and advantages of norms-as-decision-rules versus norms-as-constraints versus moral-values-as-preferences, does any one of these approaches appear more promising than the others? Second, are the major analytical difficulties likely to arise in attempting to integrate moral concerns into the economic model of the individual being squarely confronted by these three approaches? Are there promising alternative approaches that have yet to be explored? Finally, in light of the positive and normative economics issues motivating this research, does the potential for timely intellectual progress seem sufficient to make further efforts appear worthwhile?

Comparative Evaluation of Approaches

Of the three approaches identified, norms-as-decision-rules appears to hew most closely to the standard rational egoist model and, therefore, might be most appealing to many economists. Although what counts as rational behavior is not as clear in game-theoretic contexts as it is in standard rational choice models, there does not seem to be much difficulty in generating "cooperative" rules that would appeal to rationally self-seeking players. The difficulty is on the other side: the rules that emerge seem to lack many of the properties of moral rules. In particular, they seem to lack any sense of weighing the benefits to others as of similar importance to one's own, and it is difficult to see the derived rules as being sufficiently internalized to produce moral behavior with any consistency or reliability. However, this line of analysis does make how norms might emerge and be adopted under certain special conditions less mysterious.

The norms-as-constraints approach has the advantage of minimizing the problem of the instability of strategic rules by simply taking these rules or norms as givens, seemingly beyond the reach of reflective choice. However, problems of a different sort arise with this approach. The constraints typically encountered in microeconomics (such as budget constraints) are externally imposed and enforced. In the case of moral norms, however, the nature of enforcement becomes a significant issue, since moral norms are, at least in part, internally enforced. Indeed, one of the principal aims of "moral character formation" is to produce agents who will act appropriately even in the absence of external enforcement mechanisms. Moreover, since moral (as opposed to legal) rules are often described as "rules we give ourselves," and are understood to be amenable to rationally motivated change over time, interpreting moral rules as simply unquestioned constraints appears to strip them of much of their typical character.

Moral-values-as-preferences might, in some ways, appear to be a more attractive modification of the rational egoist model. Like constraints, preferences are normally taken as given and not to be questioned. However, they are also understood to be subject to shifts over time; on some occasions, even normally dominant preferences might conceivably suffer suddenly overwhelming shifts. Moreover, treating moral values as preferences has the advantage, stressed by Dewey and other moral philosophers, of not building in too strong a distinction between moral and other (natural, aesthetic, etc.) values. However, an important difficulty here is that moral values are usually seen as being arrived at through a process of reflection, employing an "idealized" standpoint in which initial preferences get tested and (to use an ancient metaphor) "purified." Such refined values would therefore seem to hold a somewhat elevated place in the pantheon of preferences; it is problematical whether/how they can be properly traded off in any simple way against other given and therefore presumably "shallower" (Hirshman uses the term *wanton*) preferences. Thus, this approach faces the problem of spelling out how the satisfaction of preferences of starkly different dimensions is carried out by the agent, and doing so in a way that sheds light on those economic behaviors (specified in the previous chapter) that this literature is trying to illuminate.

At present, then, it seems that none of the approaches has been developed successfully enough to merit singling it out as "most promising." Moreover, all the approaches appear to suffer from a certain lack of willingness to confront openly, and deal unambiguously with, some of the deeper complexities involved.

Complexities and Unexplored Alternatives

There are several major complexities surrounding moral values and norms that remain unexplored or inadequately investigated in this literature. In our view, these represent both major challenges and possibly significant opportunities for deepening the analysis. The first of these items concerns the relation between adopting moral rules and trying to serve one's (possibly long-term) self-interest. The second involves the plausibility of entering moral concerns into the rational choice model in only one basic way. The third relates to the largely unexplored territory of reconciling respect for moral rights with other aspects of the rational choice of actions significantly affecting others.

Moral Rules and Self-interest
It is an ancient question of ethics, clearly formulated at least as early as Plato's *Republic,* whether behaving morally is coincident with behaving in one's own self-interest. Those working on the incorporation of moral values or norms into the rational egoist model can hardly be required to settle this dispute, but they at least need to acknowledge that a problem exists. While some would maintain, following Kant, that choosing morally in the full sense requires that self-interest not be considered, this need not always be inconsistent with maintaining that moral behavior is consonant with self-interest in some broad sense. Thus, behavior conformable to moral requirements might conceivably be chosen for self-interested reasons. However, capturing this possibility requires some modification of the standard conception of the economic agent, usually thought of as concerned only with his or her own material welfare, and some modification of certain conceptions of what moral rule following really means.

Single-Mode Entry of Moral Values or Norms
It seems clear from the literature that economists would strongly prefer a single, unified way of introducing moral considerations into economic decision making, in the interests of parsimonious changes in the standard model.

But even given the more limited purposes economists have in mind, the history of ethics suggests that it is unlikely such an approach will be able to capture what they want. The efforts of moral philosophers over the centuries to rationalize all moral decision making in terms of a single principle or type of consideration—whether hedonistic consequences or natural law or self-realization—have been of doubtful success. Absent a major conceptual breakthrough, not in evidence in the literature reviewed, it seems likely that, in the end, a successful incorporation may require something beyond treating moral factors as *only* decision rules or *only* constraints or *only* preferences.

Further Issues of Reducibility: Rights and Rights Shifting
Largely to simplify analyzing an already complex literature, we have refrained from considering an additional level of moral concepts, that of moral rights. This simplification seemed reasonable for a first pass at the literature, since for many purposes rules of obligation and moral rights are interchangeable. However, structures of rights are clearly relevant to economic analysis. Moreover, if brought into the model at all, they serve to make it even more unlikely that moral concerns can be adequately introduced into the rational egoist model using a single mode of analysis; that is, moral rights render even more intractable the reducibility problem introduced in the preceding section (see Scanlon 1984). This is so because a rights framework tends to make certain preferences *decisive,* or nearly so, largely independent of the utilitarian evaluation of the associated outcomes. Put differently, a rights framework tends to disallow the usual straightforward trading off of preferences associated with rights against other preferences, no matter how strongly held.

There is a second issue involving the extent to which both rule-constraints and rights are taken as given. Most discussions of market exchanges presuppose a foundational structure of (legal and moral) rights, both property rights and other liberty rights (e.g., freedom to trade with anyone willing to transact without prior permission). In the standard model, only within this given framework of rights does the rational maximizer pursue his or her self-interest. But if the economic agent is genuinely self-seeking, it seems reasonable to suppose that he or she will use any means feasible to *shift* the structure of rights in ways favorable to himself or herself (and disadvantageous to others). Out of this insight has come a whole literature attempting to capture the dynamics of such rent seeking (Buchanan, Tollison, and Tullock 1980). But then the whole question of when rights will be "taken as given" versus changeable by the "selfish maximizer" strongly affects how markets undergirded by rights coordinate human interaction. Put another way, this line of reasoning challenges us to model what conditions justify a particular structure of rights compared to another in which the rights boundaries have been shifted. Within the model, it forces consideration of *when* constraints are simply taken as providing the given framework versus when they are subjected to consequentialist-maximizing reasoning and become the focus of actions aimed at altering them. That is, once rights are introduced into the picture, it seems clear that we must not only admit some kinds of nonconsequentialist reasoning into the model, but we must carefully try to relate the two modes of reasoning.

Is the Payoff of Trying to Incorporate Moral Values and Norms Large Enough to Make the Effort "Worth It"?

This is, of course, a currently unanswerable question. We believe that there probably are large payoffs to pursuing this line of inquiry, even if it ultimately proves unsuccessful. Even in that case, we believe a good deal would be learned about the underpinnings of economic theory by economists and even by philosophers along the way.

One kind of argument in favor of pursuing the incorporation of norms focuses on the nature of idealizations in economics and moral philosophy. Despite economists' willingness to make quite strenuous idealizations (in the sense of abstracting from complicating facts) about the context of market decision making, as a rule they pride themselves on being utterly "realistic" about human beings' basic selfishness. Theorists of morality, on the other hand, while also ignoring many of the complications generated by the messy imperfections in everyday choice, take pride in facing "realistically" the weightiness of the moral imperatives that oblige one no matter what others may or may not do.

Now some might be tempted to see in the effort to incorporate moral norms and values into economics a still further unwelcome idealization, that is, seeing decision making in market transactions as some might wish it to be rather than as it actually is. We suggest that the focus of the effort under review is exactly the reverse. It is precisely because it aims for a more realistic (in the sense of comprehensive) picture, one that incorporates both human limitations of knowledge and concern for others as well as the diverse ways in which humans compensate for such limitations, that something of value may emerge.

Of course it just may be that such efforts to complicate the model of economic decision making will yield a less useful framework for analysis even in "promising" situations, because it may become harder to derive definite predictions that can be usefully confronted by experience. However, even if this should turn out to be so, we would claim (see Goldfarb and Griffith, n.d.) that this would not by itself justify junking the incorporation effort. Economics as a discipline has other important roles to play besides attempting to predict, including simply helping us to grasp a well-founded picture of the world today, even if it is unable to tell us exactly what tomorrow's world will be like.

In any case, this effort toward more comprehensive understanding should, in the long run, be more important for normative than for positive economics. As we pointed out earlier, it is common to claim significant benefits from market coordination of human interaction. But if such benefits are partly due to well-functioning moral codes, it is inappropriate and potentially seriously misleading to give credit only to the first while ignoring the second.

The price of success in this analytical endeavor may be much more interdisciplinary cooperation of a concerted kind. Repeatedly we have been struck by how disciplinary blinders restrict one's reactions to familiar terms occurring in an unfamiliar context. We have also noted with dismay how borrowed conceptual frameworks may end up oddly distorted in a new usage.

Assuming that such interdisciplinary cooperation were to succeed in building a more comprehensive model of economic decision making, our conclusion is that there should be a sizable payoff. Even more important than the payoff within economics (and probably moral philosophy) would be the potential gain in our society's self-understanding of the possibilities and limitations of noncoercive social coordination. This would appear to be a goal well worth pursuing.

REFERENCES

Alchian, Armen. 1950. "Uncertainty, Evolution, and Economic Theory." *Journal of Political Economy* 58:211–21.

Axelrod, Robert. 1984. *The Evolution of Cooperation.* New York: Basic Books.

Becker, Gary. 1965. "A Theory of the Allocation of Time." *Economic Journal* 75:493–517.

Bergsten, Gordon. 1985. "On the Role of Social Norms in a Market Economy." *Public Choice* 45(2):113–37.

Braybrooke, David. 1987. "Social Contract Theory's Fanciest Flight." *Ethics* 97: 750–64.

Brennan, Timothy. 1989. "A Methodological Assessment of Multiple Utility Frameworks." *Economics and Philosophy* 5:189–208.

Brunner, Karl. 1987. "The Perception of Man and the Conception of Society: Two Approaches to Understanding Society." *Economic Inquiry* 25(3):367–89.

Buchanan, James, Robert Tollison, and Gordon Tullock, eds. 1980. *Toward a Theory of the Rent Seeking Society.* College Station, Texas: Texas A&M Press.

Campbell, Donald T. 1983. "The Two Distinct Routes beyond Kin Selection to Ultrasociality: Implications for the Humanities and Social Sciences." In *The Nature Of Prosocial Development,* ed. Diane Bridgeman. New York: Academic Press.

Coleman, James S. 1987. "Norms as Social Capital." In *Economic Imperialism,* ed. Gerald Radnitsky and Peter Bernholz. New York: Paragon House.

Elster, Jon. 1985. *Sour Grapes: Studies in the Subversion of Rationality.* Cambridge: Cambridge University Press.

Elster, Jon. 1986. "Introduction." In *Rational Choice,* ed. Jon Elster. London: Basil Blackwell.

Etzioni, Amitai. 1986. "The Case for a Multiple-Utility Conception." *Economics and Philosophy* 2:159–83.

Foreman, Frank. 1988. Review of *Morals by Agreement,* by David Gauthier. *Public Choice* 56:89–96.

Frank, Robert. 1987. "If *Homo Economicus* Could Choose His Own Utility Function, Would He Want One with a Conscience?" *American Economic Review* 77:593–604.

Gauthier, David. 1986. *Morals by Agreement.* Oxford: Oxford University Press.

Goldfarb, Robert, and William Griffith. N.d. "The Theory-as-Map Analogy and Changes in Assumption Sets in Economics." In *Socio-Economics: Toward a New Synthesis,* ed. A. Etzioni and P. Lawrence. Armonk, New York: M. E. Sharpe. In press.

Gould, Stephen Jay. 1982. *The Panda's Thumb.* New York: Norton.

Hirschman, Albert. 1985. "Against Parsimony." *Economics and Philosophy* 1:7–21.

Hirshleifer, Jack. 1985. "The Expanding Domain of Economics." *American Economic Review Directory* (December): 53–68.

Lancaster, K. J. 1966. "A New Approach to Consumer Theory." *Journal of Political Economy* 74:132–57.

Langlois, Richard, ed. 1986. *Economics as a Process.* Cambridge: Cambridge University Press.

Lumsden, Charles, and E. O. Wilson. 1981. *Genes, Mind, and Culture.* Cambridge, Mass.: Harvard University Press.

McPherson, Michael. 1984. "Limits on Self-Seeking: The Role of Morality in Economic Life." In *Neoclassical Political Economy,* ed. D. Colander. Cambridge: Ballinger.

Mueller, Dennis. 1986. "Rational Egoism Versus Adaptive Egoism as Fundamental Postulate for a Descriptive Theory of Human Behavior." *Public Choice* 51(1): 3–23.

Phelps, Edmund. 1975. "Introduction." In *Altruism, Morality, and Economic Theory,* ed. Edmund Phelps. New York: Russell Sage Foundation.

Plott, Charles. 1987. "Rational Choice in Experimental Markets." In *Rational Choice,* ed. Robin Hogarth and Melvin Reder. Chicago: University of Chicago Press.

Radner, Roy. 1986. "Can Bounded Rationality Resolve the Prisoner's Dilemma?" In *Contributions to Mathematical Economics in Honor of G. Debreu,* ed. W. Hildenbrand and A. Mas-Colell. Amsterdam: North-Holland.

Scanlon, Thomas. 1984. "Rights, Goals and Fairness." In *Theories of Rights,* ed. J. Waldron. Oxford: Oxford University Press.

Schenk, Robert E. 1987. "Altruism as a Source of Self-Interested Behavior." *Public Choice* 53:187–92.

Schotter, Andrew. 1981. *The Economic Theory of Social Institutions*. Cambridge: Cambridge University Press.

Sen, Amartya. 1974. "Choice, Orderings and Morality." In *Practical Reason*, ed. S. Korner. New Haven: Yale University Press.

Sen, Amartya. 1977. "Rational Fools: A Critique of the Behavioral Foundations of Economic Theory." *Philosophy and Public Affairs* 6:317–44.

Sen, Amartya. 1987. *On Ethics and Economics*. Oxford: Basil Blackwell.

Ullman-Margalit, Edna. 1977. *The Emergence of Norms*. Oxford: Oxford University Press.

Vanberg, Viktor. 1986. "Spontaneous Market Order and Social Rules." *Economics and Philosophy* 2:75–100.

Vanberg, Viktor. 1988. *Morality and Economics: De Moribus Est Disputandum*. Bowling Green, Ohio: Transactions Books.

The Trouble with Norms

Timothy J. Brennan

What Are Norms?

Norms, which I take here to mean behavior-guiding moral principles, figure prominently in social or political philosophy as ways to deal with the conflicts caused by the inability to satisfy everyone's interests simultaneously. The traditional normative question has been which norms to follow. The usual candidates are maximization of aggregate welfare (utilitarianism), respect for rights, self-fulfillment, efficiency, or some combination of these under various interpretations. A reflection of this tradition in economics is the formal explication of axiomatic bases for norms, examining their consequences and consistency, particularly regarding social policy choices.[1]

At a different level—I am not sure whether higher or lower—arguments for the choice of norms involve a hypothetical or actual process in a morally compelling setting. The most influential example today is Rawls's conception of justice as "fairness," in which he argues that anyone behind the "veil of ignorance," not knowing who he or she would be in the actual world, would choose to maximize liberty and the welfare of the least well-off class of persons.[2] In *Morals by Agreement*,[3] Gauthier argues that one should act in accord with the precepts that would have been chosen by rational agents when mutual cooperation would be individually beneficial. In less hypothetical veins, Nozick and Posner base moral theories on the mutual consent implicitly underlying actual transactions.[4] Nozick advocates a "process" ori-

---

The insight of Dale McCarthy into these issues is most appreciated, as are the comments of Ken Koford, Robert Goldfarb, and William Griffith. Remaining shortcomings are the sole responsibility of the author.

1. See K. Arrow, *Social Choice and Individual Values* (New York: Wiley, 1951). An example of the technique is J. Roemer, "Fairness Rules and Their Application by an Organization (WHO)." Manuscript, University of California; Davis.

2. J. Rawls, *A Theory of Justice* (Cambridge, Mass.: Harvard University Press, 1970).

3. D. Gauthier, *Morals By Agreement* (Oxford: Oxford University Press, 1986).

4. R. Nozick, *Anarchy, State, and Utopia* (New York: Basic Books, 1974); R. Posner, *The Economics of Justice* (Cambridge, Mass.: Harvard University Press, 1981), chap. 4.

entation that limits state involvement just to pursue desired patterns of wealth distribution, while Posner defends wealth maximization as a moral norm.

While these conceptions contribute to our moral intuition, the abstraction that makes them plausible bases for moral theory handicaps their ability to offer helpful guidance for behavior. This has led to two related controversies in modern moral theory about whether philosophical reasoning can contribute to ethical judgment. Within analytic philosophy, some suggest that general rules cannot reflect the richness of actual ethical life and decisions, and that devotion to rules is an improper sacrifice of one's identity.[5] Within feminism, there is a growing interest in the degree to which personal relationships and caring are neglected or ruled out by the ideal observer standpoint.[6]

Norms also have been the subject of empirical study. Much effort in the social sciences is directed toward the identification of the norms people follow, how and whether these norms influence behavior, and the processes by which these norms arise. Fields such as anthropology, political science, psychology, sociology, history, and law each have had complementary and sometimes overlapping roles to play in addressing norms.[7] More recently, biological and evolutionary models of the development of norms have been offered.[8]

Norms and Economics: What the Trouble Is Not

To economics, though, the supposed "queen" of the social sciences, norms present a puzzle. The description of that puzzle, and the methodological tension that accompanies it, is examined by Griffith and Goldfarb.[9] Initially, they derive the tension between economics and norms from the apparent

---

5. See B. Williams, *Ethics and the Limits of Philosophy* (Cambridge, Mass.: Harvard University Press, 1985); S. Wolf, "Moral Saints," *Journal of Philosophy* 79 (1982): 419–39.

6. See N. Noddings, *Caring: A Feminine Approach to Ethics and Moral Education* (Berkeley: University of California Press, 1984); J. Hardwig, "Should Women Think in Terms of Rights," *Ethics* 94 (1984): 441–55; O. Flanagan and K. Jackson, "Justice, Care, and Gender: The Kohlberg-Gilligan Debate Revisited," *Ethics* 97 (1987): 622–37; L. Blum, "Gilligan and Kohlberg: Implications for Moral Theory," *Ethics* 98 (1988): 472–91.

I note parenthetically that these writings and those cited in n. 5 run counter to William Griffith and Robert Goldfarb's claim in this volume that "the theory of morality . . . has by now produced a reasonable degree of consensus about what constitutes morality or 'the moral viewpoint.'"

7. An example of an empirical study of norms is Orbell, van de Kragt and Dawes, "Covenants without the Sword," this volume.

8. R. Frank, "Social Forces in the Workplace," this volume, and "If *Homo Economicus* Could Choose His Own Utility Function, Would He Want One with a Conscience?" *American Economic Review* 77 (1987): 593–604; R. Axelrod, *The Evolution of Cooperation* (New York: Basic Books, 1984).

9. W. Griffith and R. Goldfarb, "Amending the Economist's 'Rational Egoist' Model to Include Moral Values and Norms," this volume.

conflict between the self-interest perspective of economics and public or social good supported by norms. This tension, however, may be more apparent than real. Economic theory is quite as capable of predicting behavior according to norms as it would behavior according other preferences.[10] It can predict, probably rather accurately, that the frequency of lying goes up as its cost, relative to that of telling the truth, goes down. The "other-regarding" aspect of norms is already reflected in economic parlance as an externality. Norms may be instrumental and provide no intrinsic pleasure from their performance, but individuals perform all sorts of tasks, often burdensome, to obtain a future reward. One can "invest" in norm-based behavior; the "reward" is the benefits to others that accrue.

The origin, evolution, and acquisition of norms may be unexplained within economics, but no more so than are preferences for goods, where the consumption seems more direct. For example, I find the impulse to charity far easier to comprehend than I do the willingness to pay to sit through Gilbert and Sullivan. Moreover, economists—I should say neoclassical economists— have never aspired to predict, explain, or evaluate preferences themselves; their goal has been the prediction of behavior and the evaluation of policy and institutions based on those preferences.[11]

The difficulty in specifying just what it is about norms that is supposed to conflict with economics is illustrated by the examples of norm-based behavior offered by Griffith and Goldfarb. They explain refusal to steal a car, payment of taxes, or service on juries as "guided by explicit requirements of the law, backed by sanctions for failures to comply" as well as the potentially adverse reactions of "relatives, neighbors, and friends." If imprisonment and scorn are economic "bads," obeying the law in these instances is readily explicable as a private cost-benefit decision. Similar arguments are made about activities unrelated to legal obligations, such as help to younger siblings with college expenses, aid to an elderly person, or local charitable contributions or public service, even without invoking specific preferences, externalities, or investments. That some of the costs and benefits are neither monetary nor legal detracts not at all from the pertinence of what Griffith and Goldfarb call the economist's "rational egoist" model.

---

10. See T. Brennan, "A Methodological Assessment of Multiple Utility Frameworks," *Economics and Philosophy* 5 (1989): 189–208.

11. Since explanations or evaluations of economic phenomena that rely on changes in preference appeal, by definition, to noneconomic considerations, economists have made efforts to minimize the scope of situations in which preference change needs to be invoked. See G. Stigler and G. Becker, "De Gustibus Non Est Disputandum," *American Economic Review* 67 (1977): 76–90. They find that phenomena such as addiction, acquired "tastes," custom, advertising response, and fads can be explained without invoking changed preferences. Whether these are the best or most sensible explanations is another matter.

Griffith and Goldfarb recognize this. They suggest that economics might aid in understanding the use of norms rather than legal or monetary incentives and when the outcomes of those norms may not meet their intended goals. They warn, however, that economics may be able to incorporate norm-based behavior only at a cost of becoming either an *ex-ante*, "nontestable tautology" or an *ex-post*, "self-fulfilling prophecy." The alleged problem of irrefutability stands, I think, on a confusion between the method of economics and its content. As a method, economics may be applied to either norm-based or conventionally self-interested behavior. A failure of a specific behavioral prediction suggests not that economics should be rejected as a method, but that the underlying preferences and costs were not as originally specified. By analogy, one could say that physics, as a method of understanding natural phenomena, was not rejected in the shift from Newtonian to relativistic mechanics; rather, what was rejected was the supposition that mass was independent of velocity.

The lack of commitment of economics to a specific set of preferences, evidenced by the ability to just "stick norms in the utility function," suggests that its pretensions to predictive or explanatory usefulness are unjustified. However, economics cannot be any more regular than the underlying behaviors of economic actors. If norm-based behavior is sufficiently widespread and nonrandom to be of philosophical or methodological interest, then it can become a testable part of economic content as well, just as is the assumption of profit maximization by firms. If a narrower conception of self-interest suffices to explain and predict behavior, invoking norm-based or other-regarding preferences is unnecessary. To continue the physics analogy, the usefulness of physics follows not from the mere existence of forces in nature, but that the forces are sufficiently nonrandom to reduce a seemingly wide range of phenomena to a few categories. The "tunnel vision" that Griffith and Goldfarb rightly find typical of economists (and potentially dangerous to the extent that it minimizes the importance of norm-based behavior in securing desired ends) could and should be widened. The methods of economics and the "rational egoist" model nevertheless seem to remain intact.

To be sure, much depends upon the interpretation of *egoism*. If egoism implies a particular specification of which preferences count, that is, a claim that actions taken do not promote egoistic ends, then the egoist model may not apply. Griffith and Goldfarb do not offer such a specification. They associate egoism with "self-interest," but if a subjective concept of self-interest is intended, nothing is excluded. Nothing in the subjective conception of agency underlying economic theory rules out any preference, as long as the implicit ordering of choices meets minimal conditions of completeness and transitivity.[12] If sacrificing a nice day to help a friend makes me happy, am I

---

12. Stigler and Becker, "De Gustibus."

acting egoistically? On the other hand, an objective conception of self-interest seems inconsistent with much behavior that is uncontroversially within the purview of economics. For example, many might argue that smoking harms the smoker, but few would argue that this conflict with objective "self-interest" renders economics incapable of explaining or evaluating the behavior of tobacco markets.[13]

These observations on the trouble with norms, however, seem more evasive than responsive. To make the tension between norms and economics more precise, Griffith and Goldfarb propose three characterizations of norms—as decision rules, as behavioral constraints, and as preferences. A *decision rule* might be thought of as a rule of thumb, in which an agent is free to act in accord with preferences but chooses instead to follow a rule, trading off optimality for the benefits in not having to plan choices as carefully. To relate decision rules to other-regarding norms, Griffith and Goldfarb define decision rules as strategies to follow in interacting with others to achieve a desired result. They find that the "norms-as-decision-rules" characterization is inaccurate if norms are not motivated by self-interest. But their finding is compelling only if there is a practical way or reason to partition preferences into "self-interested" and "nonself-interested" categories. If norms are to be usefully characterized as nonself-interest-promoting behavior, such a specification is crucial.

In addition, much norm-based behavior is incomprehensible if construed strategically. Consider voting. As Griffith and Goldfarb note, voting is inexplicable if the costs of the effort involved in voting are compared to the nearly infinitesimal likelihood that one's vote will affect one's welfare. The conclusion is not premised upon an alleged lack of substantive difference between candidates, but is derived from the computation that the likelihood that a large population of voters will split *exactly* 50-50, either but for your vote (i.e., if you are the tie breaker with an odd number of votes cast) or with your vote (i.e., you are the tie maker with an even number of votes cast), is virtually zero. In these terms, commentators on election behavior should not lament low turnouts, but should instead be amazed that anybody bothers.[14]

These minimal probabilities, though, rule out not putatively self-interested motivations for voting, but strategic explanations as well. In 1980, I remember being told to vote for Jimmy Carter because "a vote for [then liberal favorite] John Anderson was a vote for Ronald Reagan." My response was

---

13. Conflicts between chosen behavior and desirable ends should call into question the worthiness of efficiency as a normative goal. See M. Sagoff, "Values and Preferences," *Ethics* 96 (1986): 301–16.

14. It is trivially easy to explain voting by invoking a preference to vote. As cited by Griffith and Goldfarb, Mueller observed in 1986 that the prediction that no one will vote was off in the 1984 presidential election by "eighty million voters or so." To paraphrase Mueller, we seem to have eighty million confirmations of the hypothesis that people like voting.

that voting makes no sense if viewed on the basis of its effect on the election, hence the strategic considerations underlying the advice was ill founded. If citizens come to value voting only for its effect on the outcome rather than as the exercise of a civic responsibility to state one's views or as a fun way to meet neighbors on a November day, then few, in fact, will vote.[15]

Griffith and Goldfarb next characterize norms as *constraints,* defined as limits on the choices agents can make. What makes constraints limiting to an agent is his or her perception that the costs of violating the constraints are large, infinite in the extreme. The "budget constraint" in basic consumer theory, for example, is a constraint only if penalties for theft are viewed as prohibitive. Viewed from this perspective, "norms-as-constraints" becomes indistinguishable from Griffith and Goldfarb's subsequent characterization of norms-as-preferences. They, too, note that the line between these characterizations is blurred. In either characterization, the "rational egoist" model can be retained, as action continues to be in accord with preferences, subject to constraints.

The major methodological question Griffith and Goldfarb leave us with is whether the economist should address the emergence of norms. Norms could be regarded as just a preference, and hence a matter more for psychology or sociology than economics. Economists can tell that, if the price of bread falls, more will be bought, but will offer no explanation for why people buy *n* loaves per year or prefer wheat to rye. If, though, formation of preferences—be they norms or anything else—affects market conduct, or if causality runs in the reverse direction, is it not the economist's responsibility to look at the genesis of "tastes"? Norms may be especially difficult for economists to neglect since they seem to provide some welfare-maximizing functions, as Sen and others have pointed out.[16] This question, important as it may be, is essentially about whether economists should study the "rational egoist's" ends, not just his or her means. The "rational egoist" model as pursuit of given ends itself still need not be rejected.[17]

---

15. Obviously, if each predicted that no one else would vote, then everyone would show up. A complete model would have to incorporate some sort of "rational" or "consistent" expectation of the behavior of others. It seems, though, that in a population where each values a (subjectively) favorable outcome more than the cost of voting, the only "rational expectation equilibria," if there are any, would involve ties.

16. The use of norms to mitigate free riding in the provision of public goods is discussed in A. K. Sen, "Rational Fools: A Critique of the Behavioral Foundations of Economic Theory," in *Choice, Welfare, and Measurement* (Cambridge, Mass.: MIT Press, 1982), 84–106. A claim that norms are wealth maximizing is made by R. Ellickson, "A Critique of Economic and Sociological Theories of Social Control," *Journal of Legal Studies* 16 (1987): 67–99.

17. For example, one might feel that advertising affects preferences, but actions taken in accord with those preference may still fit Griffith and Goldfarb's "rational egoist" conception.

What the Trouble Is—or May Be

We could conclude that there really is no tension between economics and norms, but that is not satisfying. The puzzle seems to persist; attempts to define it away or change the focus to the emergence of norms within the "rational egoist" framework leave me unsettled. One hypothesis may be that other-regarding preferences do not easily fit within the neoutilitarian welfare measure used by economists. Consider two individuals, A and B, dividing a fixed pool of resources R. Let $U^A(x)$ be the direct utility A gets from consuming x, and let $U^B(R - x)$ be B's utility from consuming the remainder of the pool. Suppose that A is a perfect utilitarian, in that he or she cares about B's direct utility as much as he or she cares about his or her own. Formally, let A's total utility be given by

$$V^A(x) = U^A(x) + U^B(R - x).$$

To see whether x is allocated efficiently, we maximize $V^A(x)$ subject to the constraint that $U^B(R - x)$ is at least as great as some value U^o. Normally A gains if and only if B loses, rendering all allocations $x \in (0,R)$ efficient, but the presence of $U^B(R - x)$ in A's total utility means that the constraint may be nonbinding; A will willingly give up x because of the utility he or she gets from making B better off. If the constraint on B's utility is nonbinding, efficiency implies that $U^A + U^B$ is maximized, seemingly implying that utilitarianism is efficient. However, the utilitarian calculus would maximize $V^A + U^B$, which equals $U^A + 2U^B$. A's altruistic perspective renders "narrow" utilitarianism efficient but apparently now not the "true" utilitarian moral standard.[18]

The double-counting conundrum may (or may not) be theoretically interesting, but it seems one of implementation, not a flaw in the rational actor model per se. The real tension between norms and economics follows, I think, from the conjunction of two potential properties of norms. The first is that norms qua norms seem to be consciously chosen, rather than just happen without reflection. But what, within a rational choice model, can it mean to choose preferences? The philosophical literature on will offers models of

---

18. Brian Barry (*Political Argument* [London: Routledge and Kegan Paul, 1970], 63–66) discusses in detail the implementation problems involved in counting "publicly oriented" wants in political decisions. Ronald Dworkin ("DeFunis v. Sweatt," in *Equality and Preferential Treatment*, ed. M. Cohen, T. Nagel, and T. Scanlon [Princeton: Princeton University Press: 1977], 63–83) finds this double counting violates the utilitarian norm to count all preferences equally. An example in a similar vein is provided in D. Friedman, "Does Altruism Produce Efficient Outcomes? Marshall versus Kaldor," *Journal of Legal Studies* 27 (1988): 1–15.

choice in which what an agent wants to do can differ from what it wants to want to do.[19] Such a distinction, however, does not easily fit within the rational maximization framework of economics.[20] Using subscripts to indicate levels of preferences (p), if p_1 at one level are chosen in accord with p_2 over p_1, p_1 would seem to be merely epiphenomenal in a "rational egoist" model. Under the economist's conception of agency, it makes no sense to say that one could have done something that one did not "want" to do.

There may be a way out. One could view adopted "preferences" as instruments to maximize welfare in accord with prior preferences. Frank provides an example of this line of reasoning.[21] Workers might find it beneficial to develop a preference not to shirk, if employers can detect which workers have this preference and can reward them accordingly. In this sense, an acquired preference to be reliable and diligent leaves the worker better off according to his or her prior preferences for things other than reliability. This rationalization, however, fails with ethical norms. As Griffith and Goldfarb point out, a defining characteristic of moral behavior is that it is not motivated merely by self-interest. It is distinctively moral to refrain from stealing when punishment would not be forthcoming, to tell the truth when lying would be beneficial, or to vote out of a sense of duty even when the likelihood of affecting the outcome is infinitesimal.

These arguments imply that norms cause trouble for economics if they are actively chosen by an agent, but that they do not maximize welfare when measured against the agents' other nonnorm-based preferences. If norms are given rather than chosen, economists could accept norms as just like other preferences. If norms are chosen only to facilitate satisfaction of given prior preferences, economists might be able to rationalize norms as indirect instrumental strategies for maximizing narrow welfare, with no intrinsic value to the agent. If norms are chosen, but not chosen to maximize prior welfare, neither of these rhetorical strategies are available. This, I think, is the root of the tension between moral behavior and the economist's "rational egoist" model.

But is this tension real? It depends upon whether one feels compelled to reject characterizing norms as just another preference. The economic turn of mind resists this rejection, not so much because of a special sense about norms but from the broader inability to accommodate the idea that any preferences can be, in some sense, willfully acquired, especially in a nonself-

---

19. See H. Frankfurt, "Freedom of Will and the Concept of a Person," in *Moral Responsibility,* ed. John M. Fisher (Ithaca: Cornell University Press, 1986), 65–80; Sen, "Rational Fools"; Brennan, "A Methodological Critique of Multiple Utility Frameworks."

20. T. Brennan, "Voluntary Exchange and Economic Claims," *Research in the History of Economic Thought and Methodology* 7 (1990): 105–24.

21. Frank, "Social Forces in the Workplace."

serving way. An agent's preferences are simply taken to be what they are revealed to be; a more complex conception is, by the "norms" of economic methodology, both empirically unnecessary and theoretically illogical.

Even if the notion of willful preference acquisition seems comprehensible, it may be inexplicable. That one's self-conception is fluid, with unclear boundaries and subject to the influence of will and experience, seems to be more a lesson from life, not scholarship. Descriptions of the processes that relate what one does to who one is can strike the analytically inclined reader as vague and romantic. For example, consider the following from Noddings.

> When I look at and think about how I am when I care, I realize that there is invariably this displacement of interest from my own reality to the reality of the other. . . . To be touched, to have aroused in me something that will disturb my own ethical reality, I must see the other's reality as a possibility for my own. This is not to say that I cannot try to see the other's reality differently. Indeed, I can. I can look at it objectively by collecting factual data; I can look at it historically. If it is heroic, I can come to admire it. But this sort of looking does not touch my own ethical reality; it may even distract me from it.[22]

As an example of the use of this line of argument, Okin argues that Rawls's theory of justice should *not* be dismissed by those who adopt an "ethic of care."[23] In her view, the ethical appeal of the "original position" derives from the sense of empathy with the station of others that could not exist without "a voice of responsibility, care, and concern for others."[24]

This "caring" approach does not yet seem capable of persuading an analytical, methodological individualist, economist or philosopher, that our preferences, that is, our identities, are open to self-initiated change, and that who we are and what we believe is a matter of will, commitment, and responsibility. It may be argued, and may well be true, that it is no more

---

22. Noddings, *Caring,* 14. This conception of personhood, exemplified by the references in nn. 9 and 10 above, is also used to criticize behavior based upon supposedly impersonal moral norms.

23. S. M. Okin, "Reason and Feeling in Thinking About Justice," *Ethics* 99 (1989): 229–49.

24. Okin, "Reason and Feeling," 230. She notes that Rawls "frequently obscures" or "is unwilling to call explicitly on the human qualities of empathy and benevolence in the working out of his principles of justice" (230). While one might wish Okin were correct regarding Rawls's underlying motivations, it still seems that his argument is the outcome of choices by strongly self-interested, highly risk-averse individuals. The outcome of decisions behind the veil of ignorance is notably lacking in any moral dimensions other than those held by mutually disinterested persons. See T. Nagel, "Rawls on Justice," in *Reading Rawls,* ed. Norman Daniels (New York: Basic Books, 1975), 1–16.

appropriate to describe this "openness of preference" in terms amenable to the "rational egoist" model than it would be to discuss Ella Fitzgerald in terms of audio frequencies. The analytic perspective has something to contribute, but somehow it misses the point. But this, I believe, is the task to accomplish if a canyon between moral norms and economic method exists and is to be bridged.

Norms versus Laws: Economic Theory and the Choice of Social Institutions

Mark A. Cohen

Although traditional economic theory has focused on the allocation of goods and services in a market economy, recent developments in economics have expanded the scope of analysis to virtually all spheres of human behavior.[1] Economists have literally invaded other disciplines in their analysis of non-market behavior and institutions such as crime and punishment, religion, marriage and family planning, history, and law.[2] Although some scholars question the relevance of the economic paradigm to nonmarket behavior,[3] few would argue with the proposition that economics has played a major role in refocusing the debate in most social science disciplines.

This essay focuses on the choice of social institutions: When does society choose social norms? When do we choose laws? Recent developments in the law and economics literature suggest that society relies on social norms for enforcement of socially desirable outcomes when it is efficient (i.e., less expensive) to do so. That is, the choice between laws and norms can be partially explained as the outcome of rational economic decisions on the part of society.

It has been suggested that one of the reasons society seldom relies on moral obligation is "the increasing dominance, in our public discourse about public policies and institutional structures, of the classical economic model of the rational individual decision maker."[4] Instead, I argue that if it is *true* that

I am grateful to Ken Koford, Jeff Miller, Pat Rettew, and Paul Rubin for their comments on earlier drafts of this essay. Of course, they do not share in the blame for any remaining errors.

1. See, for example, Gary S. Becker, *The Economic Approach to Human Behavior* (Chicago: University of Chicago Press, 1976).

2. See, for example, Richard A. Posner, "The Law and Economics Movement," *American Economic Review* 77, no. 2 (1987): 1–13.

3. See Mark Kelman, "On Democracy-Bashing: A Skeptical Look at the Theoretical and 'Empirical' Practice of the Public Choice Movement," *Virginia Law Review* 74, no. 2 (1988): 199–273.

4. William B. Griffith and Robert S. Goldfarb, "Amending the Economists's 'Rational Egoist' Model to Include Moral Values and Norms," this volume, 42.

economics is somehow to "blame" for society's not relying on social norms to solve a particular social problem, there are two possible explanations why this is so.

First, it is possible that society should *not* be relying on social norms in this particular situation; in which case economic analysis is quite correct. This would be the case when the social cost of enforcing norms exceeds the social cost of enforcing laws.[5] This is a normative statement; the economic model tells policymakers in this particular situation that they should *not* be relying solely on social norms, and that enforcing laws is preferable.

Second, it is possible that economics is not being correctly applied to the problem at hand, in which case the analyst is incorrect (not the theory). That is, society does not rely on social norms in this particular situation because to do so would "cost" more than the alternative—legal rules. This is a positive statement; the economic model suggests that the *reason* we observe laws is that social norms are inferior in this situation. Indeed, I argue here that the economic model can help us explain when society uses social norms versus laws.

The Good Samaritan versus a Duty to Rescue

Throughout this essay, I will rely on the case of the "good samaritan."[6] Consider the plight of an individual who is driving on an isolated road and spots an elderly person whose car has run off the road and needs assistance. There are five possible reasons why a passerby would stop to help the person in need.[7] Although I list them separately, it is clear that an individual may be simultaneously influenced by any or all of these factors.

1. *Pure altruism.* This implies the individual will gain nothing from the rescue other than personal satisfaction.
2. *Reciprocal altruism.* The individual expects that there is a positive probability that someday he or she will also be in a situation of similar need. Further, the fact that the individual comes to the rescue today will increase the probability that this good samaritan norm will be operative in the future, when it might be needed.

---

5. It should be noted that the "social cost" of enforcing either norms or laws includes the cost associated with individuals who do not abide by the laws or norms in addition to actual enforcement costs.

6. This case is also referred to frequently by Griffith and Goldfarb. Thus, it is a useful point of reference in comparing their approach to economic analysis to the one developed here.

7. See William M. Landes and Richard A. Posner, "Salvors, Finders, Good Samaritans, and Other Rescuers: An Economic Study of Law and Altruism," *Journal of Legal Studies* 7 (1978): 93 for a discussion of these various types of altruistic behavior. The terms *reciprocal*

3. *Recognition factor.* The fact that the individual was a good samaritan will become known among that person's peers and family. Moreover, this fact will bring some positive benefits to the good samaritan in terms of reputation, fame, etc.

4. *Informal Monetary Incentives.* The potential good samaritan may expect the person in need to offer some compensation for the assistance provided. Of course, one would need to explain how this "informal" contract would be enforced. It is quite likely that the preceding three factors that influence one to be a good samaritan would cause a person receiving assistance to offer a reward.

5. *Formal Legal Rules.* These may provide either positive or negative incentives. For example, one might envision a legally enforceable reward plan for good samaritans. Alternatively, those who are in a position to become good samaritans might be held to a legal standard requiring them to help those in need. The "punishment" for failure to rescue could be in the form of either civil or criminal liability.

Normative Considerations: The Costs and Benefits of Encouraging Good Samaritan Behavior

As mentioned earlier, an economic analysis of good samaritan laws has both normative and positive implications. First, focus on the normative aspects of this problem. In order to do so, recall the economist's fundamental tool of analysis—utility maximization. Reduced to its basics, economic theory tells us that individual optimizing decisions are based on two factors: preferences and constraints. People choose their consumption and leisure activities based on maximizing utility (i.e., personal preferences), subject to external constraints (e.g., income, wealth, time, laws). Thus, if society wishes to influence individual behavior, it must change either (or both) of these factors.

Suppose society wishes to encourage people to be good samaritans. The extent to which each of these five factors (pure altruism, reciprocal altruism, recognition factor, informal monetary sanctions, and formal legal rules) affects individual behavior depends on many other factors—some of which are more easily influenced by policymakers than others. For example, the importance of reciprocal altruism and the recognition factor are likely to be inversely related to the size of the community.[8] However, this fact offers little

---

altruism and *recognition factor* are taken from Landes and Posner, although the former term is originally attributable to the biological literature; see Richard L. Trivers, "The Evolution of Reciprocal Altruism," *Quarterly Review of Biology* 46 (March 1971): 35–57.

8. See James M. Buchanan, *Freedom in Constitutional Contract* (College Station: Texas A&M Press, 1977), chap. 11.

hope to a policymaker who wants to encourage altruistic behavior. Instead, there are two ways society can affect moral behavior—by influencing either preferences or constraints.

For example, one might attempt to change individual preferences for being a good samaritan by teaching moral values in the school, home, church, etc. This is likely to increase purely altruistic behavior. Alternatively, one might attempt to teach people to be more risk averse. Increasing people's fear of being left stranded on a highway might increase the potency of reciprocal altruism for being a good samaritan.

Economists might also help predict which approaches and under what circumstances such attempts at changing preferences are likely to be successful. For example, one is more likely to be successful teaching "moral behavior" when it can be shown that leading an ethical life will benefit the individual through an enhanced reputation, etc. It should also be noted that teaching moral values to children is entirely consistent with individual utility-maximizing behavior by parents, as parents are likely to benefit from the good reputation of their children.[9]

There are also many ways society could change the constraints facing potential good samaritans. For example, increasing peer and family pressure would increase the relative importance of the recognition factor as a constraint on individual behavior. Formal legal rules such as mandatory rewards or legal liability provide incentives through decreasing the "price" of being a good samaritan. The fact that legal rules are generally accompanied by rewards and penalties does not necessarily mean they will only be complied with when financial incentives exist. Instead, it is quite possible that many rules are complied with solely because they exist. That is, one of society's ethical norms might be compliance with existing laws. Thus, penalties and rewards might be used to increase compliance over the level that would exist in the absence of such financial incentives.

Consider the normative implications of affecting individual constraints. An economic analyst might be able to identify (and possibly quantify) the costs and benefits of a reward or punishment scheme. The costs and benefits of various enforcement mechanisms will depend on (1) the number of people who will be in need of roadside assistance, (2) the number of potential good samaritans, and (3) the cost of detecting and punishing violators. All of these variables will crucially depend on the type of enforcement mechanism chosen.

For example, the economist would likely note that a formal legal rule establishing liability for a duty to rescue will provide perverse incentives that

---

9. Gary S. Becker, *A Treatise on the Family* (Cambridge, Mass.: Harvard University Press, 1981), 193.

affect both the number of people in need and the number of good samaritans. It might encourage potential good samaritans to stay away from risky situations where they might be called upon to help and to avoid acquiring the skills necessary to help a stranded driver. It would also diminish the incentive to be a good samaritan created by the recognition factor, since one who saves another is simply obeying the law, not being a "hero."[10] For automobile drivers, a formal rule might reduce the incentive to take proper care so that they do not run off the road and find themselves in need of help.[11]

At first, it might seem that the law ought to impose legal liability for failure to rescue. After all, in many cases, the person in need of rescue is likely to value the rescue by more than the cost to the person who is in a position to offer assistance. However, legal liability for failure to rescue might actually be inefficient, due to both the perverse incentives caused by a liability rule and the cost of enforcement.[12]

Several examples of perverse incentives were discussed previously, such as people avoiding situations where they might be called upon for assistance. In addition, the cost of enforcing such a liability rule might be exorbitant— primarily due to the burden of proof likely to be required in order to bring charges against a violator of this law. First, one needs to determine if any potential rescuers were available. This might be particularly difficult in the case of a victim who has already died. Second, one needs to find the potential rescuer. Since all witnesses would also be liable for failure to rescue, the chance of locating a potential rescuer is rather slim.

Finally, one would have to prove that the potential rescuers could have assisted the victim without imposing too great a burden on themselves (either financial or at the risk of their own safety). Thus, the expected cost of bringing a suit for failure to rescue is very high, the expected benefit very low. Moreover, since the person charged with failure to rescue has a lot to lose from an unfavorable ruling, he or she is willing to spend a considerable sum defending against such a claim.

Thus, even though a formal legal rule mandating a duty to rescue might be established, it is possible that the net result will be a decrease in the number of good samaritans (due to the incentives problem) in addition to increased administrative costs to society (due to the high cost of enforcement). On the other hand, the use of less formal social norms might avoid all of these perverse incentives and costs. Depending on the circumstances, there might

---

10. See Landes and Posner, "Salvors, Finders."

11. See Donald Wittman, "Liability for Harm or Restitution for Benefit?" *Journal of Legal Studies* 13 (1984): 57–80.

12. My subsequent discussion is based primarily on the arguments set forth in Paul H. Rubin, "Costs and Benefits of a Duty to Rescue," *International Review of Law and Economics* 6 (1986): 273–76.

be more or fewer good samaritans under a social norm enforcement scheme than under a legal rule. Nevertheless, it is possible that the lower costs associated with norms would tip the scales in favor of this approach.[13] Of course, without a thorough empirical study of these costs and benefits, it is impossible to make a definitive policy recommendation. Instead, my discussion was meant to be illustrative.

Why might the use of social norms be a better solution than legal rules for dealing with the good samaritan problem? An economic rationale would be that good samaritans are generally able to internalize a good deal of the benefits otherwise conferred on the person in need. Whether the reason is purely altruistic or based on family and peer pressure, good samaritans clearly benefit from their actions. This benefit might be in the form of increased personal satisfaction (in the case of pure altruism) or in either pecuniary or nonpecuniary benefits that accrue from having a favorable reputation within one's family and community.

The reputation effect of being a good samaritan also suggests why some attempts at using social norms to influence behavior will fail. For example, an individual is much less likely to be a good samaritan if the only pressure comes from a government bureaucrat through public service announcements extolling the virtues of helping elderly motorists in need of assistance. Unless there is some reputational value to being a good samaritan, there is little benefit for the individual to internalize social norms after listening to this public service message.[14] For example, President Ford's "Whip Inflation Now," President Carter's sweaters, and President Reagan's "Just Say No to Drugs" were all dismal failures at influencing individual behavior. Without corresponding peer or family pressure, they had little chance of succeeding.

Thus, I would argue that economics does, indeed, allow for the possibility that moral obligation will affect individual behavior in socially desirable ways. However, in order to be an effective social tool, moral suasion must either directly affect individual preferences or it must be accompanied by costs or benefits that can be internalized by individual decision makers.

Positive Considerations: The Choice of Norms versus Laws

This discussion suggests that social norms can be thought of as economic institutions that force individual decision makers to internalize the exter-

---

13. James M. Buchanan (*The Limits of Liberty* [Chicago: University of Chicago Press, 1975], 117) has noted the "superiority of securing tolerable behavioral order and predictability through ethical standards," due to the lower cost of enforcement.

14. It is possible that a public service announcement increases the reputational value of being a good samaritan. For example, people who hear the public service announcement might be

nalities they create (whether positive or negative). But this raises the fundamental question that was to be the theme of this volume: "Why does society sometimes enforce its values by personal ethical standards or social norms?" In particular, why does society not recognize a legal liability for failure to rescue and, instead, rely on social norms for good samaritans? This moves us into the realm of positive economic theory.

In order to understand why society sometimes uses norms instead of rules, consider the evolutionary process by which common law tends toward efficiency.[15] The basic intuition behind the common law efficiency model is that inefficient rules are more likely to be challenged in court than efficient rules. This is because parties that value a property right highest are willing to spend more to litigate than the other party. Of course, efficiency requires that the highest valued user of a property right ultimately ends up with that right. Generally, if the highest valued user is on the "right" side of the common law doctrine, the other party will not be willing to challenge that doctrine. However, if the common law doctrine places the property right on the party that values the property right less, the highest valued user is willing to challenge the doctrine.

Although this model of common law efficiency is appealing, it has several practical limitations. In particular, it applies most directly to situations where both parties to the dispute have long-term interests in the outcome of the issue. Moreover, court precedents might be thought of as public goods— once it has been established, all potential litigants can benefit from the fact that the precedent has been established without incurring the expense of litigation. Thus, a free rider problem might arise—where all potential litigants will postpone litigation hoping that another set of potential litigants will go to court instead. In the case of a duty to rescue, it is not clear whether or not the model would fully apply. However, if liability insurance included coverage against claims for failure to rescue, the insurance industry would have a long-term interest in the outcome of this matter. Moreover, any person (and hence every insurance company) could potentially be on either side of a "failure to rescue" lawsuit. Thus, pressures toward efficiency might be adequate in this case.

---

convinced that this activity is socially desirable; hence, they look more favorably on those who do this good deed.

15. This discussion is based on the model developed by Paul H. Rubin, "Why is the Common Law Efficient," *Journal of Legal Studies* 6 (1977): 51–63. A good discussion of the common law efficiency model is also contained in Robert Cooter and Thomas Ulen, *Law and Economics* (Glenview, Ill.: Scott Foresman, 1988), 492–96. For a critique of this literature, see Lewis Kornhauser, "A Guide to the Perplexed Claims of Efficiency in the Law," *Hofstra Law Review* 8 (1980): 627–33; John Byrne and Steven M. Hoffman, "Efficient Corporate Harm: A Chicago Metaphysic," in *Corrigible Corporations and Unruly Law,* ed. Brent Fisse and Peter A. French (San Antonio: Trinity University Press, 1985), 125–31.

If the common law refuses to impose liability for failure to rescue, why do we ever see good samaritans? The answer, of course, lies in the realm of social norms. In particular, the first four factors listed earlier (pure altruism, reciprocal altruism, recognition factor, and informal monetary incentives) provide incentives for people to be good samaritans. Of course, there will always be some people who will decline to be good samaritans when the occasion arises. For these people, the incentives simply are not strong enough.[16]

Thus, if one believes the models of common law efficiency, we might expect the common law to decline to impose legal liability for failure to rescue, because the cost of a legal liability for failure to rescue exceeds its benefits. Simply put, since it is "cheaper" to use social norms than legal rules in this case, society relies upon social norms. I argue that society generally chooses between norms and rules by choosing the least costly solution.[17] In other words, society chooses the most efficient enforcement mechanism— whether it be norms or legal rules.

Although the focus of my discussion has been on the duty to rescue, the general principle applies to other norms as well. Posner has noted that "the law of contracts, for example, enforces only a limited subset of prom- ises . . . but this is because the scope of the law is limited by the costs of administering it. The costs of legally enforcing all promises would exceed the gains because many promises do not enhance value significantly, and some that do may be made in circumstances where the costs of legal error outweigh the benefits from enforcing the promise in the form made. . . ."[18]

---

16. A somewhat related argument that relies on different mechanisms for achieving effi- cient norms can be found in the realm of "evolutionary economics." See Robert H. Frank, "Social Forces in the Workplace," this volume.

17. The "cost" of a law or norm includes, (1) establishing the law or norm, (2) enforcement of the norm or law, and (3) external costs such as the victim who is not rescued since some people do not comply with the norm or law. It is much more costly to establish a social norm than it is to create a law. However, it is much cheaper to enforce a social norm once it is in place.

18. Richard A. Posner, *Economic Analysis of Law* (Boston: Little, Brown, 1986), 239.

Comments

Dennis C. Mueller

Griffith and Goldfarb have done us a tremendous service in bringing together a huge and amorphous literature to shed light on several important methodological issues in economics. My comments are intended as amplifications of some of the points Griffith and Goldfarb make, and of my own position on these issues as originally outlined in the 1986 article they cite.

It is important, particularly when discussing the introduction of norms, rights, altruism, and the like into economic analysis, to keep in mind whether one is interested in using the economic methodology for positive or normative analysis. Failure to take into account norms, rights, and altruism has been cited both in criticism of the predictive and explanatory powers of economics and in criticism of the vacuous normative content of neoclassical welfare economics. Consider the first criticism.

It is true that concepts of preferences or a utility function are sufficiently general as to be able to incorporate moral and altruistic types of behavior. Indeed, one can assume that an individual's utility goes up if he or she experiences pleasure or if he or she experiences pain (masochism), if he or she observes others experiencing pleasure (empathy) or pain (sadism), if one reduces certain risks, or if one increases them. The concepts of preferences and utility are sufficiently pliable that no action need be ruled out as the best possible choice from a set of alternatives for some set of preferences or utility function.

But such pliability is as much a liability as an advantage in developing refutable hypotheses. To sharpen our predictions, narrower specifications of preferences and utility are needed. Most economists work with quite narrow definitions, that is, an individual's utility is a function of only his or her *own* consumption, leisure, income, and the like. By and large, such assumptions serve us well, but in some areas, as in predicting criminal acts, charity, and voting, the narrow definition of utility assumption leads to predictions that correspond poorly to observed behavior. The question then arises of how best to modify the economist's behavioral model to improve its capacity to predict human behavior.

To see the issues, consider the following example. Two students from a class are picked at random and told to write down a distribution of \$20. How much of the \$20 each wants to go to himself or herself, how much to the other person. No discussion is allowed and the students do not show one another their proposals. A coin flip is used to pick one of the proposals, and the \$20 is distributed in accordance with the dictates of the chosen proposal.

What proposals would the students make? Here the beauty of the narrow view of preferences economists usually assume is apparent. If the students maximize their own income, each student proposes \$20 for himself or herself and nothing for the other student. A sharper prediction one could not ask for. But it is also a prediction that is likely to be falsified in a large fraction of the cases. If so, then considerations other than the narrowly selfish maximization of own income are at work. Considerations of fairness or altruism or some such would appear to be involved.

As Griffith and Goldfarb correctly point out, one can introduce norms as alterations to the constraints within which the decision problem is set. The narrow, self-interest modeling of the problem would see individual 1 as choosing a Y_1 and Y_2 to maximize $U_1(Y_1)$, subject to the constraint $20 = Y_1 + Y_2$, with the trivial solution being $Y_1 = 20$ and $Y_2 = 0$. The first modification Y_2, with the trivial solution being $Y_1 = 20$ and $Y_2 = 0$. The first modification to the problem one can make is to assume that it is the preferences of the individual that need changing. One gets utility from 2's having income, $U_1(Y_1, Y_2)$. Under this assumption, 1's "selfish" utility maximization decision leads him or her to propose some fraction of the \$20 for 2 (assuming $\partial U_1/\partial Y_2$ is large enough).

Alternatively, one can assume that individual 1 views himself or herself as being in the kind of social context requiring a different decision rule, say the quasi-utilitarian rule of maximizing:

$$W = U_1(Y_1) + \alpha U_2(Y_2) \tag{1}$$

As a third alternative, 1 may be thought to choose to maximize his or her narrowly defined utility ($U_1[Y_1]$), subject to some sort of fairness or equity constraint such as:

$$Y_2 \geq \bar{Y}; \tag{2}$$

$$Y_2 = \beta Y_1; \tag{3}$$

or

$$U_2(Y_2) = \gamma U_1(Y_1). \tag{4}$$

All of these modifications can lead to 1's choosing to assign some fraction of the $20 to 2 in his or her proposal. By appropriate choice of the $U(\cdot)$'s and the other parameters, these three alternatives can lead to 1's selecting identical proposals. For example, if $U_1(Y_1, Y_2)$ is assumed separable in Y_1 and Y_2, then maximizing this utility function, and maximizing an additive welfare function like equation 1 are one and the same. Similarly, maximizing $U_1(Y_1)$ with equation 4 as a constraint yields the same outcome as maximization of equation 1 does, if $\alpha = \lambda/(1 - \lambda\gamma)$, where λ is the Lagrangian constant assigned to equation 4. Thus, whether one modifies the preference function of an individual, the decision rule, or the constraints to the problem is largely a matter of mathematical convenience.

More substantive issues arise when one tries to predict which individuals choose to assign part of the $20 to the other person, and how much they assign. One expects that an individual will assign more to the other person, if the two students happen to be friends. A student used to sharing with others, say a student from a large family, might assign more to the other party than someone not in the habit of sharing, say an only child. It is here that the disciplines of psychology and sociology have the most to contribute to the modeling of behavior by telling us what variables to look for in an individual's background that may help us predict his or her future.

This backward-looking aspect of human behavior is the biggest difference between the economist's usual modeling of individual behavior and a broader, psychological-based modeling. For the economist, bygones are bygones and the rational, self-interested individual considers only the future payoffs from various actions. But past experiences are not a psychological equivalent to sunk costs—something an individual can ignore, even when to do so might be to his or her narrow advantage. To predict which individuals contribute to charities, vote, commit crimes, and engage in other forms of socially interactive behavior, we need to know more than just the probabilities and dollar entries in the payoff matrix at the time of decision. We need to know how the individual's preferences (read decision rule, read psychological constraints) have been shaped.

It should be noted that some of the philosophical distinctions that concern Griffith and Goldfarb—rights, norms, altruism—however important for a normative evaluation of individual actions, *may be* less relevant for developing a predictive behavioral theory. The latter may require only a knowledge of particular environmental variables in a person's background.

In closing, let me clarify my position on the evolution of norms. I am struck by the central role the selfish behavior postulate plays in biology, psychology, economics, and the work of some sociologists and anthropologists. If the public choice methodology continues to conquer political science, and sociologists and anthropologists coalesce on a selfish-based theory, all of the social sciences could be working from a common methodological stem.

Social biology is concerned with the evolution of the species and gene structures. To understand the appearance and disappearance of norms one needs to rely on psychology, sociology, and anthropology.

It is easy to imagine, based on behavioral psychology, how superstitions and taboos begin. A savage, driven half-mad by a prolonged drought, goes into a frenzied dance. Soon thereafter it rains. The gods have rewarded the savage's dance with rain, and he is called upon to dance the next time there is a drought. We know from behavioral psychology that habits can be sustained with only occasional reinforcement. So long as it rains once in a while following the rainmaker's dance, his powers in the eyes of the other members of the tribe are preserved.

The more often a primitive people can check a casual relationship, the more likely it is to be founded in fact. The chance recovery of a sick person following consumption of a particular herb may lead to the herb's being regarded as a cure for the illness, even when it has no curative effect. But for common herbs and illnesses, it will be only efficacious herbs that remain in use. That primitive peoples have discovered which herbs cure which diseases is not so terribly surprising.

Similar arguments apply to religious taboos and norms. One presumes that the prohibition of the eating of pork by the Jews came about as the Jews in the Middle East observed that people who ate pork frequently became sick afterwards. That this religious taboo only exists in parts of the world that are very hot, and thus conducive to the development of the trichana worm, is again not totally coincidental.

One expects other behavioral norms to evolve in a similar way. Chance may keep some norms alive that do not promote the welfare of the group or are even dysfunctional, but one expects behavioral restraints that make people better off to have higher survival properties than those that do not.

If the latter is true, then the modeling of norm selection might take place by assuming that social institutions (norms, laws, etc.) evolve *as if* they were designed to maximize the welfare of the community, defined perhaps as a Benthamite or some other social welfare function. Such a theory would allow one to predict which norms and mores emerge, and when they might disappear. Such a theory would help one to link a group's ethical and legal institutions to characteristics in its physical, economic, and social environment.

Response to Our Commentators

William B. Griffith and Robert S. Goldfarb

We consider ourselves fortunate to have elicited three such interesting and useful comments. While there are places where we strongly disagree with each commentator, each of the responses helps to advance the intellectual conversation about the issues in question.

Especially salutory is Brennan's careful working through of the variety of "obvious" replies an economist might make to our argument. He shows how these replies, for the most part, fail to meet the challenges posed head-on and concludes wryly with the observation that "the root of the tension between moral behavior and the economist's 'rational egoist' model is the possibility that norms are chosen, but not chosen to maximize prior welfare."

A valuable feature of Cohen's comment is the suggestion that the question of the rationality of norm-selection should be sought at the societal rather than at the individual level. He argues that the system of legal institutions can be viewed as representing a societal decision, rationalizable on efficiency grounds. This choice involves whether to promote specified ends by relying informally on a given distribution of tendencies toward altruism in the population, or instead to foster these ends by means of explicit legal restrictions.

Mueller develops an instructive example representative of situations in which an economist should admit that the agent is considering something beyond "narrowly selfish maximization of own income." He uses this example to show that our distinction between modifying preferences or modifying constraints may not be meaningful, as long as the analyst's attention is limited to the goal of predicting behavior.

Rather than debating particular points of disagreement, we will try to emphasize and clarify some broad features of our position. These features appear to have been overlooked or underappreciated by our commentators or else represent differing fundamental assumptions that need to be underlined about the standard economic model or the nature of morality.

The Concept of an Economic Approach

The concept of the *standard economic approach* we are using differs, at times, from the one being used by the commentators. We are using a relatively rich or elaborate notion, akin to a Kuhnian paradigm or a Lakatosian research program, while Brennan and sometimes Cohen and Mueller seem to be using a much more spare notion that sees economics as a toolbox in which particular tools, such as a quite narrowly defined utility function, can be readily discarded in favor of (for example) a utility function with broadly altruistic elements. When Cohen asserts that economic theory "does indeed allow for the possibility that moral obligation will affect individual behavior in socially desirable ways," or when Brennan seems to accuse us of a "confusion between the method of economics and its content," they are focusing on this toolbox concept, rather than our starting point of the rational egoist model; this model is, we would argue, a standard and widely used paradigmatic approach in economics. Indeed, Mueller seems to implicitly agree with this assertion when he notes that "most economists work with quite narrow definitions, that is, an individual's utility is a function of only his or her *own* consumption, leisure, income, and the like."

But what is the argument for starting from a relatively rich or elaborate conception of economic theory akin to a paradigm in the sense of Kuhn or research program in the sense of Lakatos? While we cannot fully argue the case here, there is convincing evidence from the history and sociology of science that academic training in a discipline includes much more than absorbing a set of analytical tools or theory claims. It also involves learning to imitate what Kuhn calls models of eminently successful work in the discipline and to avoid approaches seen as "wrong turns" by the discipline. Lakatos calls these aspects of ongoing disciplinary research programs their positive and negative heuristics: "dos and don'ts" that are communicated along with the analytic techniques or formal theory postulates to novice members of the profession.

To tie this to the point at issue here, our view is that the professional socialization of young economists includes the positive heuristic to try to use the rational egoist model as much as possible in generating explanatory schemes. It also includes the negative heuristic that any forced, unavoidable departure from this basic model should be in as minimal a way as possible. If this minimal departure assertion is correct, one can expect to find that the (relatively limited) movement within the profession to incorporate moral concerns will tend to proceed in ways that are consistently trying to minimize the actual differences between their alternative approaches and the standard rational egoist model and also will try to play down the consequences of the suggested modifications for the concept of *rational* or the concept of *egoist*.

Our examination of this literature reveals that it does indeed have these characteristics (the reader searching for a particularly revealing example should read Hirshleifer 1985). Thus, we would maintain that economics, as it is understood by practitioners, is not so amenable to change in its basic structure as Brennan's remarks suggest; our review of the literature suggests that economists would give up on either the full rationality or the full egoism of the individual economic decision maker only as a last resort, and will try hard, at first, to modify or bend concepts and propositions coming from outside the discipline to fit the mainstream economic model with the most minimal adjustments to it.

We have two additional comments on the relevance of the standard paradigmatic approach versus the toolbox approach. First, while Brennan and Cohen seem to be implying that moving away from the standard rational egoist version of the economic model involves no great inconvenience or sacrifice, this neglects the fact that the standard welfare economics results (that many economists appear to be so fond of) seem to depend on minimizing departures from the standard rational egoist assumptions. Second, Brennan's toolbox approach seems to suggest using the method of economics but not being enamored of the restricted content used in the past. But if he believes that, how can he also argue the following: "The origin, evolution, and acquisition of norms may be unexplained within economics, but no more so than are preferences for goods where the consumption seems more direct. . . . Moreover . . . neoclassical economists have never aspired to . . . explain . . . preferences." This statement is absolutely correct as a positive description of the activities of neoclassical economists. But if Brennan thinks that the toolbox, rather than the paradigm, approach is right, why should he then hold up past (paradigmatic) practice as compelling evidence indicating how researchers should behave? Indeed, our point was precisely that this unconcern with the origin and evolution of preferences may not be appropriate in the case of moral preferences, while it is appropriate in the case of "ordinary preferences for goods." (This proposition of ours, it should be noted, draws heavily on Hirschman 1985.) Indeed, Brennan's discussion in the last part of his comment focuses on the possibly distinctive differences between moral and "ordinary goods" preferences in a way quite consistent with our point that unconcern with evolution of preferences may not be appropriate for moral preferences.

Characteristics of Moral Norms versus Moral Values

While it is apparently not sufficiently clarified or emphasized, our two essays are meant to reflect the idea that the concepts of moral norms and moral values cannot be treated as identical without significant loss of understanding. A large philosophical literature criticizing recurrent attempts to reduce values to norms (and vice versa) provides testimony to the widely held perception among ethical theorists that a successful fundamental reduction has not been achieved.

In contrast to the situation in the philosophy literature, popular usage often conflates norms and values, at times indiscriminately using one for the other, as though they were, for all practical purposes, perfect substitutes. Some of our commentators appear not to distinguish norms from values at all, or at least to assume that these terms are interchangeable or reducible for the limited purposes for which economists might need to appeal to concepts of morality.

We would stress that our position, as developed in Part 1 of the essay, is that including *only* norms or *only* values would leave the incorporation project seriously incomplete. It is apparently not clear why we hold that position; clarifying our reasons may make it clearer why we strongly disagree with some of our commentator's sometimes implicit suggestions that we have mistakenly failed to adopt seemingly easy reductionist solutions to problems of incorporating norms and values.

We would argue that norms (sometimes equivalent to *rules* or *principles*) function differently in moral discourse and argument than values do. Deontological moral theorists have typically held this view, and even some of the most important writers in the consequentialist tradition, such as John Stuart Mill, have acknowledged its validity.

Consider an example involving the incorporation of altruism into the economic model. If one views this as the only essential element in introducing moral concerns into the economic model, it seems natural to see morality as simply another value to be included in preferences. Seen in this way, it is to be weighed against other values, such as one's own material interests, as more or less important depending on the particular context of choice. Mueller's discussion of the sharing experiment brings out how naturally this way of looking at choice fits the economist's modeling framework. (However, as Brennan suggests, unless we have some way of analyzing the "costliness" of altruism, this incorporation may have very limited predictive power, at most.)

But norms function in a different way than values in moral discourse and argument. Thus, an agent who only held moral values (as described in the preceding paragraph) might well be subject on occasion to accusations of immorality in the sense of having violated moral norms relevant to a particular context. This possibility arises because moral norms suggest particular *standards* or *threshholds* below which action is immoral; above the threshhold, the same action is not immoral, though it might be criticizable as weak.

It may be helpful to illustrate these contrasting features of values versus norms with an example. Critics of the typical economic view of the firm sometimes assert that employers may, at times, behave altruistically in ways not consistent with profit maximization. This claim about employer behavior may or may not be correct, but our interest is in the implicit view of morality it involves, not in its factual accuracy. Suppose the claimed altruistic behavior involves providing day-care for employees' children in a way allegedly not reducible to profit maximization (such as the employer's interest in the profitability of having an optimally productive work force). Such a claim does not include the implication that individual employers have some kind of moral obligation to provide such facilities, such that failure to do so would count as "immoral behavior." Nor is it suggested that there is some minimum standard of concern for employee welfare from which any comparable moral obligation could be "derived."

Contrast this day-care example with another situation. Critics of the typical economic view of the firm also sometimes suggest that firms may, at times, heed moral *norms* in their actions and policies. When a firm, though not legally required to, provides workers with safety devices for dealing with dangerous production activities, there is an implication that *standards* of behavior are involved. In this case, in contrast to the day-care example, there is the notion that the firm has a moral obligation with respect to the risk the worker is being subjected to. A firm's concern for slipping profit levels would not justify placing workers in an "unacceptably high" risk situation, even though it is well understood that a risk free workplace is not attainable. In contrast, unacceptably low profit levels certainly would be expected to enter the pro-day-care employer's decision about whether to indulge his altruistic instincts and provide day-care, and no moral opprobrium would be attached to this calculation.

If this distinction between moral norms and moral values is correct, then incorporating only one of the two concepts would seem to leave the analysis incomplete, and it would not be surprising if some of the phenomena we might be interested in analyzing with the expanded economic model were beyond its capabilities.

One final note concerns Brennan's suggestion that norms might be seen as indistinguishable from preferences because their effectiveness depends upon the agent perceiving the costs of violating the constraint as "large, infinite in the extreme." In our view, this way of reducing norms to values also fails, although for a different reason. As we have argued, one defining characteristic of moral constraints in Western thought is their character as self-imposed and internalized, so that they are not tied solely to external sanctions, to be ignored whenever detection of violations can be avoided. Hence the only way costs can be interpreted that makes sense of this notion of an internalized constraint would be psychological and metaphorical: "costs to self-respect," "costs to integrity," etc. But then we might as well say that norms are constraining because they are accepted as norms, and leave the psychological-metaphorical explanation in terms of costs to a background problem of explaining the psychological motivation for adherence to norms, rather than trying to incorporate these costs into the model directly.

Analysis at the Individual versus Group Level

Our attempt to summarize alternative approaches to incorporating moral norms and values into the microeconomic model focused on the individual. That is, we were trying to incorporate moral concerns into the economic model of the individual agent. In contrast, Cohen's entire analysis and one of the two major components of Mueller's analysis is at the societal level, rather than at the level of the individual. Thus, Cohen asks how society decides whether to use legal sanctions rather than the existing distribution of norms, and Mueller spins out evolutionary scenarios about the appearance and disappearance of norms in society. It is important to recognize that this is a fundamental difference in emphasis. Thus, when Cohen, for example, asserts that "the choice between laws and norms can be partially explained as the outcome of rational economic decisions on the part of society," he is posing and answering a quite different question than the one we address: how might moral concerns be conceptualized as entering the individual's (or individual firm's) decision framework. Moreover, his use of the term *rational* at society's level has very little connection to the notion of rationality at the individual level (as in *rational egoist*) that we (and most discussions in economics that use the term *rational*) focus on.

Why does this difference in focus need to be stressed? While, as indicated above, we think that both Cohen and Mueller provide very useful insights, we also think that their (sometimes) ignoring of the individual level produces implications that may be incomplete or misleading. In Cohen's case, his contribution is best understood as an analysis of choosing between the use of legal devices versus norms, given the current degree of "altruistic content" of preferences. But people like Brunner, Phelps, and Bergsten argue that markets may function better under some moral regimes (sets of moral preferences) than others, and the moral or altruistic content of preferences may be subject to change over time. If there is something to this line of argument, then an analysis such as Cohen's that seems aimed at reassuring us that society is making rational choices about modes of enforcement given the stock and distribution of moral preferences among individuals may be diverting our analytical attention from a possibly serious and analytically worthy problem: what causes individual moral preferences to change over time, and are these changes likely to be consistent with or antithetical to a "better-functioning economy"?

In Mueller's case, he provides further elaboration of his 1986 argument that the emergence of norms may be modelable by "assuming that social institutions (norms, laws, etc.) evolve as if they were designed to maximize the welfare of the community, defined perhaps as a Benthamite or other social welfare function." He reasons that superstitions or taboos might develop from coincidental linking of events ("A savage . . . goes into frenzied dance. Soon thereafter, it rains.") But the more often such supposed causal relationships can be checked, the more likely are surviving ones to be "founded in fact." Thus, Mueller argues that those social norms whose benefits are founded in fact will be more likely to survive.

Mueller's examples—efficacious herbs, avoiding pork—certainly are plausible, but he has chosen examples that avoid a potentially important stumbling block for this "as if" argument. The examples given are cases where the benefit to the individual is clear (avoidance or curing of a disease), so that the rule is likely to be attractive to individuals. Even more crucially, what is beneficial for the individual seems to be obviously beneficial for the group. Thus, not only are information problems minimized, but there is no conflict between individual and group benefit. If the individual adopts it because it is good for him or her, it is, by implicit assumption in Mueller's argument, also good for the group. This allows Mueller to talk about social institutions being chosen "to maximize the welfare of the community"—that is, the group—on the basis of examples in which norms are chosen because they are attractive to individuals. But it is surely plausible that there are norms that individuals may find attractive, and therefore conceivably adopt, that have deleterious group effects. Indeed, Hirshleifer (1985, 62) refers to this problem of conflict between what is good for the individual and the group as a major source of difficulty with the kind of modeling principle Mueller is advocating. Vanberg's (1986) more extended argument about the gap between norms attractive to the individual and those advantageous to the group is discussed in Part 2 of our essay.

This response has stressed apparent differences between us and our commentators in three areas: how to specify the "standard economics approach"; the importance of the distinction between norms and values; and a focus on the individual agent versus a focus on the societal level. We hope that our efforts to highlight these differences helps to clarify and advance the discussion of these important issues.

REFERENCES

Hirshleifer, Jack. 1985. "The Expanding Domain of Economics." *American Economic Review Directory,* December, 53–68.
Hirschman, Albert. 1985. "Against Parsimony." *Economics and Philosophy* 1:7–21.
Vanberg, Viktor. 1986. "Spontaneous Market Order and Social Rule." *Economics and Philosophy* 2:75–100.

Part 3
Experimental Evidence on the Nature of Social Norms

The nature of social norms, like most empirical phenomena, is most likely to be found through empirical examination. One valuable empirical approach is through laboratory experimentation. A precise situation can be devised, and subjects' reactions to the situation can be elicited and examined. If questions about the specific method arise, the experiments can be modified and rerun. Experiments are particularly valuable when the phenomenon to be examined is relatively subtle.

Part 3 begins with Orbell, van de Kragt, and Dawes's "Covenants without the Sword: The Role of Promises in Social Dilemma Circumstances." They examine behavior in "social dilemmas"—circumstances in which people's individual incentives are to shirk in the provision of a public good. The experiments are carefully crafted to be certain that the subjects really are facing social dilemmas, and that they do not misunderstand the situation. In that case, their maximum payoff, which they should choose if they are purely self-interested, comes from shirking. However, in fact, many or most subjects do not shirk despite their clear self-interest. This striking result demands explanation. Altruism would be the explanation that fits most nearly into economists' models, but Orbell, van de Kragt, and Dawes are able to show that the experimental data reject altruism. Rather, the data support the idea that people look for mutual promises in these social dilemma situations. When they receive enough mutual commitments, they willingly carry out actions that benefit others at their own expense.

In "Alternative Social Science Perspectives on 'Social Dilemma' Laboratory Research," Richard M. Weiss looks at the experiments from the standpoints of sociology, social psychology, and organization theory. Each of these perspectives raises questions about the use of such experiments, questions that further experiments may be able to answer. Weiss also points out that social norms of hard work or cooperation may be manipulated by organizations to take advantage of people. Thus, people may properly be suspicious of norms set up by such organizations.

Robert P. Inman's "Comment" shows that one can be quite confident (statistically) in Orbell, van de Kragt and Dawes's conclusion that cooperation was caused by multilateral promises and not altruism. He then emphasizes how these results are contrary to standard economic reasoning. People fail to follow a "best" strategy where they could make promises and then cheat. He suggests that it is people's experience with reputation effects—mathematically, the repeated play of a game—that leads them to cooperate.

Covenants without the Sword: The Role of Promises in Social Dilemma Circumstances

John M. Orbell, Alphons J. van de Kragt, and Robyn M. Dawes

David Hume's (1948) justification of promise making as an institution is still the classic one. Naturally selfish people, he argues, can benefit from the actions of others who are themselves naturally selfish, but the desired beneficial actions from those other people will not be forthcoming without assurances of reciprocal advantage.

> Were we, therefore, to follow the natural course of our passions and inclinations, we should perform but few actions for the advantage of others from disinterested views, because we are naturally very limited in our kindness and affection; and we should perform as few of that kind out of regard to interest, because we cannot depend upon their gratitude. Here, then, is the mutual commerce of good offices in a manner lost among mankind, and everyone reduced to his own skill and industry for his well-being and subsistence. (85)

It is to our mutual advantage, therefore, if we can devise some mechanism that will ensure such reciprocal giving, and promise making does the trick. It is a human invention "founded on the necessities and interests of society" by which individuals accept an obligation to deliver future benefits for the advantage of some other individual or individuals. It is an invention that, clearly, will be generally valued because it is a means to general advantage.[1]

The research reported here was developed with support from the National Science Foundation under grant #SES-8605284. Support was also given by Carnegie-Mellon University and Utah State University. Any opinions, findings, and conclusions or recommendations expressed in this essay are those of the authors and do not necessarily reflect the views of the National Science Foundation or the sponsoring universities.

1. Perhaps the strongest assertion that promise making is fundamental to human society and, indeed, human nature comes from Nietzsche in his *On the Genealogy of Morals* (second

Of course, to say that the institution of promise making works to the general advantage is not to provide a reason for selfish individuals actually to keep their promises. In fact, the assumption of selfishness clearly predicts that people will break their promises when it is to their net advantage to do so, and Hobbe's well-known conclusion is that, absent the sword of Leviathan to enforce compliance, such promises are empty:

> If a covenant be made, wherein neither of the parties performe presently, but trust one another; in the condition of meer Nature, (which is a condition of Warre of every man against every man), upon any reasonable suspicion, it is Voyd. . . . For he that performeth first, has no assurance the other will performe after. . . . And therefore he which performeth first, does but betray himselfe to his enemy; contrary to the Right (he can never abandon) of defending his life, and means of living. ([1651] 1947, 70)

Hume recognizes this problem, but finds incentives sufficient to ensure promise keeping short of Leviathan in reputation that can ensure the promise keeper gains from future exchanges that would be precluded to one who earns a reputation from promise breaking:

> After these signs [the form of words by which an individual makes a promise] are instituted, whoever uses them is immediately bound by his interest to execute his engagements, and must never expect to be trusted any more if he refuse to perform what he promised (Hume 1948, 87).

Hume thus differs from Hobbes with respect to promise keeping only insofar as he identifies reputation as a source of private incentives sufficient to induce compliance over an iterated series, and does not believe the institution must rest entirely on some centralized Leviathan. He is quite consistent with Hobbes in his insistence that the institution must be supported by private incentives, despite the general benefits that it provides.

Modern analysts agree. While there has been remarkably little empirical study of promise keeping, individual interest is what is normally said to account for several closely related behaviors. Thus:

—Janis and Mann (1977), writing about why people keep their commitments (a broader concept than promises) emphasize the private costs

---

essay, [1888] 1967, 57) where he asks: "To breed an animal *with the right to make promises*—is not this the paradoxical task that nature has set itself in the case of man? Is it not the real problem regarding man?"

of welshing, notably "the stigma of being known as erratic and unstable" (280).

—Ainslie (1975), writing about impulse control when short-term incentives support the impulse, identifies commitments as rearrangements of external contingencies so that the person stands to lose more by not performing the action than by performing it (see also Brickman 1987; Cialdini 1984; Kiesler 1971).

—Schelling (1960 and 1984) makes the game-theoretic point that having one's promise backed by the threat of being sued can actually be to one's private advantage; my self-interested reason for keeping my promise persuades other, no less self-interested people (with whom I would like to consummate a profitable exchange) that I am actually to be trusted.

Of course people normally do keep promises when it is in their private interest to keep them. And, certainly, it is easy to defend the position that institutions supported by individual self-interest are more firmly rooted than those that are not.

But to concede that egoistic cost-benefit calculations can explain promise keeping does not concede that such calculations are necessary for it. In fact, showing that people keep promises when it is to their private advantage to do so does not require that they would not also have kept them, for whatever reason, had their private incentives been to the contrary.

Our interest is in promise keeping without the Hobbesian "sword" of self-interest to back it up, particularly in multilateral promise keeping when the issue is the keeping of promises made to a group, not to a single, other contracting party. The ethical issue of when people are obliged to keep promises is logically distinct from the empirical one of when they actually do so, but the two are related insofar as feelings of obligation motivate and direct actual behavior; we will look briefly at the problem of ethical obligation in the multilateral case. Then we will review an experimental study of promise keeping whose findings are consistent with people's feeling ethical obligation in multilateral cases only in highly specific circumstances. The study is conducted within the social dilemma (Dawes 1980) experimental paradigm in which: (1) there is a dominant incentive confronting each individual in some group of individuals; (2) there is a suboptimal equilibrium associated with that dominant incentive; and (3) all plausible material and interpersonal sidepayments supporting both cooperation and promise keeping have been eliminated.

As many authors (e.g., Buchanan 1975; Gauthier 1967; Orbell and Rutherford 1973) have pointed out, the logic of Hobbes's state of nature is essentially social dilemma logic, involving a dominant incentive (act in a predatory manner) and a suboptimal equilibrium associated with that incentive (mutual predation). The social dilemma experimental paradigm, therefore, permits a test of predictions about behavior in such circumstances, not the least of which is the prediction that promises to cooperate in the absence of private, egoistic sidepayments supporting such promises will not be kept.

When Is a Promise Not a Promise?

Philosophers and linguists define promises in terms that are characteristically formalizations of everyday usage. Searle's (1969) list of the necessary conditions for recognizing a promise, for example, includes most importantly the following: The promisor and the promisee must be in effective communication with each other; the promise must concern some future act under the control of the promisor; the promisee wants the promisor to do that act; the act would not obviously happen in the normal course of events; and the promisor uses phrases (conventionally "I promise to . . .") that are generally understood to place him or her under an obligation to do that act (for similar definitions, see Atiyah 1981; von Wright 1983).

But when does a promise, defined in such a reasonable manner, acquire ethical force? Simply having uttered the magic words certainly is not sufficient; coerced promises are not binding in law or ethics, and both law and ethics recognize that certain changes of circumstance can free an individual from obligation. We find Atiyah's (1981) discussion useful. After carefully reviewing (and rejecting) various arguments about the conditions of promissory obligation, he argues (189–91) that most situations involving promises can be broken down into two elements:

1. consent to the terms of the proposed exchange, and
2. the binding commitment to consummate the exchange. These really are quite separate things. . . . Now so far as the first of these elements is concerned, it seems to be still the case that each promise is nothing more than an indication of the party's willingness to exchange on the terms proposed. . . . The promises are not commitments to consummate the exchange, but admissions of the fairness of the terms proposed, and therefore of the obligation that each will come under, if and when the other's performance is accepted.

For Atiyah, therefore, obligation does not derive from the words per se, but from both parties to the proposed exchange having accepted the terms as proposed. The words per se do not create obligation, but they do indicate acceptance of the terms of exchange—which acceptance, when it is mutual, is what creates obligation.

Atiyah's proposal does resolve a lot of problems with others' efforts to specify the basis of promissory obligation, but it does not provide a ready argument about the basis of obligation in the multilateral promising case that concerns us. Consistency with the bilateral case requires that a lone individual who promises cooperative behavior (indicating willingness to abide by a "contract to cooperate") not be bound when everybody else withholds their promises. But it would seem reasonable to take the same position for a second promisor—and a third, and fourth, and so on. We might specify some number or proportion of the population that must have promised for the contract to be ethically binding but, with a single exception, such a solution would be arbitrary and artificial.

The exception is requiring everyone to have promised. When that has happened, the situation is formally identical with the situation in the bilateral case when both parties have promised, and Atiyah's dichotomy gives us a clear argument: an individual promising in the multilateral case is ethically bound to keep the promise only when everyone else in the group has also promised. By this argument, promises to cooperate in social dilemma situations are, in the first place, indications that people buy into the cooperative solution, but only become binding obligations to act cooperatively when everyone has explicitly bought into it.

This is an uncomfortable argument insofar as it frees promisors from an obligation to keep their promises when even a single individual withholds his or her promise. And it is a conclusion that gets progressively more uncomfortable as the size of groups increases, giving a single individual the capacity to undermine the otherwise consensual promise making of his or her fellows. We will return to the problem after having reviewed recent experimental findings about the circumstances under which people *behave* as if their promises are, and are not, ethically binding.

Empirical Findings

Background

For the past ten years, we have been conducting laboratory experiments investigating the circumstances under which people cooperate in social dilemma situations. Our tactic has been to provide subjects with monetary incentives that match the defining criteria of social dilemmas (dominant incentive, suboptimal group equilibrium) and to observe differences in the incidence of cooperation that are associated with different experimental conditions. These are what Brewer (1985) calls "analogue experiments," involving an experimental design that replicates the essential features of theoretically interesting, natural-world situations. Whether or not the findings can be extrapolated to particular natural-world situations, of course, remains problematic; that is something that must be argued on a case-by-case basis. It is important to note, however, that the situation confronting subjects is a real dilemma, involving real money; it is, therefore, no less real than dilemmas in natural situations— and differences we observe between experimental conditions in the laboratory are differences that can be expected in natural situations with comparable incentive structures.

The findings to be reported are from a larger study (Orbell, van de Kragt, and Dawes 1988) investigating reasons for the well-recognized capacity of a period of group discussion to greatly increase cooperation rates. Experiment 1 of that study tested and rejected the hypothesis that discussion triggers generalized norms favoring cooperation (discussion among members of one group does not increase cooperation vis-à-vis subjects in a different group), and experiment 2 of that study—described in detail below—was designed, among other things, to permit systematic investigation of the serendipitous observation of frequent promise making among members of cooperative groups.

Hypotheses

A first hypothesis about promise keeping is the simple Hobbesian one: promises will not be kept in the absence of private incentives supporting them. This is, of course, a strong hypothesis and a small number of individuals keeping their promises in the absence of such private incentives would not invalidate its spirit; indeed, Hobbes argued that promises would not be sufficient to solve problems in the State of Nature, not that no individuals would keep their promises.

A second hypothesis is the expectations one: expectations about others' promising is a crucial explanatory variable between the number of others promising to cooperate and one's own cooperation. Thus, (1) the more people in one's group promise to cooperate, the more people are expected to do so; and (2) the more people are expected to cooperate, the more people keep their promises to do so.

The hypothesis requires that—the Hobbesian hypothesis notwithstanding—people are somewhat disposed to keep their promises, but whether or not they do so depends on their expectations of others' behavior. While in a (symmetric) social dilemma situation the incentive to defect remains constant regardless of the number cooperating, the absolute payoff from cooperation increases with the number cooperating. Therefore, the more others make promises to cooperate, and the more the individual believes that those promises will be kept, the higher the expected payoff from cooperation. As Dawes (1980) puts it:

If others cooperate, then the expected payoff for cooperation is not too low, even though—in a uniform game, for example, the *difference* between the payoff for cooperation and that for defection is quite large. People may be greedy, may prefer more to less, but their greed is not "insatiable" when other utilities are involved. (191)

Thus, the hypothesis depends on the plausible assumptions of some constant, nonmonetary utility from cooperation ("doing the right thing") and diminishing utility from monetary gains (cf. Kahneman and Tversky 1982).

By this hypothesis, notice, promise keeping becomes a self-fulfilling hypothesis to the extent promises are believed. The appearance that group members will keep their promises can lead them actually to do so.

One of the most replicated findings from social dilemma experimental research is of a strong positive correlation between expectations of others' cooperation and one's own cooperation (notably, Dawes, McTavish, and Shaklee 1977) and, contrary to the model now being discussed, there is evidence that expectations often occur *subsequent to* one's own choice, rather than prior to it. Critical to this expectations hypothesis, however, is the positive correlation between the number promising in a subject's group and his or her expectations about others' cooperation.

A third hypothesis we call the consensual promising one. It is a behavioral extrapolation from the ethical argument, sketched above, that finds a clear basis for obligation in the multilateral case (such as subjects confronted in our experimental situation) only when everyone in a discussing group has promised to cooperate. By it, people will not feel that their promises to cooperate are ethically binding unless and until everyone in the group has promised—and thereby indicated acceptance of the contract to cooperate. Short of that, having promised will not be regarded as ethically binding, being only a "speech act" indicating willingness to abide by such a contract, if consummated, and will be, therefore, behaviorally void.

Method

Subjects were recruited by advertisements in the Logan, Utah, daily newspaper and in Utah State University's student newspaper; the advertisement promised $4.00 for keeping an appointment, and said that subjects could make between $0.00 and $38.00 extra from the experiment itself "depending on their own decisions and the simultaneous decisions of others in the experiment."

Initial contact was by telephone. Subjects—about two-thirds of whom were students—were assigned to time slots according to their convenience and the availability of slots, and these slots were later randomly assigned to the several experimental conditions. On arrival, subjects were checked in, signed standard consent forms, and were seated by lot around a fourteen-person table in a large room; seats were designated by letters *A* through *N*. Subjects were asked not to talk among themselves before the experiment began. An experimenter sat at the head of the table, and two observers sat in the corners of the room opposite him.

When all were seated, the experimenter read instructions emphasizing at several points that all decisions the subjects made would be in strict privacy—that nobody else in the group would know what they had done, they would leave the experiment room one by one in order to be paid, and after that they would leave the general area one by one. The experimenter also emphasized that there was absolutely no deception in the experiment and that we would be at pains to ensure that everyone understood what was going on; anyone who did not understand any part of the instructions should feel free to ask questions.

In front of each subject was a clipboard with a "promissory note" for $5.00 attached. Subjects were told that, after ten minutes of free (taped) discussion among themselves, they would be divided by lot into two, seven-person groups and that each individual would have to make a choice between: (1) keeping the $5.00 endowment for himself or herself; (2) giving it to the other six members of his or her own seven-person group—in which case each other individual gets $2.00 as a consequence for a total group benefit of $12.00; or (3) giving it to the seven members of the other group—in which case each individual in the other group gets $3.00 as a consequence for a total benefit to that group of $21.00.

Because the payoff schedule was complex, we could not present it to subjects in a matrix. Instead, we used the form we would later use for figuring individual payoffs at the end of the experiment to take them through six important examples of what might happen; we encouraged questions at this time, and are confident that subjects fully understood the dollar consequences of those choices for themselves and for others in the experiment.

This incentive structure defines what Schwartz-Shea and Simmons (1988) call a "layered" Prisoners' Dilemma—one in which separate dilemma relationships exist between different subsets of the population. Thus, there is a dilemma between individuals and their seven-person groups, one between individuals and the wider, fourteen-person population, and one between the two seven-person groups qua groups.

Promise making is not something that can be readily manipulated in standard experimental ways. Promises that are coerced are, rightly, not re-garded as binding in law, and we cannot expect subjects to respond to promises that are required by an experimenter in the same way they would respond to promises that are voluntarily made. (In fact, Dawes, McTavish, and Shaklee [1977] found that a formal procedure for promise making following discussion led to no higher rates of cooperation than did discussion alone.)

Accordingly, we placed three observers in different parts of the room during this initial fourteen-person discussion period, and they recorded on charts of the room's seating any instances they saw of promises to give to the other group. (Because subjects were seated in a U-shaped pattern, with the experimenter at the top, and because promises often came rapidly and jointly, it was difficult for any one observer to be confident of identifying individuals who did make promises.) Consistent with standard definitions discussed above, a "promise" was recognized operationally as an explicit statement or indication that a subject would give to the other group when the time came for choice. Thus, the statements "I will give to the other group" (if made in response to an explicit request for a promise), "yes I'll give," or "I promise to give" were counted as promises, as was the raising of a hand in response to questions such as "who promises to give to the other group?" We coded only promises to give to the other group, not commitments to keep or promises to give to one's own seven-person group—which, of course, had not yet been designated.

In half of our replications we gave both seven-person subgroups a further ten minutes of free discussion and in the other half we required the same amount of "quiet time." When occasional subjects asked whether there would be discussion in the seven-person rooms, they were told "You will get further instructions when you get there."

Subjects recorded their decisions on a "decision form" on their clipboard. (They were told not to return the promissory note physically, due to the likely violation of privacy that would have involved.) After making their choice and while the experimenters were figuring out the result, subjects filled out a questionnaire that, among other items, asked them to record their expectations about the number of others keeping their endowment, and the percent of those who did not keep who would give to the other group.

Because promise making was not under experimental control, we stratified within levels of promise making in an effort to obtain equal numbers of groups in which: (*a*) in the fourteen-person discussion all subjects promised to give to the other group, and (*b*) not all did so. The stratification device was largely, but not entirely, successful: We ended with seven pairs in a subsequent discussion with universal promising condition; six in a no subsequent discussion with universal promising condition; six in a subsequent discussion with less than universal promising condition (having an average of 7.8 promisors; and five in a no subsequent discussion with less than universal promising condition (having an average of 4.0 promisors). We were unable to run enough replications to assure equal samples in each cell by randomly eliminating groups with universal promising. We ran a total of twenty-four, fourteen-person groups; there was universal promise making in fourteen.

Results

Promise making was a quite frequent behavior: Ignoring the subsequent seven-person group discussion versus no discussion manipulation,[2] 249 of 336 subjects did promise to give to the other group (74.1 percent) during the fourteen-person discussion periods. Further, such promises were often kept: 193 of the 249 (77.5 percent) who promised to give to the other group actually did so when the time came. This is significantly more than the 49 of 87 (56.3 percent) who gave to the other group after not having promised to do so. ($\chi^2 = 13.33$; $p < .001$; $\phi = r = .21$.)[3]

Remembering that the game was not iterated (so that there was no reason to expect private benefits in future plays from one's current cooperation) and remembering also our care to ensure that subjects' choices were anonymous (and they fully understood that fact), these data are inconsistent with the strong Hobbesian hypothesis that promises in the absence of "the sword" of private incentives will not be kept.

The expectations hypothesis postulates a sequence from number of others making a promise in one's fourteen-person group, through expectations about others' cooperation, to the subject's own cooperation. There is, in fact, a correlation of .25 ($p < .001$) between the first two of these variables, and a correlation of .58 ($p < .001$) between the latter two. The model does not work, however, when we consider only the replications in which less than fourteen promised: the correlation between the number of others promising and expectations is only .10 (n.s.). And the correlation between the number of others promising and one's own choice is only .03 (n.s.).

Among these replications, there is still a significant correlation between expectations and one's own choice (.53, $p < .001$), but that is not sufficient to sustain the hypothesis. (We will discuss the issue of causality between these two variables later.) From these data we can reject, at least, the hypothesis of

---

2. The presence or absence of discussion in the seven-person groups had no effect on promise-making, which happened before the split into seven-person groups ($F = 1.15, p = .29$). The effect of discussion in seven-person groups on giving to the other group was not significant when analyzed with the other experimental manipulation (all vs. not all promise). Only the latter's main effect was significant ($F = 31.62, p < .001$). Therefore, we do not address the seven-person discussion variable in subsequent analyses.

3. Here and in the subsequent discussion, promising is coded as 1 = promised to give to the other group, 0 = did not so promise; choice is coded as 1 = giving to the other group, 0 did not so give (viz., either kept for oneself or gave to others in one's own seven-person group).

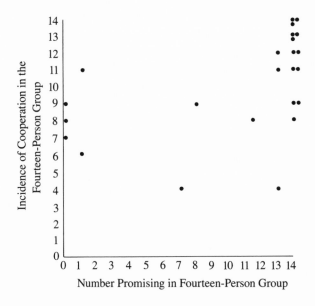

Fig. 1. Number promising and the incidence of cooperation in fourteen-person groups

a linear relationship between number promising to cooperate and expectations about others' cooperating.

The consensual promising hypothesis is supported, however. Giving to the other group is significantly more frequent when everyone in a group promised to do so than when less than everyone did (84.1 percent and 57.8 percent respectively; $\chi^2 = 27.3$, $p < .001$; $\phi = r = .29$; 59.7 percent of promise makers in the latter condition kept their promises). Figure 1 plots the relationship between number promising in a fourteen-person group and the incidence of cooperation among members of that group; a probit analysis of these data indicates that a step-level function gives a good model fit ($\chi^2 = 79.03$, $p < .0001$).

Discussion

Our three hypotheses translate into three different stories. At the outset all three are the same: discussion provides an opportunity for subjects to confirm (as already explained in our instructions) that there is an opportunity for a "cooperative surplus" (Gauthier 1986); subjects recognize the possible uses of promising as a way to ensure cooperative behavior; and promises are extracted from at least some group members.

At this point the stories diverge. In the Hobbesian story, subjects who have promised (as well as those who have not) assess the incentives confronting them and, recognizing the dominance of the defect alternative, reject cooperation—whether or not they have promised. While this story might describe the behavior of some subjects in our study, our data show that it was not characteristic.

The expectations story involves a more complex weighing of moral pressures from promising, the behavior of others, and possible private payoffs. By it, individuals who have promised to give to the other group assess the number of others they expect to keep their promises to do so—and the payoffs that number implies should they personally keep or not keep their promises. Granted they attach some utility to keeping their own promises, and granted that they become less interested in the gains available from defection as the payoffs available from cooperation mount, cooperation becomes, in net, the more attractive personal option after some number of others can be counted on to cooperate.

But the insignificant correlations among the replications where less than all promised between the number of others promising and expectations about others behavior, and between the number of others promising and cooperation do not support this story.

By the consensual promising story, promising individuals monitor the number of others who have promised, and when and only when everybody else has promised, they accept that their own promise represents a binding commitment—and behave accordingly. A deal is a deal; consensual promising makes it a deal, but less than consensual promising does not. The data are broadly consistent with this story.

Note that this story does involve individuals calculating their private interest insofar as they recognize the general advantage from everybody giving; promises are "invented" as a means to that general advantage. But the keeping of promises hinges more on accepting that a deal has been made than it does on the expected value of keeping a promise. In fact, even when there has been consensual promising in the fourteen-person group, the cooperators—normally more optimistic about others' cooperation than defectors—still expect significantly less than universal giving (10.41 compared to the thirteen others possible; $z = 9.59$, $p < .001$). Consensual contracting does not work because people expect everyone to adhere to the contract. It works, we believe, because people do not feel bound by their promise unless everyone else has also promised.

Accidents of leadership and initiative in the various groups appeared to have something to do with why some groups made consensual promises and some did not. Almost invariably, after subjects spent the first few minutes of the discussion period seemingly assuring themselves and each other that there was a common understanding of what was going on, in some groups some individuals pushed the idea of getting explicit promises from everybody—often with success. When no individual was willing or assertive enough to do this (or considered the possibility), promise making seemed much less likely to happen. We also observed strong interpersonal pressures toward promising in some groups, pressures whose effectiveness is suggested (albeit, not conclusively demonstrated) by the second-order correlation of .85 ($p < .001$) between the number of other subjects in one's fourteen-person group who promise and one's own promise making.[4]

Finally, we believe that the best (endogenous) explanation for expectations about others' choices is that they derive from the subject's own choice. Dawes, McTavish, and Shaklee (1977) report data supporting the possibility, and several theoretical perspectives are compatible with it. First, dissonance theory shows how behaving in a particular way can produce beliefs compatible with that behavior. Second, behavioral decision theory has demonstrated the importance of "anchoring and adjustment" (Kahneman and Tversky 1973), a strategy by which individuals base judgments on an initial cue (the "anchor") from which adjustments are made. Perhaps players in social dilemma games use their own behavior as an anchor, from which they make only relatively modest adjustments when assessing the likely behavior of others.

Conclusions

People do keep their promises to cooperate in multilateral social dilemma situations that have the same logic as the Hobbesian state of nature, but they can only be relied on to do so when promise making has been consensual among group members. The data are consistent with a consensual contracting model by which a promise serves, in the first place, as an indication that the promising individual buys into the "cooperative solution," and only in the second place—after everyone is understood, by their promises, to have bought into that solution—as a source of obligation on the individual actually to cooperate. The contingency of cooperation on the unanimity of contracting in these multilateral situations parallels Atiyah's (1981) argument about the contingency of obligation on both parties having indicated acceptance of the contract in bilateral situations.

---

4. Some individuals did publicly resist the pressures to make promises, indicating that they did not want to be bound to give their endowment away. If such individuals did eventually give in and make a promise along with everyone else, the experimenters (from their privileged position) saw most of them keep their promises. In one noteworthy case, a single individual argued successfully against general promise making on the grounds that such promises "wouldn't mean anything, and we are all going to give anyway." He then organized his seven-person group into giving to each other—and did so himself.

This essay does not provide an explanation for the behavioral importance of consensual contracting, but we offer two speculations. The first is a cognitive one. As Kahneman and Tversky (1973) demonstrate, outcomes that are particularly "available"—readily imaginable or retrieved from memory—are likely to be fixed upon in our thinking even if their availability is unrelated, or negatively related, to their objective probability. "Everyone promises and everyone keeps their promise" seems a particularly available outcome, and subjects could well fix on that and be particularly sensitive to shortfalls from it when deciding whether or not a group contract has been made, and whether or not, therefore, they should personally cooperate. Such availability might be reinforced by subjects extrapolating from the more frequent bilateral case (where "the other person promises" and "the other person does not promise" are the only possible circumstances) to the more complex multilateral one.

The second speculation involves social solidarity and is raised by a provocative article by Korn and Korn (1983) on Tonga. In the context of arguments that promise making is a universal institution, they cite Tonga as a society in which that institution does not exist. There, they say, a "promise" that one will deliver something in the future is not assumed to have created an obligation actually to deliver; it is, rather, "an expression of solidarity and concern" (448) for the recipient's need. Obligation exists in Tonga but it is based, they claim, on social solidarity (and an associated norm for reciprocity), rather than on an institution of promise making in the usual sense of that term.

It is not new to propose that social solidarity can create obligation in the absence of promise making. Hume recognized it explicitly:

> But though this self-interested commerce of men [which serves to justify promise making] begins to take place and to predominate in society, it does not entirely abolish the more generous and noble intercourse of friendship and good offices. I may still do services to such persons as I love and am more particularly acquainted with, without any prospect of advantage; and they may make me a return in the same manner, without any view but that of recompensing my past services. (1948, 87)

But we speculate further that universality of promise making becomes behaviorally important because it is a trigger for solidarity—which then becomes the immediate cause of cooperation. Caporael et al. (1989) have argued that pressures within small groups in Plio-Pleistocene conditions placed a premium on the evolution of cognitive/affective mechanisms (notably the potential for solidarity) sensitive and responsive to social stimuli; these mechanisms, in turn, supported development and maintenance of group membership and the conduct of social interaction. Perhaps separate individuals start thinking of themselves as a group, and start acting cooperatively, after they come to accept—as a consequence of universal promise making—that there is general agreement among themselves on a joint strategy for responding to their common problem. Notice that this second speculation has the implication that consensual promise making will not work if, for some reason, it does not produce at least some substantial measure of group solidarity.

Speculating about solidarity's involvement raises the further possibility that there is *no* causal relationship between consensual promise making and cooperation, mediated or otherwise. The important "minimal group" literature in social psychology has shown the extreme ease with which feelings of group identity (or solidarity) can be produced and its power to influence allocative tasks very much like cooperation.[5] The ten-minute period of group discussion that provided our subjects with the opportunity for promise making is a substantially less minimal manipulation than many described in this literature. Thus, it is quite possible that feelings of group identity generated by this manipulation produced the increase of cooperation we observed, and that the promises we also observed had no independent effect at all—whether proximate or remote. Separating the effects of consensual promise making and group identity is, clearly, an important agenda item for further empirical research.

The size of group seems an important parameter. On the one hand, the requirement that acceptance of the contract be universal before promises acquire felt ethical force (or that there be expressed consensus of purpose before group identity or solidarity is forthcoming) is a requirement that will be progressively difficult to meet as group size increases. Clearly, extracting promises to cooperate from all members of a 14-person group will be easier than doing so from all members of a 100-person group. (And we should remember that only about half of our 14-person experimental groups were successful.) On the other hand, as group size increases the probability of an effective leader emerging would seem to increase, and our experience was that leadership had a lot to do with whether or not everyone in a group did end up promising.

It is possible that the requirement relaxes as size increases, so very large groups can generate obligation even though some considerable absolute number do withhold their promises. It is also possible that some structural patterns can carry the potential of consensual promise making to very large groups. For example, sets of groups that have solved their intragroup dilemmas and

---

5. For example, by telling subjects (randomly) that they are either "overestimators" or "underestimators" of the number of dots on a page of dots—after which, they show a significant proclivity to favor those (supposedly) like themselves in an allocation task.

now confront *intergroup* dilemmas might be able to communicate something functionally the same as consensual promise making through representatives at a negotiating table (related to this latter possibility, see Coleman 1986). Or clusters of bilateral promises might, under some circumstances, aggregate to more general understandings about obligations taken and given—and bypass, thereby, the necessity for multilateral promises and their attendant difficulties.

These are speculations, however. We have demonstrated one circumstance in which "covenants without the sword" are reliably kept, but the implications of our finding for the satisfactory resolution of large-number, multilateral social dilemmas cannot be decided by a priori theorizing alone.

REFERENCES

Ainslie, G. 1975. "Specious Reward: A Behavioral Theory of Impulsiveness and Impulse Control." *Psychological Bulletin* 82:463–96.
Atiyah, P. 1981. *Promises, Morals, and Law.* New York: Oxford University Press.
Brickman, P. 1987. *Commitment, Conflict, and Caring.* Englewood Cliffs, N.J.: Prentice-Hall.
Brewer, M. 1985. "Experimental Research and Social Policy: Must it Be Rigor versus Relevance?" *Journal of Social Issues* 41:159–76.
Buchanan, J. 1975. *The Limits of Liberty.* Chicago: University of Chicago Press.
Caporael, L., J. Orbell, R. Dawes, and A. van de Kragt. 1989. "Selfishness Examined: Cooperation in the Absence of Egoistic Incentives." *Behavioral and Brain Sciences* 12:683–98.
Cialdini, R. 1984. *Influence: How and Why People Agree to Do Things.* New York: Morrow.
Coleman, J. 1986. "Psychological Structure and Social Structure in Economic Models." In *Rational Choice,* ed. R. Hogarth and M. Reder. Chicago: University of Chicago Press.
Dawes, R. 1980. "Social Dilemmas." *Annual Review of Psychology* 31:169–93.
Dawes, R., J. McTavish, and H. Shaklee. 1977. "Behavior, Communication and Assumptions about Other Peoples' Behavior in a Commons Dilemma Situation." *Journal of Personality and Social Psychology* 35:1–11.
Gauthier, D. 1967. "Morality and Advantage." *Philosophical Review* 76:460–75.
Gauthier, D. 1986. *Morals By Agreement.* New York: Oxford University Press.
Hobbes, T. [1651] 1947. *Leviathan.* London: J. M. Dent and Sons.
Hume, D. 1948. "A Treatise of Human Nature, part 2: Of Justice and Injustice." In *Hume: Moral and Political Philosophy,* ed. H. Aiken. New York: Collier Macmillan.
Janis, I., and L. Mann. 1977. *Decision Making: A Psychological Analysis of Conflict, Choice, and Commitment.* New York: Free Press.
Kahneman, D., and A. Tversky. 1973. "Availability: A Heuristic for Judging Frequency and Probability." *Cognitive Psychology* 5:207–32.

Kahneman, D., and A. Tversky. 1982. "The Psychology of Preferences." *Scientific American* 246:160–73.

Kiesler, C. 1971. *The Psychology of Commitment*. New York: Academic Press.

Korn, F., and S. Korn. 1983. "Where People Don't Promise." *Ethics* 93:445–50.

Nietzsche, Friedrich. [1887] 1967. *On the Genealogy of Morals*. Second Essay, Sec. 1, trans. W. Kaufman and R. J. Hollingdale and ed. W. Kaufman. New York: Vintage Books.

Orbell, J., A. van de Kragt, and R. Dawes. 1988. "Explaining Discussion-induced Cooperation." *Journal of Personality and Social Psychology* 54:811–19.

Orbell, J., and B. Rutherford. 1973. "Social Peace as a Collective Good." *British Journal of Political Science* 4:501–10.

Schelling, T. 1960. *The Strategy of Conflict*. Cambridge, Mass.: Harvard University Press.

Schelling, T. 1984. "Ethics, Law, and the Exercise of Self-command." In *Choice and Consequences*. Cambridge, Mass.: Harvard University Press.

Schwartz-Shea, P., and R. Simmons. 1988. "Ingroups, Outgroups, and the LPD: Experiments in the Layered Prisoner's Dilemma." Presented at the annual meeting of the Public Choice Association, San Francisco.

Searle, J. 1969. *Speech Acts: An Essay in the Philosophy of Language*. New York: Cambridge University Press.

von Wright, G. 1983. *Practical Reason*. Ithaca, N.Y.: Cornell University Press.

Alternative Social Science Perspectives on "Social Dilemma" Laboratory Research

Richard M. Weiss

Orbell, van de Kragt, and Dawes report on the latest findings from a decade-long stream of empirical research that has continuously refined methods and hypotheses for investigating a central issue in the history of Western thought. For those of us who believe that this is what social science is supposed to be about, the persistence and rigor of this endeavor is as impressive as its uncommonness is discouraging. Although the design of the particular experimental game described in the essay is "one-shot," that could hardly be said of the authors' research program.

The comments that follow are offered from the perspective of three academic disciplines that otherwise are unrepresented in this volume. I will suggest some alternative explanations for the Orbell, van de Kragt, and Dawes findings from the social psychology literature and then attempt to broaden the focus somewhat by bringing in the literature of organizational psychology. This commentary will conclude with some remarks from a sociologist's perspective in which I raise some caveats regarding Orbell, van de Kragt, and Dawes's speculations on the potential applicability of their findings on the effects of promising. The sincerity of my complimentary introductory comments notwithstanding, I would like to begin with some cautionary remarks regarding the details of the design of the experiments reported here by Orbell and his associates.

A Social Psychology Perspective on Theory and Method

The validity of the manipulations employed in these experiments is a bit uncertain. Although Orbell, van de Kragt, and Dawes are likely to be far less guilty of these errors than the following comments imply, I will take this opportunity to discuss some considerations that are well recognized by social psychologists but that may be less familiar to economists and political scientists.

The authors contend that the subjects' behaviors were relatively unlikely to have been influenced by concerns over appearing deceitful to their fellow subjects. The fact that they each knew that they would be participating in only one Prisoner's Dilemma–type game, and that demonstrating trustworthiness was therefore not instrumental to their outcomes, certainly is consistent with that view. The authors also report various specific precautions taken to ensure anonymity, such as letting subjects out of the experiment one at a time. Nevertheless, what matters is whether the subjects *believe* they will not be identifiable. If there is any lesson that has been learned by social psychologists, it is that the intentions underlying our behaviors are not necessarily perceived by others in the same way (see, for example, Tagiuri 1969). That is, although we may design an experimental procedure in a manner that we feel signals an intention to ensure anonymity, others do not necessarily interpret the signal accurately, find it credible, or, for that matter, even notice it. Thus, the subjects in this study might have wondered whether members of the experimental team (with whom the subjects had to meet after the experiment to collect their payment) would be aware of who had engaged in embarrassingly selfish behavior. Or subjects might have imagined that the other subjects would be congregating outside of the building in which the study was conducted, discussing among themselves what had happened, and figuring out who had "cheated" all of them—for a miserable five dollars!

Social psychologists deal with this problem primarily through debriefing subjects after they participate in an experiment. This is done not only to explain the nature and purpose of the experiment and why it had been necessary to employ deception (as is often the case), but also to learn from the subjects whether they had experienced the experiment as it had been intended (Carlsmith, Ellsworth, and Aronson 1976). This process sometimes itself involves some initial deception, as illustrated by the debrief in a study of behavioral contagion in which I played the role of the researcher. After having subjects cool their heels in a waiting room for half an hour, I had to enter and very brusquely tell one of those waiting (actually a confederate) that the experimental apparatus had broken, that he should leave, and that he would not be receiving any payment. I reappeared after another half-hour and made the same extremely rude speech to the actual subject. To check whether the subjects actually had believed they were waiting to participate in an experiment (in fact there was none beyond what they had experienced), that equipment had broken, and so on, we positioned another member of the research team a few feet down the hallway outside the lab. When the angry subjects stomped out, they were approached by this researcher, who said "Pardon me. I'm doing a survey for the department chairman on the use of students as research subjects. Have you had any experiences with researchers that you could tell us about." It is with mixed emotions that I can report that each subject responded with something like "Have I? Let me tell you about the son of a bitch back in that room!"

In the case of the experiments reported by Orbell, van de Kragt, and Dawes, it is not entirely certain that their subjects' perceptions of the game are consistent with the authors' interpretation of why the subjects acted as they did. Although these experiments *may* demonstrate that promising leads to relatively spontaneous, noncoerced cooperative behavior, their design does not allow us to rule out completely somewhat more parsimonious alternative explanations for these findings from the social psychology literature.

Much of social psychology has focused on how the behavior, attitudes, and so on of individuals and groups may influence the behavior, attitudes, and so on of other individuals, group members, and other groups. Analyses of this topic, social influence, frequently have suggested that there are two categories of such influence, *informational* and *normative* (Deutsch and Gerard 1955). The first of these terms refers to influence exerted by providing information, and is particularly relevant in the wide range of circumstances in which the target of the influence attempt has imperfect information on which to base a decision. The second term refers to influence attempts that capitalize on individuals' desire for positive regard from others.

The finding by Orbell, van de Kragt, and Dawes of an association between cooperation and the expressed belief that others will cooperate could be interpreted as resulting from normative social influences. This particular finding may be attributable not to any behavior of the cooperators, but to that of subjects at the opposite end of the cooperate-defect dimension. Specifically, defectors' anxieties over the experimenters' potentially disapproving reaction to their behavior might have motivated them to claim that they acted as they did only because they expected others to defect as well.

Additional support for this alternative interpretation is provided by a related body of literature in social psychology that focuses on how individuals attempt "to affect the perceptions of her or him by another person" (Schneider 1981, 25). This work on "impression management" has demonstrated, for example, that subjects in experiments are very concerned about being seen as honest and cooperative (Shulman and Berman 1975). Indeed, findings such as this are part of a fairly extensive empirical literature on the social psychology of experiments that attempts to assess the effects of individuals' reactions to the artificialities of laboratory experimentation (see Page 1981).

What I take to be the central finding of the Orbell, van de Kragt, and Dawes study, that publicly expressing a promise to cooperate leads to cooperation when group members are unanimous in committing to that promise, also may be interpreted in terms of the existing literature of social psychology.

Beginning in the 1930s (Sherif 1935), conformity was the subject of extensive laboratory research. A well-known finding of that research was that if a subject is made to believe that he or she is part of a group that holds unanimously to a certain position, that subject has a very high likelihood of conforming. If, however, the subject notices even one individual violating that consensus, the likelihood of the group's exacting conformity from him or her, while still statistically significant, is greatly lessened (Asch 1951). Originally, this finding was interpreted as demonstrating the potency of normative social influence. The study was replicated on a number of occasions, however, under conditions in which the subject was anonymous, so that conforming could neither enhance nor diminish his or her regard among peers. Although the level of conformity achieved in these studies was not as great, it still occurred significantly, suggesting that informational influence also played a role (Crutchfield 1955; Deutsch and Gerard 1955).

I would suggest the possibility that unanimity in the Orbell, van de Kragt, and Dawes study created a consensually held norm, to which the cooperators were conforming. The authors claim that this condition is necessary for a "promissory obligation" to exist, as they contend is demonstrated by the absence of support for the linear expectations model. In contrast, the evidence from the social psychology literature indicates that, although the extent of conformity is lessened when unanimity breaks down, it is still significant. The scattergram that Orbell, van de Kragt, and Dawes present as figure 1 certainly is consistent with their interpretation; however, it by no means disconfirms this alternative view. Despite a relatively small number of data points, the figure suggests that the rate of cooperation may not be an entirely discontinuous phenomenon, with very high cooperation under unanimity and virtually none otherwise; rather, the extent to which others will cooperate may indeed have some degree of linear association with the extent of promising.

An Organizational Psychology Perspective

In this study, Orbell and his associates addressed Hume's question of whether we are "naturally very limited in our kindness and affection," acting, instead, out of self-interest. Self-interest has been defined here as maximizing one's economic gain, and selflessness and "affection" as cooperating with others. The research evidence on what motivates people in organizations, however, suggests that questions of how humans behave "naturally" are insensitive to the important differences among us. In 1954, Abraham Maslow published his well-known theory of a five-stage hierarchy of human needs. He posited that the opportunity to satisfy physiological needs is the only motivating factor for individuals who are deficient in such needs, that only when those needs are satisfied will the opportunity to satisfy security and safety needs be motivating, that only when they in turn are satisfied will fulfillment of social needs be motivating, and so on. This process was presumed to continue until the only way to motivate an individual was to provide the opportunity for "self-actualization"—reaching one's fullest potential as a human being (when asked how many people actually do achieve self-actualization, Maslow named himself and an extremely short list of others).

Unfortunately, what is a good deal less well known than the outline of his theory is that in the thirty-five years since its publication there have been a number of efforts directed to empirically investigating its validity. This research has indicated that there is, indeed, a hierarchy of needs that works much as Maslow suggested; however, there are three or perhaps two discriminable stages in the hierarchy rather than the five he posited. For example, Alderfer (whose mentor, Argyris, was a proselytizer for Maslow's perspective and—no doubt coincidentally—one of those on Maslow's short list of the self-actualized) presented data that indicated three steps in the hierarchy, which he labeled existence, relatedness, and growth (Alderfer 1969). Existence needs (for things like food and shelter) can be satisfied by money. Alderfer's data (and those of other researchers) indicate that when these most basic needs have been satisfied, rewards that can satisfy those needs are not as motivating as are rewards that can satisfy the need for social "relatedness" with others, such as functioning as part of a team instead of separately. He found that individuals can satiate on relatedness rewards eventually, and will then be motivated by the opportunity for psychological "growth" (a term that is meant to be akin to, but somewhat broader than, self-actualization).

In light of this body of evidence, whether people act in a self-interested or in a cooperative manner seems less the issue than the conditions under which those similarly "natural" tendencies will be elicited. If individuals feel a deficiency of basic need satisfaction, we should not expect them to do anything but attempt to maximize the likelihood of acquiring for themselves the wherewithal to reduce that deficiency. If, on the other hand, individuals have satisfied their lower-level needs, the motivations to have rewarding social relations and be well regarded by one's fellows may be quite powerful, and high levels of conformity to a norm of cooperation are likely.

Problematically, however, laboratory experiments typically do not employ a sufficiently powerful manipulation to activate motives such as these—and this is probably true for the studies conducted by Orbell and his associates. If their subjects were sufficiently in need of money, and if the amounts of money were great enough to be seen by them as affecting their ability to satisfy their existence needs, the normative social influence on their behavior probably would have been a good deal less. That is, hungry individuals are not likely to be deterred from earning money for food by the thought that people whom they will never again meet may disapprove of their behavior.

A View from Sociology

Orbell, van de Kragt, and Dawes conclude with an appropriately modest view of the direct applicability of this laboratory research on promise making to resolving social dilemmas. Whereas many social psychologists would categorize the social interactions examined in their work as a form of social influence process, among sociologists the mechanisms by which society influences individual behavior have been referred to as social controls. This concept has a long and distinguished history in sociology, originating with a series of articles by E. A. Ross published in the *American Journal of Sociology* around the turn of the century in which he analyzed the major institutions of social control, such as the family, organized religion, and education. Ross and other members of the Chicago school viewed them as mechanisms to combat the alienation, normlessness, and criminality associated with the newly urbanizing and industrializing social order. That individuals should be made less alienated, anomic, or criminally deviant were norms with which most all could agree.

To a great extent, however, interactions of individuals and small groups with the larger society now are mediated through organizations of one form or another, and an analysis that appears entirely benign in the context of the overall society may have different ramifications when applied to work organizations, for example. The notion that social controls in typical work organizations are salutary suggests the encouragement of conformity to norms that have not been established by any sort of democratic political process, but by a small elite whose interests may or may not coincide with those of either the organization's work force or that of society in general. Not surprisingly, the only advocacy for applying the Chicago school social control perspective to organizations has been from two management professors (Trice and Beyer 1982).

More significantly, it was also from a university school of business management that a highly influential theory of organizations emerged, which, in emphasizing the centrality of cooperation, has much the same potential for bias as does a social control perspective. In his highly influential book, *The Functions of the Executive* (1938), Chester Barnard, a business executive who participated in a seminar on Pareto's social thought at the Harvard Business School during the 1930s, defined organizations as systems of cooperation and argued that because they were based on cooperative endeavor, their outputs necessarily were moral. As the antonym of conflict, cooperation is seemingly a desirable state of social relations; nevertheless, strings of letters such as KKK, PLO, and ACLU remind us that there are organizations whose activities are not universally regarded as moral, despite the commitment of their members to cooperating in those organizations' activities. Barnard's critics (e.g.,

Perrow 1986) argue that he ignored issues of interest: cooperation on whose terms and toward what ends?

Appropriately, in light of such limiting conditions, Professor Orbell and his associates are extremely sensitive to the difficulty of generalizing the findings of their investigations beyond small groups. As a further stage of their research program, they suggest a set of studies to examine structural patterns that might extend their work to larger social systems. I hope that in pursuing that very worthwhile agenda they may consider some of the perspectives upon which I have commented here.

REFERENCES

Asch, S. E. 1951. "Effects of Group Pressure on the Modification and Distortion of Judgments." In *Groups, Leadership, and Men,* ed. H. Guetzkow. Pittsburgh: Carnegie.

Alderfer, C. P. 1969. *Existence, Relatedness, and Growth.* New York: Free Press.

Barnard, C. I. 1938. *The Functions of the Executive.* Cambridge, Mass.: Harvard University Press.

Carlsmith, J. M., P. C. Ellsworth, and E. Aronson. 1976. *Methods of Research in Social Psychology.* Reading, Mass.: Addison-Wesley.

Crutchfield, R. S. 1955. "Conformity and Character." *American Psychologist* 10:191–98.

Deutsch, M. and H. B. Gerard. 1955. "A Study of Normative and Informational Social Influences." *Journal of Abnormal and Social Psychology* 51:629–36.

Maslow, A. H. 1954. *Motivation and Personality.* New York: Harper and Row.

Page, M. M. 1981. "Demand Compliance in Laboratory Experiments." In *Impression Management Theory and Social Psychological Research,* ed. J. T. Tedeschi. New York: Academic Press.

Perrow, C. 1986. *Complex Organizations.* New York: Random House.

Schneider, D. J. 1981. "Tactical Self-presentations: Toward a Broader Conception." In *Impression Management Theory and Social Psychological Research,* ed. J. T. Tedeschi. New York: Academic Press.

Sherif, M. 1935. "A Study of Some Social Factors in Perception." *Archives of Psychology* 27 (187).

Shulman, A. D., and H. J. Berman. 1975. "Role Expectations about Subjects and Experimenters in Psychological Research." *Journal of Personality and Social Psychology* 32:368–80.

Tagiuri, R. 1969. "Person Perception." In *Handbook of Social Psychology,* ed. G. Lindzey and E. Aronson. Reading, Mass.: Addison-Wesley.

Trice, H. M., and J. M. Beyer. 1982. "Social Control in Worksettings: Using the Constructive Confrontation Strategy with Problem-Drinking Employees." *Journal of Drug Issues* 12:21–43.

Comment on "Covenants without the Sword"

Robert P. Inman

Whether in the halls of government, the marketplace, or the family circle, cooperation is essential for mutually beneficial human interactions. Working or playing "together" enhances the welfare of all freely participating parties. Despite the obvious rewards from cooperative activity, achieving cooperation can be exceedingly difficult. More often than not, cooperative behavior provides its largest rewards just where the individual incentives to cooperate are least compelling. We would all be better off if worldwide disarmament could be achieved, but no one nation has the incentive to disarm without credible assurances that all others will follow suit. We are all better off when a "fair day's work" earns a "fair day's pay" but the worker has a private incentive to be lazy and the employer gains if he or she can shortchange employees. Even in affairs of love, where the gains are sweetest and the losses most deeply felt, "cheating hearts" are common. To encourage and preserve cooperation when private incentives dictate otherwise, we strive to fashion enforceable agreements—treaties, contracts, and marriage vows—but not always with success. When the "sword" behind such contracts fails, then we must look elsewhere for enforcement: to covenants without swords.

How can cooperation be achieved without an externally enforceable agreement when all individuals have incentives to violate the terms of cooperation? This question is the core issue of the social sciences to many.[1] Each social science has its suggestion: economics relies upon repeated interactions and the value of reputation (see Holmstrom 1985), psychology upon human needs (Weiss's comment in this volume), and political science, sociology, and anthropology upon conformance to group or societal norms of behavior (see Elster 1989). As this volume of essays attests, there is no more important, or interesting, issue than trying to understand how competing individuals come to first establish and then enforce a cooperative relationship.

The essay by John Orbell, Alphons van de Kragt, and Robyn Dawes

---

1. Indeed, the issue presents itself even if the sword successfully enforces the cooperative agreement, for how do we assure the cooperation of the "armed" enforcer?

addresses this question using the methodology of small-group experiments. The experiments reported here are "one-shot" games in which players interact for ten minutes, are allowed to make nonbinding (i.e., no "sword") agreements with each other, and are then given a chance to cheat on those agreements in private, after which individual rewards are determined. Final rewards are private information, so cheating cannot be easily detected. The reward for cheating is $5. The gains from full cooperation for each individual can be as high as $33. A cheater who is fortunate enough, or clever enough, to be paired with a group of all (other) cooperators can earn $38, advertised by the experimenters as a participant's maximum reward from the experiment. The optimal private strategy then is to persuade all others to cooperate during the ten-minute period of group interaction, and to then cheat on the group itself when it comes time to make one's final contribution.

Orbell, van de Kragt, and Dawes focus on the effectiveness of one mechanism for cooperative behavior in these groups—an individual's promise to the group not to cheat. They ask the question: when do promises foster cooperative behavior? Their answer: when everyone else in the group also promises to cooperate.[2] Without the unanimity of promises, however, promises alone do not appear to be a binding restriction on individual behavior; individuals in groups where promise making was virtually absent (i.e., groups with 0 or 1 promisers) were no more likely to cooperate than individuals in groups where some promising occurred.[3]

---

2. The validity of the conclusion can be seen from their figure 1. The figure indicates the number in each group who promised to cooperate (on the horizontal axis) and the number in each group who finally did cooperate (on the vertical axis). It is clear that when all fourteen group members promised to cooperate, more members of the group actually did cooperate. In the thirteen groups where all fourteen members promised to cooperate, 84.1 percent of those groups' members did cooperate (153 cooperators/182 total players in those thirteen groups). In contrast, in the seven groups where only a few (eight or less), or perhaps no one, promised to cooperate, the rate of final cooperation was 55.1 percent (54 cooperators/98 total players in those seven groups). This difference in the rate of cooperation is statistically significant at a .99 level of confidence.

Individuals in groups with twelve or thirteen promisors can be analyzed separately and their final behavior compared to those in the two sets above. Individuals in groups with twelve or thirteen promisors—almost unanimity—behaved much more like individuals in groups with only a few promisors than they did like individuals in groups with all promisors; the rate of final cooperation is 62.3 percent, which is not statistically distinguishable from the rate of cooperation found in those groups with only a few promisors. It is significantly less than the rate found in groups with all promisors, however.

3. Comparing the rate of final cooperation by individuals in groups that had 0 or 1 promisors to the rate of final cooperation in groups with several (more than one but less than fourteen) promisors shows no significantly different rates of final cooperation: 55.4 percent in the no promise groups vs. 57.1 percent in the some promise groups.

In the one special circumstance when everyone in the group promised to cooperate, however, promises did appear to encourage cooperative behavior. How did unanimous promising foster such cooperation? Orbell, van de Kragt, and Dawes suggest the following plausible process. First, the stating of a promise to cooperate by any one individual established that individual's willingness to participate in a contract that shared the benefits of cooperation. If all other members of the group agreed and also promised to participate in the contract to cooperate, then the contract was "struck" and a cooperative agreement was *established*. Second, once a contract to cooperate had been agreed to, each player (acting in private) then decided to either follow (act cooperatively) or deviate (cheat) from the agreement. Most (84.1 percent) kept their promise and agreed to cooperate. The economic payoff to the typical cooperating member of these groups was thereby higher, since cooperation increased rewards; of course, the 15.9 percent who cheated in these groups did better still. Importantly, the promise to cooperate also seemed to help *enforce* the contract to cooperate. Together, unanimous promising—what Orbell, van de Kragt, and Dawes call "consensual promising"—significantly encouraged cooperative behavior.

Why does consensual promising work in these experiments? The answer has to be found in a theory of "norms" or a theory of "needs." Since the game, by its structure, is played only once, the economists' favorite explanation for cooperative behavior, built upon the private advantages of reputation, cannot apply. Reputation has value only in repeated games. What norms or needs might then apply? Professor Weiss suggests that the *need* to belong to a group and to be "well regarded by one's fellows" might explain the high rate of cooperation observed here, and that is surely part of the story. The reward from cheating in this experiment was only $5. Many of us pay a good deal more than that to feel part of a group, even a group as anonymous as the attenders at a sporting event that we all could watch for free on television. In the Orbell, van de Kragt, and Dawes experiment, even groups with no promises to cooperate showed an average rate of cooperation of 57.1 percent.[4]

---

4. For the three groups where no one promised, the rate of final cooperation was 57.1 percent (24 cooperators/42 total members of the three groups).

Of course, one wants to ask what could induce such a high rate of cooperation among strangers, even when the group could develop no clearly articulated goal. There is an implicit goal of any participant in an experimental setting, however: to make some money. In this experiment, it is also clear that cooperation will allow the group to make more money. If one wants to belong to the group, and the implicitly understood goal of the group is to take as much money as possible from the experimenter, then those who wish to belong to the group will cooperate. Perhaps this is the motivation for the comment by one subject given in n. 4 of Orbell, van de Kragt, and Dawes: Promises "wouldn't mean anything, and we are all going to give [i.e., cooperate] anyway."

The psychological need to be part of a group surely accounts for some of the cooperative behavior observed here.

But meeting "needs" cannot be the whole explanation. The experiment also reveals that individuals are more likely to cooperate when, and only when, everyone in the group promises to cooperate—that is, when consensual promising applies. Two effects must be at work here. First, promising must fashion a multilateral, implicit (i.e., without external enforcement) contract to cooperate among all players. Importantly, under consensual contracting such a contract is *established* only when all players agree. Second, individuals generally conform to the terms of this implicit contract, even though breaking that contract cannot be detected and it is in the private interests of each player to do so. Only a norm can *enforce* such behavior (see Elster 1989). What norm might apply here? It cannot be just the personal norm of keeping one's promise, for then there would be a simple linear relationship in figure 1 between the number in each group who promise and the number who finally cooperate. That is clearly not observed in the data. The likely norm of behavior here is one that requires us to stand behind our contracts. It is here that consensual promising differs from just promising; consensual promising elevates each individual promise to the status of a contract. In our society a contract counts.

To social scientists searching for effective institutions to foster cooperative behavior, these results are heartening. If we accept the essay's central conclusion, then the norm of fulfilling one's contractual obligations coupled with some good heart-to-heart discussion of at least ten minutes seems to go a good way toward solving the social dilemma of free riding. We need to be cautious with our optimism.

First, note that the experiment is presented as a one-play game. It is important to know what will happen to the power of consensual promising when the game is played repeatedly. Since not everyone finally cooperates, even with consensual promising, and the cheaters do earn more, one wonders if the next play for such a game with the same participants might show a consensus much harder to achieve. Without consensus, the promise to cooperate loses the advantage—its only advantage—of becoming contractual. One expects contracting—and thus cooperation—to be more difficult when there are known to be "cheaters" at the table. But then, if cooperative contracting becomes more difficult when there is evidence of prior cheating, might not repeat play actually encourage cooperative behavior when consensual promising has been achieved? With consensual promising, each player pays a high (present value) penalty for cheating if such behavior undermines the ability to "write" a future beneficial implicit contract. It is not clear, a priori, what repeat play will do to the power of consensual promising. But it is important to know, for most social institutions in which the strategy might be employed (firms, legislatures, and families) require ongoing, repeating interactions.

Second, as I have noted, the decision to cheat in this experiment hardly offers a big reward—neither absolutely ($5) nor relative to the aggregate possible payoffs (just 13 percent).[5] In real life, however, cheating the group often brings with it very substantial absolute and relative financial rewards. Would these subjects cooperate so readily if they could earn an extra $100 or $1000 by cheating? That norms of behavior might have a price is an important issue that must be explored, though it is probably not possible to do so on a modest NSF-funded budget. We need to look to controlled situations in the real world—and to the methodologies of economics, anthropology, and sociology—for answers to this question.

Finally, consensual promising is a useful tool for inducing cooperative behavior only if a consensus can be achieved. One of the more interesting findings from the Orbell, van de Kragt, and Dawes experiments was the importance of group leaders to the process of consensus building. But why did such individuals emerge in some groups and not in others? Did every consensual group have a clear leader? Do recognized leaders become more important as group size increases? How did the leaders fashion the consensus, particularly in these one-play games in which he or she had no sanctions over the players to force agreement? We all know from personal experiences that strong personalities can foster cooperative behavior when it is in everyone's interest to cheat, but is it their argument or their ardor that wins the day? Orbell, van de Kragt, and Dawes have the tapes to provide us with some answers.

All this said, our caution with their conclusions need not dampen our appreciation for Orbell, van de Kragt, and Dawes's thoughtful study—a study even now more timely than when it was first presented. For if it is true that cooperative behavior can best be enforced by covenants with swords or by consensual promises tied to the norms of "contracting," then surely the fall of the communist regimes in Eastern Europe leaves those peoples dangerously exposed to the Hobbesian "void." Without their communist Leviathan or our capitalist norms of contracting to lean upon, how will cooperation in these societies now be achieved? Now, there is an experiment well worthy of our close study!

---

5. The maximum payoff is $38. The small relative reward for cheating is in contrast to what typically is observed in two-player Prisoner's Dilemma experiments where the cheater can capture all or nearly all the positive surplus of the game. If subjects play such experiments not only to earn money but to win, earning an extra $5 dollars when everyone else gets at least $33 is hardly a "smashing" victory, particularly since no one else knows you won!

REFERENCES

Elster, J. 1989. "Social Norms and Economic Theory." *Journal of Economic Perspectives* 3 (Fall): 99–117.

Holmstrom, B. 1985. "The Provision of Services in a Market Economy." In *Managing the Service Economy: Prospects and Problems,* ed. R. P. Inman. New York: Cambridge University Press.

Part 4
Evolutionary Selection
of Social Norms

In "Social Forces in the Workplace," Robert H. Frank points out that humans have certain inherent moral traits. He shows how these moral values can be understood as equilibrium results under conditions of natural selection. Typically, when people act upon moral values they are giving up the alternative of following narrow self-interest. That should be a losing strategy, and so it would be selected against in an evolutionary setting. However, Frank points out that moral values could be signaled by some external sign. In that case, people with moral values might gain from interacting with each other, and they could be better off as a group than people without moral values.

If it is costly to tell whether a person has moral values, then there can be a natural selection equilibrium in which some people will have moral values and others will not. The people with moral values will seek out others with moral values, but the gain from cooperating will be just balanced out by the cost of determining whether others have moral values. That allows the less moral types to survive in a natural selection process.

Frank goes on to apply this framework to a number of problems in the social norms of firms. People try to find accurate signals of others' character. Other people try to make it difficult to read their character as less ethical. Some cultures have stronger rules for socialization into moral values and better means of monitoring others' character. A variety of traits that seem inconsistent with self-interest, such as the desire for revenge or "getting even," can be explained in terms of natural selection.

Kenneth J. Koford examines some problems with the use of equilibrium evolutionary models in "Biological versus Cultural Indicators of Ability and Honesty." Since human natural selection involves both genetic and cultural evolution, it is not likely that both will be in equilibrium in the modern world. In general, cultural evolution moves much more quickly, but even cultural evolution may be unable to adjust to the rapid changes of the past few centuries. Koford's essay also examines the stability of dynamic models like Frank's. If adjustment is slow, it is hard to reach equilibrium; if adjustment is rapid, overshooting and dynamic instability are likely.

Social Forces in the Workplace

Robert H. Frank

It was once common for economists to attribute other-regarding motives to economic agents. Fairness, pride of workmanship, trustworthiness, sympathy, and other similar motives are still discussed widely in the literature on organizational behavior. But many modern economists find these notions hopelessly muddled and vague, and they have by now all but disappeared from the neoclassical lexicon. In this essay, I will survey recent research that suggests that a variety of other-regarding motives can be brought squarely within the neoclassical tent. And that to do so implies very substantial changes in the traditional model's portrayal of behavior in the workplace.

A Brief History

In 1950, UCLA economist Armen Alchian published a paper entitled "Uncertainty, Evolution, and Economic Theory," in which he argued that maximizing behavior on the part of economic agents is the result—often wholly unintended—of selection pressures in the marketplace. Alchian's argument borrows heavily from Charles Darwin's explanation of the origin of species. It begins with the premise that there is variation in the way economic agents behave in any given situation. Some linen sellers, for example, have white sales each January, others do not; some airlines hire only college graduates, others have less stringent cutoffs; some firms have formal employee grievance procedures, others do not; and so on. In a given environment, certain of these alternatives lead to higher net revenues than others, and in the long run there is a tendency for those behaviors that are most adaptive to proliferate. Their spread can occur either through relatively faster growth of the firms that employ them, or through imitation on the part of competing firms.

Firms need not understand *why* the successful practices work. Ask a linen retailer why he or she has white sales in January and he or she will likely respond that that is simply the way it's done in the industry. Alchian's argument allows room for maximizing behavior that results from the purposeful calculations of economic agents. But the important point is that it does not *require* such calculations. Self-serving behavior will emerge spontaneously from the struggle to survive.

Similar environmental forces are thought to mold efficient behavior on the part of consumers. Of course, selection pressures are less intense with respect to consumers than firms—after all, a firm that fails to maximize goes bankrupt, whereas an inefficient consumer can usually muddle along. Even in the consumer realm, however, it is clear that successful behaviors are often imitated where they can be, and that better methods, in time, tend to drive out worse. Here again, "successful" methods are understood to be those that maximize the individual consumer's wealth.

More than any other piece of modern research, Alchian's paper (and its strategic deployment by Milton Friedman and others) has been responsible for the egoistic orientation of modern neoclassical economists. Alchian was, of course, by no means the first to assert self-interest as an important human motive. But largely through his influence, we have inherited the modern presumption that self-interest is the only motive that will ultimately survive in a bitterly competitive material world.

I will argue, however, that Alchian's Darwinian argument is also consistent with a rich variety of less narrowly egoistic motives. Paradoxically, in order for an economic agent to do well in the material world, it is often necessary to set aside the strict pursuit of self-interest.

The Commitment Model

One of the most frequently discussed examples of the conflict between rationality and self-interest is the familiar prisoner's dilemma.[1] Thomas Schelling (1960) provides another vivid illustration of a class of problems in which the purely rational, self-interested person fares poorly. Schelling describes a kidnapper who suddenly gets cold feet. He wants to set his victim free, but is afraid the victim will go to the police. In return for his freedom, the victim gladly promises not to do so. The problem, however, is that both realize it will no longer be in the victim's interest to keep this promise once he is free. And so the kidnapper reluctantly concludes that he must kill him. The kidnapper's belief that the victim will act in a rational, self-interested way spells apparent doom for the victim.

Schelling suggests the following way out of the dilemma: "If the victim has committed an act whose disclosure could lead to blackmail, he may confess it; if not, he might commit one in the presence of his captor, to create a bond that will ensure his silence" (1960, 43–44). (Perhaps the victim could

---

1. The material in this section is drawn from Frank 1988. On rationality and self-interest, see, for example, Sen 1977.

allow the kidnapper to photograph him in the process of committing some unspeakably degrading act.) The blackmailable act serves here as a *commitment device,* something that provides the victim with an incentive to keep his promise. Keeping it will still be unpleasant for him once he is freed; but clearly less so than not being able to make a credible promise in the first place.

In everyday economic and social interaction, we repeatedly encounter commitment problems like the prisoner's dilemma, or like the one confronting Schelling's kidnapper and victim. The solution suggested by Schelling tries to eliminate the problem by altering the relevant material incentives. Unfortunately, however, this approach will not always be practical.

An alternative approach is to alter the psychological rewards that govern behavior. Emotions that urge people to behave in non-self-interested ways can sometimes accomplish this. Suppose, for example, the kidnap victim was known to be a person who would feel bad if he broke a promise. Such a feeling, if sufficiently strong, would deter him from going to the police even after it became in his material interests to do so.

Some further examples of commitment problems and of how emotional predispositions can help solve them.

The Cheating Problem. Two persons, Smith and Jones, can engage in a potentially profitable venture, say, a restaurant. Their potential for gain arises from the natural advantages inherent in the division and specialization of labor. Smith is a talented cook, but is shy and an incompetent manager. Jones, by contrast, cannot boil an egg, but is charming and has shrewd business judgment. Together, they have the necessary skills to launch a successful venture. Working alone, however, their potential is much more limited.

Their problem is this: each will have opportunities to cheat without possibility of detection. Jones can skim from the cash drawer without Smith's knowledge. Smith, for his part, can take kickbacks from food suppliers.

If only one of them cheats, he does very well. The noncheater does poorly, but isn't sure why. His low return is not a reliable sign of having been cheated, since there are many benign explanations why a business might do poorly. If the victim also cheats, he, too, can escape detection, and will do better than by not cheating; but still not nearly so well as if both had been honest. Once the venture is under way, self-interest unambiguously dictates cheating. If both Smith and Jones were emotionally predisposed not to cheat—that is, if they were honest—they would both be better off.

The Deterrence Problem. Now suppose Jones has a $200 leather briefcase that Smith covets. If Smith steals it, Jones must decide whether to press charges. If he does, he will have to go to court. He will get his briefcase back and Smith will spend sixty days in jail, but the day in court will cost him $300 in lost earnings. Since this is more than the briefcase is worth, it would clearly not be in his material interest to press charges. (To eliminate an obvious complication, suppose Jones is about to move to a distant city, so there is no point in his adopting a tough stance in order to deter future theft.) Thus, if Smith knows Jones is a purely rational, self-interested person, he is free to steal the briefcase with impunity. Jones may threaten to press charges, but his threat would be empty.

But now suppose that Jones is *not* a pure rationalist; that if Smith steals his briefcase, he will become outraged and think nothing of losing a day's earnings, or even a week's, in order to see justice done. If Smith knows this, he will let the briefcase be. If people *expect* us to respond irrationally to the theft of our property, we will seldom *need* to, because it will not be in their interests to steal it. Being predisposed to respond irrationally serves much better here than being guided only by material self-interest.

The Bargaining Problem. In this example, Smith and Jones again face the opportunity of a profitable joint venture. There is some task that they alone can do, which will net them $1000 total. Suppose Jones has no pressing need for extra money, but Smith has important bills to pay. It is a fundamental principle of bargaining theory that the party who needs the transaction least is in the strongest position. The difference in their circumstances thus gives Jones the advantage. Needing the gain less, he can threaten, credibly, to walk away from the transaction unless he gets the lion's share of the take, say $800. Rather than see the transaction fall through, it will then be in Smith's interest to capitulate.

But suppose Jones knows that Smith cares not only about how much money he receives in absolute terms, but also about how the total is divided between them. More specifically, suppose Jones knows that Smith is committed to a norm of fairness that calls for the total to be divided evenly. If Smith's emotional commitment to this norm is sufficiently strong, he will refuse Jones's one-sided offer, even though he would do better, in purely material terms, by accepting it. The irony is that if Jones knows this, he will not confront Smith with a one-sided offer in the first place.

The problems described in these examples are by no means contrived or unimportant. In joint ventures, practical difficulties almost always stand in the way of being able to monitor other people's performance. Again and again, cheating on all sides leads to a worse outcome for everyone. In these situations, having the means to make binding commitments not to cheat would benefit every party. In competitive environments, similarly, opportunities for predation are widespread. And where such opportunities exist, there is a ready supply of cynical people to exploit them. To be able to solve the deterrence problem would be an asset of the first magnitude. Bargaining problems, finally, are no less important. People must repeatedly negotiate with one another about how to divide the fruits of their collective efforts. Those who can deal successfully with these problems would have an obvious advantage.

Being known to experience certain emotions enables us to make commitments that would otherwise not be credible. The clear irony here is that this ability, which springs from a *failure* to pursue self-interest, confers genuine advantages. Granted, following through on these commitments will always involve avoidable losses—not cheating when there is a chance to, retaliating at great cost even after the damage is done, and so on. The problem, however, is that being unable to make credible commitments will often be even more costly. Confronted with the commitment problem, a purely rational, self-interested person fares poorly.

By themselves, however, emotional predispositions are not sufficient to solve the commitment problem. In order for noncheaters to benefit in material terms, others must thus be able to recognize them as such, and they, in turn, must be able to recognize other noncheaters. Otherwise, they have no way to protect themselves from being exploited by cheaters. The impulse to seek revenge or justice is likewise counterproductive unless others have some way of discerning that one has it. The person in whom this sentiment lies undetected will fail to deter potential predators. And if one is going to be victimized anyway, it is better *not* to desire revenge. It is the worst of both worlds, after all, to end up spending $300 to recover a $200 briefcase. For similar reasons, a commitment to fairness will not yield material payoffs unless it can be somehow communicated clearly to others.

But how to communicate something so subjective as a person's innermost feelings? Surely it is insufficient merely to *declare* them ("I am honest. Trust me."). The essential ingredients of one potential means of communication are nicely captured in the Frank Modell drawing reproduced in figure 1. The wary couple must decide whether to buy a pencil from the gentleman with the whip. If they believe him to be a fully rational, self-interested person, the presence of the whip should make no difference. The man would realize that no amount of added pencil sales could possibly compensate him for the jail term he would get if he actually used it. But if they believe he is *not* in full control, the whip will matter. It will then be in their interests to buy a pencil whether they want one or not. And in that event, the man gets the extra sale without so much as lifting the whip from his side.

Note that the sign around the man's neck is not the only, or even a very good, signal that he is not fully rational. On the contrary, that he seems to have realized the sign might serve his purposes can only detract from its ability to do so. It is the expression on his face that really makes his point. People who are fully in control of themselves just don't often look like that.

Posture, the rate of respiration, the pitch and timbre of the voice, perspiration, facial muscle tone and expression, movement of the eyes, and a host of other signals guide us in making inferences about people's feelings. We quickly surmise, for example, that someone with clenched jaws and a

Fig. 1. The extortionist. Drawing by Modell; © 1971 The New Yorker Magazine, Inc.

purple face is enraged, even when we do not know what, exactly, may have triggered his or her anger. And we apparently know, even if we cannot articulate, how a forced smile differs from one that is heartfelt.

At least partly on the basis of such clues, we form judgments about the emotional makeup of the people with whom we deal. Some people we feel we can trust, but of others we remain ever wary. Some we feel can be taken advantage of, others we know instinctively not to provoke.

Being able to make such judgments accurately has always been an obvious advantage. But it is often no less an advantage that others be able to make similar assessments about our own predispositions. A blush may reveal a lie and cause great embarrassment at the moment, but in circumstances that require trust, there can be great advantage in being known to be a blusher.

The Problem of Mimicry

If there are genuine advantages in being vengeful or trustworthy and perceived as such, there are even greater advantages in appearing to have, but not actually having, these qualities. A liar who appears trustworthy will have better opportunities than one who glances about furtively, sweats profusely, speaks in a quavering voice, and has difficulty making eye contact.

In most people, at least some of the outwardly visible symptoms of emotion are beyond deliberate control. We do know, however, that there are people who can lie convincingly. Adolf Hitler was apparently such a person.

In a September 1938 meeting, Hitler promised British Prime Minister Neville Chamberlain that he would not go to war if the borders of Czechoslovakia were redrawn to meet his demands. Following that meeting, Chamberlain wrote in a letter to his sister: ". . . in spite of the hardness and ruthlessness I thought I saw in his face, I got the impression that here was a man who could be relied upon when he gave his word . . ." (Ekman 1985, 15–16).

Clues to behavioral predispositions are obviously not perfect. Even with the aid of all of their sophisticated machinery, experienced professional polygraph experts cannot be sure when someone is lying. Some emotions are more difficult to simulate than others. Someone who feigns outrage, for example, is apparently easier to catch than someone who pretends to feel joyful. But no matter what the emotion, we can almost never be certain.

Indeed, the forces at work are such that it will always be possible for at least *some* people to succeed at deception. In a world in which no one cheated, no one would be on the lookout. A climate thus lacking in vigilance would obviously create profitable opportunities for cheaters. So there will inevitably be a niche for at least some of them.

Useful lessons about the nature of this problem are contained in the similar instances of mimicry that abound in nature. There are butterflies, such as the monarch, whose strategy for defending themselves against predators is to have developed a foul taste. This taste would be useless unless predators had some way of telling which butterflies to avoid. Predators have learned to interpret the monarch's distinctive wing markings for this purpose. This has created a profitable opportunity for other butterflies, such as the viceroy, who bear similar wing markings but lack the bad taste that normally accompanies them. Merely by looking like the unpalatable monarchs, viceroys have escaped predation without having had to expend the bodily resources needed to produce the objectionable taste itself.

In such instances, it is clear that if mimics could perfectly simulate the wing marking with neither cost nor delay, the entire edifice would crumble: the comparatively efficient mimics would eventually overwhelm the others, and the predators' original reason for avoiding that particular marking would vanish. So in cases where mimics coexist alongside the genuine article for extended periods, we may infer that perfect mimicry either takes time or entails substantial costs. The fact that the bearer of the genuine trait has the first move in this game will often prove a decisive advantage.

Similar considerations apply in the case of those who mimic emotional traits. If the signals we use for detecting these traits had no value, we would have long since ceased to rely on them. And yet, by their very nature, they cannot be perfect. For if they were, it would never pay anyone to cheat, and so no one would spend the effort required to scrutinize them. In which case, again, it *would* pay to cheat.

The inevitable result is an uneasy balance between people who really possess these traits and others who merely seem to. Those who are adept at reading the relevant signals will be more successful than others. There is also a payoff to those who are able to send effective signals about their own behavioral predispositions. And, sad to say, there will also be a niche for those who are skillful at pretending to have feelings they really lack.

Indeed, at first glance it might appear that the largest payoff of all will go to the shameless liar—the person who can lie with a straight face. In specific instances, this may well be true, but we must also bear in mind the special contempt we reserve for such persons. Most of us will go to great trouble to inform others when we stumble upon someone who lies with apparent sincerity. Even if such persons are caught only very rarely, it is far from clear that they command any special advantage.

Illustration: The Cheating Problem

To help see more clearly the nature of the economic forces at work, let us consider a specific illustration of the cheating problem in which X and Y face the decision of whether to open a restaurant. Again, they have the options of cheating or not, which gives rise to four possible combinations of behavior. For the sake of concreteness, suppose the payoffs to these combinations are as summarized in table 1. The terms *defect* and *cooperate* are used to represent "cheat" and "not cheat," respectively.

The payoffs in table 1 present X and Y with a Prisoner's Dilemma. X gets a higher payoff by defecting, no matter what Y does, and the same is true for Y. If X believes Y will behave in a self-interested way, he will predict that Y will defect. And if only to protect himself, he will likely feel compelled to defect as well. When both defect, each gets only a two-unit payoff. The frustration, as in all dilemmas of this sort, is that both could have easily done much better. Had they cooperated, each would have gotten a four-unit payoff.

Now suppose we have not just X and Y but a large population. Pairs of people again form joint ventures and the relationship between behavior and payoffs for the members of each pair is again as given in table 1. Suppose, further, that everyone in the population is of one of two types—cooperator or defector. A cooperator is someone who is emotionally predisposed to cooperate, regardless of the material incentives. A defector is someone who lacks this predisposition and, therefore, always defects.

In this scheme, cooperators refrain from cheating even when there is no possibility of being detected, and this behavior is clearly contrary to their material interests. Defectors, by contrast, are pure opportunists. They always make whatever choice will maximize their personal payoff. What will happen

TABLE 1. Monetary Payoffs in a Joint Venture

	X Cooperates	X Defects
Y Cooperates	4,4	0,6
Y Defects	6,0	2,2

when people from these two groups are thrown into a survival struggle against one another?

Population Movements When Cooperators and Defectors Look Alike

Suppose, for argument's sake, that cooperators and defectors look exactly alike. In this hypothetical ecology, this means they will pair at random. Naturally, cooperators (and defectors, for that matter) would like nothing better than to pair with cooperators, but they have no choice in the matter. Because everyone looks the same, they must take their chances. The expected payoffs to both defectors and cooperators therefore depend on the likelihood of pairing with a cooperator, which in turn depends on the proportion of cooperators in the population.

Suppose, for example, the population consists almost entirely of cooperators. A cooperator is then virtually certain to have a cooperator for a partner, and so expects a payoff of nearly four units. The rare defector in this population is similarly almost certain to get a cooperator for a partner, and can expect a payoff of nearly six units. (The defector's unlucky partner, of course, gets a payoff of zero, but his lone misfortune does not significantly affect the average payoff for cooperators as a group.)

Alternatively, suppose the population consists of half cooperators, half defectors. Each person is then just as likely to pair with a defector as with a cooperator. Cooperators thus have equal chances of receiving either zero or four units, which gives them an average payoff of two units. Defectors, in turn, have equal chances of receiving two or six units, so their average payoff will be four units. In general, the average payoffs for each type will rise with the proportion of cooperators in the population—the cooperator's because he is less likely to be exploited by a defector, the defector's because he is more likely to find a cooperator he can exploit. The exact relationships for the particular payoffs assumed in this illustration are shown in figure 2.

When cooperators and defectors look exactly the same, how will the population evolve over time? In evolutionary models, each individual repro-

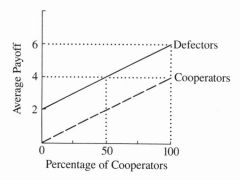

Fig. 2. Average payoffs when cooperators and defectors look alike

duces in proportion to its average payoff: those with larger material payoffs have the resources necessary to raise larger numbers of offspring.[2] Since defectors always receive a higher average payoff here, their share of the population will grow over time. Cooperators, even if they make up almost the entire population to begin with, are thus destined for extinction. When cooperators and defectors look alike, genuine cooperation cannot emerge. In a crude way, this case epitomizes the traditional economic view of self-interested behavior.

Population Movements When Cooperators are Easily Identified

Now suppose everything is just as before except that cooperators and defectors are perfectly distinguishable from each other. Imagine that cooperators are born with a red C on their foreheads, defectors with a red D. Suddenly the tables are completely turned. Cooperators can now interact selectively with one another and be assured of a payoff of four units. No cooperator need ever interact with a defector. Defectors are left to interact with one another, for which they get a payoff of only two units.

Since all elements of chance have been removed from the interaction process, payoffs no longer depend on the proportion of cooperators in the population (see fig. 3). Cooperators always get four, defectors always get two.

---

2. In very recent times, of course, there has been a negative relationship between income and family size. But if sentiments were forged by natural selection, the relationship that matters is the one that existed during most of evolutionary history. And that relationship was undisputedly positive: periods of famine were frequent and individuals with greater material resources saw many more of their children reach adulthood. Moreover, most early societies were polygynous—their most wealthy members usually claimed several wives, leaving many of the poor with none.

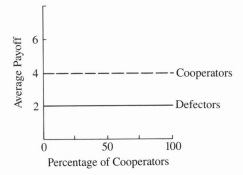

Fig. 3. Average payoffs when cooperators and defectors are perfectly distinguishable

This time the cooperators' larger payoffs enable them to raise larger families, which means they will make up an ever-growing share of the population. When cooperators can be easily identified, it is the defectors who face extinction.

Mimicry without Cost or Delay

The defectors need not go quietly into the night, however. Suppose there arises a mutant strain of defectors, one that behaves exactly like other defectors, but in which each individual has not a red D on his forehead but a red C. Since this particular strain of defectors looks exactly the same as cooperators, it is impossible for cooperators to discriminate against them. Each imposter is therefore just as likely to interact with a cooperator as a genuine cooperator is. This, in turn, means that the mutant defectors will have a higher expected payoff than the cooperators.

The nonmutant defectors—those who continue to bear the red D—will have a lower payoff than both of these groups and, as before, are destined for extinction. But unless the cooperators adapt in some way, they too face the same fate. When defectors can perfectly mimic the distinguishing feature of cooperators with neither cost nor delay, the feature loses all power to distinguish. Cooperators and the surviving defectors again look exactly alike, which again spells doom for the cooperators.

Imperfect Mimicry and the Costs of Scrutiny

Defectors, of course, have no monopoly on the power to adapt. If random mutations alter the cooperators' distinguishing characteristic, the defectors will be faced with a moving target. Imagine that the red C by which cooperators originally managed to distinguish themselves has evolved over time into a generally ruddy complexion—a blush of sorts—and that some defectors have a ruddy complexion as well. But because cooperators actually experience the emotions that motivate cooperation, they have a more intense blush, on the average.

In general, we might expect a continuum of intensity of blushes for both groups. For the sake of simplicity, however, suppose that complexions take one of only two discrete types: (1) heavy blush, and (2) light blush. Those with heavy blushes are cooperators, those with light blushes, defectors. If the two types could be distinguished at a glance, defectors would again be doomed. But suppose it requires effort to inspect the intensity of a person's blush. For concreteness, suppose inspection costs one unit. Paying this cost is like buying a pair of glasses that enable cooperators and defectors to be distinguished at a glance. For those who do not pay, the two types remain perfectly indistinguishable.

To see what happens this time, suppose the payoffs are again as given in table 1 and consider the decision facing a cooperator who is trying to decide whether to pay the cost of scrutiny. If he pays it, he can be assured of interacting with another cooperator, and will thus get a payoff of $4 - 1 = 3$ units. If he does not, his payoff is uncertain. Cooperators and defectors will look exactly alike to him and he must take his chances. If he happens to interact with another cooperator, he will get 4 units. But if he interacts with a defector, he will get zero. Whether it makes sense to pay the 1-unit cost of scrutiny thus depends on the likelihood of these two outcomes.

Suppose the population share of cooperators is 90 percent. By not paying the cost of scrutiny, a cooperator will interact with another cooperator 90 percent of the time, with a defector only 10 percent. His payoff will thus have an average value of $(.9 \times 4) + (.1 \times 0) = 3.6$. Since this is higher than the 3-unit net payoff he would get if he paid the cost of scrutiny, it is clearly better not to pay it.

Now suppose the population share of cooperators is not 90 percent, but 50 percent. If our cooperator does not pay the cost of scrutiny, he will now have only a 50-50 chance of interacting with a defector. His average payoff will thus be only two units, or one unit less than if he had paid the cost. On these odds, it would clearly be better to pay.

The numbers in this example imply a "break-even point" when the population share of cooperators is 75 percent. At that share, the expected payoff for a cooperator who does not pay the cost of scrutiny is $4 (.75) + 0 (.25) = 3$, the same as if he had paid the cost. When the population share of cooperators is below (above) 75 percent, it will always (never) be better for a cooperator to pay the cost of scrutiny.

With this rule in mind, we can now say something about how the popula-

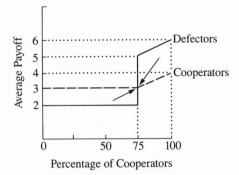

Fig. 4. Average payoffs with costs of scrutiny

tion will evolve over time. When the population share of cooperators is below 75 percent, cooperators will all pay the cost of scrutiny and get a payoff of three units by cooperating with one another. It will not be in the interests of defectors to bear this cost, because the keen-eyed cooperators would not interact with them anyway. The defectors are left to interact with one another, and get a payoff of only two units. Thus, if we start with a population share of cooperators less than 75 percent, the cooperators will get a higher average payoff, which means that their share of the population will grow.

In populations that consist of more than 75 percent cooperators, the tables are turned. Now it no longer makes sense to pay the cost of scrutiny. Cooperators and defectors will thus interact at random, which means that defectors will have a higher average payoff. This difference in payoffs, in turn, will cause the population share of cooperators to shrink.

For the values assumed in this example, the average payoff schedules for the two groups are plotted in figure 4. As noted, the cooperators' schedule lies above the defectors' for shares smaller than 75 percent, but below it for larger shares. The sharp discontinuity in the defectors' schedule reflects the fact that, to the left of 75 percent, all cooperators pay to scrutinize while, to the right of 75 percent, none of them does. Once the population share of cooperators passes 75 percent, defectors suddenly gain access to their victims. The evolutionary rule, once again, is that higher relative payoffs result in a growing population share. This rule makes it clear that the population in this example will stabilize at 75 percent cooperators.

Now, there is obviously nothing magic about this 75 percent figure. Had the cost of scrutiny been lower than one unit, for example, the population share of cooperators would have been larger. An increase in the payoff when cooperators pair with one another would have a similar effect on the equilibrium population shares. The point of the example is that when there are costs of scrutiny, there will be pressures that pull the population toward some stable mix of cooperators and defectors. Once the population settles at this mix, members of both groups have the same average payoff and are therefore equally likely to survive. There is an ecological niche, in other words, for both groups. This result stands in stark contrast to the view that only opportunism can survive in a bitterly competitive material world.

The critical assumption in this example is that people can make reasonable inferences about character traits in others. How plausible is this assumption? Perhaps a simple thought experiment will be helpful in coaxing out your beliefs on this issue.

Imagine you have just gotten home from a crowded concert and discover you have lost $1000 in cash. The cash had been in your coat pocket in a plain envelope with your name written on it. Do you know anyone, not related to you by blood or marriage, who you feel certain would return it to you if he or she found it?

For the sake of discussion, I will assume that you are not in the unenviable position of having to answer "no." Think for a moment about the person you are sure would return your cash; call her "Virtue." Try to explain *why* you feel so confident about her. Note that the situation was one where, if she had kept the cash, you could not have known it. On the basis of your other experiences with her, the most you could possibly know is that she did not cheat you in every such instance in the past. Even if, for example, she returned some lost money of yours in the past, that would not prove she did not cheat you on some other occasion. (After all, if she had cheated you in a similar situation, you wouldn't know it.) In any event, you almost certainly have no logical basis in experience for inferring that Virtue would not cheat you now. If you are like most participants in this thought experiment, you simply believe you can fathom her inner motives: you are sure she would return your cash because you are sure she would feel terrible if she did not.

For emotional predispositions to serve as commitment devices, it is not necessary to be able to predict other people's emotional predispositions with certainty. Just as a weather forecast of 20 percent chance of rain can be invaluable to someone who must plan outdoor activities, so can probabilistic assessments of character traits be of use to people who must choose someone to trust. It would obviously be nice to be accurate in every instance. But it will often suffice to be right only a fraction of the time. And most people firmly believe they can make reasonably accurate character judgments about people they know well. If you share this belief, you are in a position to see clearly why the unbridled pursuit of self-interest will often be a self-defeating strategy.

For convenience, I will use the term *commitment model* as shorthand for the notion that seemingly irrational behavior is sometimes explained by emotional predispositions that help solve commitment problems. The model describes an equilibrium in which there is an ecological balance between more and less opportunistic strategies. This balance is at once in harmony with the view that self-interest underlies all action and with the opposing view that people often transcend their selfish tendencies. As Zen masters have known all along, the best outcome is sometimes possible only when people abandon the chase.

The Importance of Tastes

The self-interest model is widely used by economists and other social scientists, game theorists, military strategists, philosophers, and others. Its results influence decisions that affect all of us. In its standard form, it assumes purely self-interested tastes; namely, for present and future consumption goods of various sorts, leisure, and so on. Envy, guilt, rage, honor, sympathy, love, and the like typically play no role.

The examples I have discussed, in contrast, emphasize the role of these emotions in behavior. The rationalists speak of tastes, not emotions, but for analytical purposes, the two play exactly parallel roles. Thus, for example, a person who is motivated to avoid the emotion of guilt may be equivalently described as someone with a "taste" for honest behavior.

Tastes have important consequences for action. The inclusion of tastes that help solve commitment problems substantially alters the predictions of self-interest models. This claim is very clearly borne out with respect to a variety of important behaviors in the workplace.

Shirking on the Job

In the workplace, as in other areas of life, there are frequent opportunities to cheat and shirk. In recent decades, economists have written at length about this issue under the rubric of the so-called principal-agent problem.[3] In the standard treatment, the firm (principal) has some task it wants the worker—its agent—to perform. The problem is that it is costly to monitor the worker's performance.

Economists have focused on the design of contracts that provide material incentives not to shirk. One ingenious proposal makes use of the observation that firms can often rank the performance of different workers even when they cannot measure exactly how much each produces.[4] Under these circum-

---

3. Grossman and Hart 1983; Harris and Raviv 1978; Holmstrom 1979 and 1982; Milgrom and Weber 1982; Pratt and Zeckhauser 1985; Radner 1981; Riley 1975; Rothschild and Stiglitz 1976; Shavell 1979.

4. Lazear and Rosen 1981.

stances, firms can elicit better performance by making part of each worker's pay depend on his or her rank in the productivity ordering.

But even the most sophisticated of these contracts is limited by the fact that behavior is often virtually impossible to monitor. Workers often confront "golden opportunities" to shirk, ones that are altogether beyond the reach of material incentive contracts. In the modern industrial firm, people tend to work in teams rather than as individuals. The classical monitoring problem is that while the firm can easily discover how much a team produces, it has little way of knowing how much each individual contributes to this total. The self-interest model emphasizes that each worker thus has an incentive to free ride on the efforts of his or her coworkers.

The commitment model suggests two approaches for solving this problem—one rather obvious, the other somewhat less so. The first is to hire workers who feel bad when they shirk. How can firms do this? Although it is not possible to observe what a worker does when confronted with a golden opportunity to shirk, his or her reputation may nonetheless provide useful clues. Sometimes even learning the groups to which people belong will provide relevant information (consider the New York City couples who advertise for governesses in Salt Lake City newspapers). Firms that encounter serious monitoring problems are well advised to gather information about the reputations of job candidates, and most of them of course already do so.

Despite this widespread practice on the part of employers, some neoclassicists assert that there is little point in trying to find out how someone has behaved in past situations. The difficulty, in Lester Telser's view, is not that we rarely observe situations that test people's character but that people have no character to test.

> . . . people seek information about the reliability of those with whom they deal. Reliability, however, is not an inherent personality trait. A person is reliable if and only if it is more advantageous to him than being unreliable. Therefore, the information about someone's return to being reliable is pertinent in judging the likelihood of his being reliable. For example, an itinerant is less likely to be reliable if it is more costly to impose penalties on him. . . . [S]omeone is honest only if honesty, or the appearance of honesty, pays more than dishonesty. (Telser 1980, 28–29)

By suggesting that character is not as empty a notion as Telser seems to think, the commitment model validates the firm's decision to gather information about the trustworthiness of prospective employees.

Where the commitment model may offer more novel insight is in suggesting ways to increase a given worker's propensity to cooperate. Most people have at least some capacity to experience the emotions that support cooperation. The extent to which they actually experience them depends strongly on environmental factors. The practical problem confronting the firm is to design a working environment that will encourage these emotions. A useful starting point is the observation that feelings of moral responsibility are much more focused on people with whom we have close personal ties. This suggests that shirking might be attacked by creating a work environment that fosters closer personal ties between coworkers.

Exactly this strategy has been followed by many successful firms in Japan. In the typical Japanese corporation, the worker "is a member of the company in a way resembling that in which persons are members of families, fraternal organizations, and other intimate and personal organizations in the United States" (Abegglen 1973, 62). Many Japanese companies provide housing and athletic and medical facilities for their workers, and educate their children in company schools. Co-workers vacation together in mountain or shore retreats maintained by the company. In contrast to the typical American worker, who works for many different firms during his or her lifetime, the Japanese ideal is lifetime tenure with a single employer.

This pattern enables the Japanese firm to solve monitoring problems in a way that the typical American firm cannot. Because of the close ties that exist between Japanese co-workers, their employers can link pay to the group's performance and rely on feelings of co-worker solidarity to overcome the inherent free rider problem.[5] In contrast, the pay schemes suggested by the self-interest model, which focus on individual performance, not only do not encourage cooperation, they actively militate against it.

This is not to say that the particular solutions adopted by Japanese firms will always be appropriate in the United States, where we place such a high premium on individuality and mobility. On the contrary, firms that blindly imitate the behavior of Japanese firms, as many American companies have begun to do, are not likely to prosper. If the commitment model is useful here, it is because it suggests the specific purpose the Japanese practices serve, namely, to encourage the emotions that support cooperation. The successful firms will be those that find ways of solving this problem in the American context. The self-interest model, with its exclusive focus on material incentives, steers management's attention in entirely different directions.

Profit-Sharing and Other Group Reward Plans

Profit-sharing plans are a favorite device in the corporate culture literature for motivating workers not to shirk their responsibilities. The argument offered in support of these plans is that workers will be reluctant to shirk for fear their

---

5. For a detailed and illuminating discussion of how Japanese firms deal with free rider problems, see Leibenstein 1987.

behavior will lessen their own compensation. Neoclassicists are quick to point out, however, that this argument overlooks the free rider that makes shirking a problem in the first place. The shirking of any individual member of a large work force, after all, will cause an all but imperceptible reduction in the firm's total profits. And since this reduction will be shared equally by the participants in the profit-sharing plan, the material incentives for any one worker not to shirk appear far too weak to matter.

The commitment model, in contrast, suggests a different interpretation of the role of profit-sharing plans. Under such plans, the injury caused by an act of shirking affects not only the shareholders of the firm, but also the shirker's co-workers. Individual workers who care about their co-workers will be reluctant to impose these costs. And this will be true even when it is impossible for co-workers to observe the act of shirking.

Fairness and Wage Bargaining

The commitment model also suggests that the wage bargain is governed by a broader set of forces than allowed for in traditional neoclassical models. The rationalists, as noted, complain that fairness is a hopelessly vague notion. And yet, as we will see, there is a reasonably simple definition that captures much of what people seem to mean by it. More important, we will see that concerns about fairness often profoundly transform behavior in the workplace.

Fairness almost always refers to the terms of a transaction (not necessarily an economic one) that occurs between people. To give the notion of fairness a working definition, it is thus useful to introduce some simple terminology concerning transactions first.

A transaction occurs when two parties exchange something. A gives B a dollar, B gives A a pineapple. When a transaction takes place voluntarily, it is conventional to assume both parties benefit. In the illustrative example, we infer that the pineapple is worth more than a dollar to A (else he would not have bought it), less than a dollar to B (else he would not have sold it).

In any transaction, there is a "reservation price" for both the buyer and seller. For the buyer, it is the most he would have paid. Had he been charged more, he would have walked away from the transaction. The seller's reservation price is the smallest amount he would have accepted.

The "surplus" from any transaction is the difference between the buyer's and seller's reservation prices. In the pineapple example, if these reservation prices are, say, $1.20 and $0.80 respectively, the resulting surplus is $0.40.

The traditional economic model says that exchange will occur if and only if there is a positive surplus—that is, if and only if the buyer's reservation price exceeds the seller's. Whenever an exchange does occur, the total surplus is divided between the buyer and seller. For the particular values assumed in the pineapple illustration, the surplus was allocated equally, both parties receiving $0.20 or 50 percent of the total.

In the self-interest model, the reservation price for one party to a transaction is defined independently of the circumstances of the other. It makes no difference to the seller, in traditional theory, whether the buyer is rich or poor; nor is the buyer assumed to care how much the seller might have paid for the thing he is now trying to sell. It is as if we imagined people who conduct all of their business with vending or purchasing machines. Each transactor is viewed in isolation, facing a take-it-or-leave-it decision that depends only on what the product itself is worth to him.

Using the notions of reservation price and surplus, we can construct the following operational definition of a fair transaction: A *fair transaction* is one in which the surplus is divided (approximately) equally. The transaction becomes increasingly *unfair* as the division increasingly deviates from equality. Simple as this definition seems, it is not always easy to apply. The most immediate problem is that reservation prices are often difficult to discern in practice. The art of bargaining, as most of us eventually learn, is, in large part, the art of sending misleading messages about them. But in many circumstances, the parties will have reasonably accurate knowledge of one another's reservation prices.

Suppose we assume that buyers care strongly about fairness as defined here. In particular, suppose they have a strong aversion to receiving less than 50 percent of the surplus. My simple definition of fairness, coupled with the assumed aversion to unfairness, yields a *fairness model* with the following specific prediction: people will sometimes reject transactions in which the other party gets the lion's share of the surplus, even though the price at which the product sells may compare favorably with their own reservation price.

In the self-interest model, of course, this can never happen. There, the division of the surplus simply plays no role in determining whether a transaction will take place. It will occur provided each party gets some positive share of the surplus, no matter how small. Yet, as we will see, concerns about fairness repeatedly cause people to reject transactions with a positive surplus.

The commitment model argues that an intrinsic concern about fairness can be advantageous, even though it may sometimes lead people to reject one-sided, but nonetheless profitable, transactions. German economists Werner Guth, Rolf Schmittberger, and Bernd Schwarze have performed an elegant test of this hypothesis (1982).

Their basic experiment is the so-called ultimatum bargaining game, which involves two players, an "allocator" and a "receiver." It begins by giving the allocator a fixed sum of money, say $20. The allocator must then make a proposal about how the money should be allocated between him and the receiver—for example, he might propose $10 for himself and $10 for the receiver. The receiver's task is then either to accept or reject the proposal. If he accepts it, then they each receive the amounts proposed. If he rejects it, however, each player receives nothing. The $20 simply reverts to the experimenters. The players in the game are strangers to one another and will play the game only once.

What does the self-interest model predict will happen here? To answer this question, we begin by assuming that each of the players cares only about his or her final wealth level, not about how much the other player gets. Now suppose the allocator proposes to keep P_A and give the remaining $20 - P_A$ to the receiver, and that the receiver accepts this proposal. If M_A and M_R were their respective wealth levels before the experiment, their final wealth levels will then be $M_A + P_A$ and $M_R + (\$20 - P_A)$.

If, on the other hand, the receiver rejects the allocator's proposal, then their final wealth levels will be M_A and M_R. Knowing this, the allocator can conclude that the receiver will get a higher wealth level by accepting the proposal than by rejecting it, provided only that P_A is less than $20. If the money cannot be divided into intervals any smaller than $0.01, the self-interest model thus predicts unequivocally that the allocator will propose to keep $19.99 and give the remaining $0.01 to the receiver. The receiver may not be pleased about this one-sided offer, but the self-interest model says he or she will accept it nonetheless because $M_R + \$0.01 > M_R$. By the logic of the self-interest model, the receiver reasons that while a gain of one cent isn't much, it is better than nothing, which is what he or she would get if the offer were refused. Because the game is played only once, there is no point in refusing in the hope of encouraging a more favorable offer the next time.

The findings from one version of their experiment are reproduced in table 2, which shows that the allocator rarely employed the rational strategy. That is, he or she almost never proposed an extremely one-sided division. A 50-50 split was the most common allocation proposed, and in only 6 of 51 cases did the allocator demand more than 90 percent of the total. On the occasions when the allocator did claim an egregiously large share for himself or herself, the receiver usually responded not as a self-interested rationalist, but in the manner predicted by the commitment model. In five of the six cases where the allocator claimed more than 90 percent, for example, the receiver chose to settle for nothing.

Actions motivated by concerns about fairness are by no means limited to participants in laboratory experiments. As we will see in the next sections, they appear to influence the terms of trade in virtually every labor contract.[6]

---

6. Fairness concerns also pervade a variety of transactions outside the labor market. See, for example, Kahneman, Knetsch, and Thaler 1986a and 1986b.

TABLE 2. The Ultimatum Bargaining Game

	N	Actual Percentage	Percentage Predicted by Rational Choice Model
Average demanded by allocator	51	67.1	99+
Proposed 50-50 splits	13	25.5	0
Proposals rejected by receiver	11	21.5	0
Average demanded by allocator in rejected proposals	11	85.3	100
Average demanded by allocator in accepted proposals	40	61.0	99+
Allocator demands greater than 90 percent of total	6	11.8	100

Source: Compiled from Guth, Schmittberger, and Schwarze 1982, tables 3–5.

Wages and Profits

On the average, firms with higher profit rates pay higher wages. Economists have been aware of this correlation for many decades.[7] The difficulty is that the self-interest model states unequivocally that profit rates should *not* affect wages. Workers, under the self-interest model, are supposed to be paid the value of what they produce. Those who produce a lot should get high wages and vice versa. This should be true no matter whether their employers' profits are above or below average.

The logic behind the self-interest model's prediction seems compelling. If a firm paid less than the value of what a worker produced, it should eventually lose him or her to a competitor. And if it paid more, it would earn lower profits than if it had not hired the worker in the first place. The self-interest model would predict that if highly profitable firms paid more, workers from less profitable firms would apply to them in droves; the resulting movements would tend to equalize wages, thus eliminating any correlation with profit rates. Because the self-interest model states so clearly that profit rates should not matter, many economists who study wage movements simply omit any mention of profits. The problem, which refuses to go away, is that profits clearly do seem to matter.

Here, too, the incompatibility between theory and observation seems to have something to do with concerns about fairness. Recall that the employment transaction resembles others in that both parties have their respective

---

7. Krueger and Summers 1986; Seidman 1979; Stigler 1946.

reservation prices. For the worker, it is the lowest wage he or she would accept before going off in search of work elsewhere. For the firm, it is the highest wage it could pay before becoming unprofitable. Everyone concedes that the unusually profitable firm has the ability to pay higher wages. The difference between the two reservation prices, which is the total surplus available for the firm and its workers to divide, will thus increase with the firm's profitability.

Although the more profitable firm has the ability to pay higher wages, the self-interest model perceives no motive for it to do so. The fairness model, however, suggests one. Note that if the firm with a strong market position pays only as much as other firms do, it will garner a disproportionate share of the total surplus—an unfair share in terms of my simple definition. Thus, if workers care strongly about the fairness of the labor contract, as other evidence suggests, they will require a wage premium for working for the more profitable firm. The other side of this coin is that they are often content to work for less when the employer has lower than average profits. The fairness model implies that workers are willing to give up income in the name of fairness, and it is this willingness that forces the more profitable firm to pay higher wages.

The correlation between wage and profit rates shows no signs of going away. It will continue to embarrass economists who insist that concerns about fairness never translate into costly actions.

The Internal Wage Structure

Another powerful illustration of how changes in tastes alter what transpires in the workplace is the case of the wage structure within competitive firms. Concerns about fairness are here reflected in the sacrifices that workers must make in order to occupy high-ranked positions among their co-workers. The traditional model, which assumes that workers do not care about the wages earned by their co-workers, says that each employee will be paid the value of his or her marginal product. Once we introduce concerns about relative wages, however, this conclusion no longer follows.[8] The argument rests on two simple assumptions: (1) most people prefer high-ranked to low-ranked positions among their co-workers; and (2) no one can be forced to remain in a firm against his or her wishes.

By the laws of simple arithmetic, not everyone's preference for high rank can be satisfied. After all, only 50 percent of the members of any group can be in the top half. But if people are free to associate with whomever they please,

---

8. The discussion that follows is developed more fully in Frank 1985.

why are the lesser-ranked members of groups content to remain? Why don't they all leave to form new groups of their own in which they would no longer be near the bottom? Many workers undoubtedly do precisely that. And yet we also observe many stable, heterogeneous groups. Not all accountants at General Motors are equally talented; and in every law firm, some partners attract much more new business than others. If everyone prefers to be near the top of his or her group of co-workers, what holds these heterogeneous groups together?

The apparent answer is that the low-ranked members receive extra compensation. If they were to leave, they would gain by no longer having to endure low status. By the same token, however, the top-ranked members would lose. They would no longer enjoy high status. If their gains from having high rank are larger than the costs borne by members with low rank, it does not make sense for the group to disband. Everyone can do better if the top-ranked workers induce their lesser-ranked colleagues to remain by sharing some of their pay with them.

Not everyone assigns the same value to having high rank. Those who care relatively less about it will do best to join firms in which most workers are more productive than themselves. As lesser-ranked members in these firms, they will receive extra compensation. People who care most strongly about rank, in contrast, will want to join firms in which most other workers are less productive than themselves. For the privilege of occupying top-ranked positions in those firms, they will have to work for less than the value of what they produce.

Workers are thus able to sort themselves among a hierarchy of firms in accordance with their demands for within-firm status. Figure 5 depicts the menu of choices confronting workers whose productivity takes a given value, M. The heavy lines represent the wage schedules offered by three different firms. They tell how much a worker with a given productivity would be paid in each firm. The average productivity level is highest in firm 3, next highest in firm 2, and lowest in firm 1. The problem facing persons with productivity level M is to choose which of these three firms to work for.

Workers who care most about status will want to "purchase" high-ranked positions like the one labeled A in firm 1. In such positions, they work for less than the value of what they produce. In contrast, those who care least about status will elect to receive wage premiums by working in low-ranked positions like the one labeled C in firm 3. Workers with moderate concerns about local rank will be attracted to intermediate positions like the one labeled B in firm 2, for which they neither pay nor receive any compensation for local rank.

Note also in figure 5 that, even though not every worker in each firm is paid the value of what he or she produces, workers taken as a group nonethe-

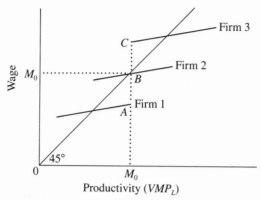

Fig. 5. The wage structure when local status matters

less do receive the value of what they produce. The extra compensation received by each firm's low-ranked workers is exactly offset by the shortfall in pay of its high-ranked workers.

The self-interest model, in contrast, says that every worker is paid the value of what he or she produces. Yet in every firm and occupation for which the relevant data are available, high-ranked workers are paid less—often substantially less—than the value of what they produce, while low-ranked workers are paid more. The difference, in large measure, represents the price a high- or low-ranked worker pays or receives for the position he or she occupies in the firm's internal hierarchy.

Segregating the Most Productive Employees

Concerns about relative wages also appear to account for the common practice of segregating the most productive employees away from their less productive co-workers. Consider, for example, the electric utility companies that employ large staffs of in-house attorneys to handle routine legal matters before the regulatory commissions that govern their operations. Simultaneously, many of these same companies contract with private law firms to supply an elite staff of highly talented attorneys to handle their most important cases. These outside attorneys often devote all of their time to the electric utility cases, raising the question of why the utilities do not simply hire them directly, thereby avoiding the substantial overhead charges imposed by the law firms. A plausible answer is that keeping the high-priced attorneys separate helps to avoid invidious comparisons between their salaries and those of their in-house counterparts.

Similar reasoning suggests why the most talented exploration geologists often operate as independent contractors. Someone who is good at finding oil is worth a great deal, much more, certainly, than the top executives of the company that extracts the oil from the earth. In purely physical terms, it would surely make sense to have the geologists serve as fully integrated staff members of the large companies that make use of their services. But the understandable awkwardness of paying a staff member several times more than the chief executive may well stand in the way of such an arrangement.

In the last decade, Cornell University has been one of the most successful institutions in the United States at raising donations from alumni and private corporations. One important reason was the leadership of its former director of development. By any conservative estimate, her contribution to the university's annual fund-raising effort was measured in the millions. Of course, it would have been impossible for the university to have paid any of its employees even a small fraction of that amount. Cornell's development director recently resigned her post and now serves as an independent fund-raising consultant to Cornell. I have no idea how much she is paid in that capacity. But it is easy to imagine that the university is now able to pay her much more than it used to.

Traditional labor market models have difficulty accounting for the widespread practice of segregating the most highly productive employees. Once we admit that relative wages matter, however, this pattern is no longer puzzling.

The Unpopularity of Piece Rates

The commitment model makes clear that people who care only about absolute wealth will be less effective bargainers than those who care also about how gains are divided. The emotion of envy acts as a commitment device that prevents people from accepting profitable, but one-sided, transactions. Envious persons often behave irrationally, but there is genuine material advantage in being an effective bargainer.

But here an emotion solves one commitment problem only to create others. To experience the emotion of envy is to feel concern about relative position in some hierarchy. Such concerns distort our decisions about a variety of important decisions, including the one of how hard to work (Duesenberry 1949). And in the process, they help explain the breadth and depth of worker resistance to piece rate pay schemes.

In the standard labor market model, the piece rate emerges as an almost ideal device for solving the shirking dilemma associated with hourly wage rates. Under piece rates, workers can continue to shirk if they like, but their pay will reflect their lower productivity. And sure enough, where piece rates have been implemented, the effect has invariably been a dramatic increase in output per worker.

Monotonously often, however, labor resists this kind of pay scheme, and employs elaborate strategies to reduce the rate of production. The occasional ratebuster is an object of intense social ostracism, and seldom survives for long on the shop floor.[9] Under the standard formulation of the neoclassical model, this resistance is a puzzle, for the piece rate scheme appears to provide a Pareto-superior alternative.

The difficulty confronting the piece rate becomes intelligible once we allow for the presence of concerns about relative wages. The piece rate induces the worker to give up some leisure in return for a higher wage, just as the traditional model predicts. Part of the lure of the higher pay is the absolute value of the goods and services it will buy in the marketplace. Indeed, in the traditional model, this is the only lure. But if relative position matters, another prospective benefit of working harder is to have higher *relative* earnings.

The catch, however, is that individual decisions to work harder fail to alter the distribution of relative wages. The worker puts out additional effort only to find his or her position the same as before. Collectively, workers may well prefer to work at a slower pace and earn lower salaries. But each individual worker on a piece rate confronts very different incentives.

Positional Concerns and Fringe Benefits

Unions and legislatures impose significant constraints on the labor compensation packages offered by private firms. The conventional explanation is that they act to prevent workers from being exploited by firms with excessive market power. There is no doubt that much of the moral force behind the early trade union movement and legislative initiatives had to do with the widespread existence of conditions like the ones in the Chicago meat factories described by Upton Sinclair at the turn of the century.

> Some worked at the stamping machines, and it was very seldom that one could work long there at the pace that was set, and not give out and forget himself, and have a part of his hand chopped off. There were the "hoisters," as they were called, whose task it was to press the lever which lifted the dead cattle off the floor. They ran along upon a rafter, peering down through the damp and the steam; and as old Durham's architect had not built the killing-room for the convenience of the hoisters, at every few feet they would have to stoop under a beam, say four feet above the one they ran on; which got them into the habit of stooping, so that in a few years they would be walking like chimpanzees. Worst of any, however, were the fertilizer-men, and those who served in the cooking

---

9. See, for example, the classic study by Donald Roy (1972).

rooms. These people could not be shown to the visitors,—for the odor of the fertilizer-man would scare any ordinary visitor at a hundred yards, and as for the other men, who worked in tank-rooms full of steam, and in some of which there were open vats near the level of the floor, their peculiar trouble was that they fell into the vats; and when they were fished out, there was never enough of them left to be worth exhibiting,— sometimes they would be overlooked for days, till all but the bones of them had gone out the world as Durham's Pure Leaf Lard. (Sinclair 1906, 106)

When the conspicuously high living standards of the factory owners were juxtaposed with the miserable living conditions of the workers, it was perhaps all but inevitable that many people would conclude that the former were exploiting the latter. But the existence of concerns about relative position can lead to similar outcomes, even in labor markets that are fully informed and perfectly competitive (Frank 1985, chaps. 7–8).

Consider, for example, the case of safety. Hoping to move forward in relative terms, people often skimp on the amounts they devote to safety. As in the case of piece rate work decisions, however, the payoffs here too are much smaller in the aggregate than they appear to individuals. For when everyone works in a riskier job, no one moves forward in relative terms. The problem is again one of simple arithmetic: no matter what risks we take on the job, only 10 percent of us can be in the top 10 percent of the income distribution.

The commitment model suggests that workplace safety standards and various other labor laws and union demands—regulating hours, wages, savings, and insurance—may be interpreted as commitment devices that help solve prisoner's dilemmas arising out of concerns about position. If these institutions are helpful, it is not because firms have too much power or because workers are incompetent—the reasons traditionally offered—but because concerns about relative position are such an important component of human nature.

Concluding Remarks

Self-interest is an undeniably important human motive. The egoistic utility functions employed in most neoclassical models have taught us a great deal about what happens in the workplace. But there are many important phenomena these models cannot accommodate. I have argued that other-regarding motives such as sympathy, anger, or concerns about fairness and relative position are important for their functional role in helping to solve commitment problems. Once we modify the utility function to include such concerns, we modify the conclusions of traditional models in fundamental ways. We see, for example, that material incentive contracts are often counterproductive as solutions to shirking problems; that profits may influence wages even in the long run; that profit-sharing plans and other group incentive schemes are often unexpectedly effective; that wages depend not only on productivity, but also on position in the internal wage hierarchy; that piece rates may be inefficient, even though they increase productivity substantially; that it may often pay to segregate the most productive workers; and that collective action to alter the composition of the compensation package is rooted less in power imbalances between workers and firms than in competition among workers for relative economic position. Social forces in the workplace have been all but ignored by neoclassical economists. The reason for this neglect has almost certainly been the belief that social forces do not lend themselves readily to economic analysis. I have attempted to show, however, that these forces spring from individual motives that ought to be perfectly intelligible to modern economists. The analytical power of the neoclassical model, properly focused, will have much to say about social behavior in the workplace.

REFERENCES

Abegglen, James. 1973. *Management and Worker*. Tokyo: Sophia University.
Alchian, Armen. 1950. "Uncertainty, Evolution, and Economic Theory." *Journal of Political Economy* 58:211–21.
Duesenberry, James. 1949. *Income, Saving, and the Theory of Consumer Behavior*. Cambridge, Mass.: Harvard University Press.
Ekman, Paul. 1985. *Telling Lies*. New York: Norton.
Frank, Robert H. 1985. *Choosing the Right Pond*. New York: Oxford University Press.
Frank, Robert H. 1988. *Passions within Reason: The Strategic Role of the Emotions*. New York: Norton.
Grossman, S., and O. Hart. 1983. "An Analysis of the Principal-Agent Problem." *Econometrica* 51:7–45.
Guth, Werner, Rolf Schmittberger, and Bernd Schwarze. 1982. "An Experimental Analysis of Ultimatum Bargaining." *Journal of Economic Behavior and Organization* 3:367–88.
Harris, M., and A. Raviv. 1978. "Some Results on Incentive Contracts." *American Economic Review* 68:20–30.
Holmstrom, Bengt. 1979. "Moral Hazard and Observability." *Bell Journal of Economics* 10:74–91.
Holmstrom, Bengt. 1982. "Moral Hazard in Teams." *Bell Journal of Economics* 13:24–40.
Kahneman, Daniel, Jack Knetsch, and Richard Thaler. 1986a. "Fairness and the Assumptions of Economics." *Journal of Business* 59:5285–5300.
Kahneman, Daniel, Jack Knetsch, and Richard Thaler. 1986b. "Perceptions of Unfairness: Constraints on Wealth Seeking." *American Economic Review* 76:728–41.

Krueger, Alan B., and Lawrence Summers. 1986. "Reflections on the Interindustry Wage Structure." NBER Working Paper no. 1968.

Lazear, E., and S. Rosen. 1981. "Rank Order Tournaments as Optimal Labor Contracts." *Journal of Political Economy* 89:1261–84.

Leibenstein, Harvey. 1987. *Inside the Firm.* Cambridge, Mass.: Harvard University Press.

Milgrom, P., and R. Weber. 1982. "A Theory of Auctions and Competitive Bidding." *Econometrica* 50:1089–1122.

Pratt, John, and Richard Zeckhauser. 1985. *Principals and Agents: The Structure of Business.* Boston: Harvard Business School Press.

Radner, Roy. 1981. "Monitoring Cooperative Agreements in a Repeated Principal-Agent Relationship." *Econometrica* 49:1127–48.

Riley, John. 1975. "Competitive Signaling." *Journal of Economic Theory* 10:174–86.

Rothschild, M., and J. Stiglitz. 1976. "Equilibrium in Competitive Insurance Markets." *Quarterly Journal of Economics* 80:629–49.

Roy, Donald. 1972. "Quota Restriction and Goldbricking in a Machine Shop." In *Payment Systems,* ed. Tom Lupton. Middlesex, England: Penguin Books.

Schelling, Thomas. 1960. *The Strategy of Conflict.* Cambridge, Mass.: Harvard University Press.

Seidman, Laurence. 1979. "The Return of the Profit Rate to the Wage Equation." *Review of Economics and Statistics* 61:139–42.

Sen, Amartya. 1977. "Rational Fools." *Philosophy and Public Affairs* 6:317–44.

Shavell, S. 1979. "Risk Sharing and Incentives in the Principal and Agent Relationship." *Bell Journal of Economics* 10:55–73.

Sinclair, Upton. 1906. *The Jungle.* New York: Sinclair.

Stigler, George. 1946. "The Economics of Minimum Wage Legislation." *American Economic Review* 36:358–65.

Telser, Lester. 1980. "A Theory of Self-enforcing Agreements." *Journal of Business* 53:27–44.

Biological versus Cultural Indicators
of Ability and Honesty

Kenneth J. Koford

Psychological, sociological, and biological facts can be useful in the analysis of strictly *economic* problems. Great payoffs have come from the hypothesis that human beings are generic utility maximizers, but economists are beginning to see gains from including more specific information about our biological and cultural natures. When economists assume that families care for each other and that parents have goals for their children, they rely upon such facts. People's demand for food, clothing, and shelter are also usually analyzed using information about human biology and culture.

Adding specific noneconomic information about humans to economic analysis could be a highly valuable research program. For economics to obtain specific quantitative findings—beyond qualitative comparative static results—it must find fundamental underlying regularities of human behavior. Such regularities can come from the large-number coordination processes of markets or the large-number principles of statistics. They can be found in engineering principles that can be included in production functions and geographical facts that can be included in spatial models. Until quite recently, however, economists have not used the other social sciences or biology to provide specific regularities. Now, discoveries by psychologists about choice under uncertainty are changing our understanding of rational choice. The social and biological context of decisions can also be used to give more precise insight into economic choices. Robert Frank's work has been in the forefront of this research, and his work has indicated some specific approaches that are both insightful and potentially very fruitful lines for further work. I examine several problems of detail in his work and describe some possible solutions.

Frank develops several models in which people hold internalized values or norms to varying degrees. Observers have some indication of an individ-

Jeffrey Miller made numerous critical and helpful comments, but is not responsible for the outcome. I am also indebted to Tom Ray and Mary Williams for helpful ideas and conversations.

181

ual's values, which is valuable in deciding who to work with or to trust. I begin by showing how social norms of the sort that Frank is discussing could have many applications in economics. I then discuss how such norms might have developed and how they could be maintained. I argue that cultural influences should be emphasized and that such an approach avoids some difficulties of purely genetic models. Thus, Frank's equilibrium with several different types of agents cannot easily reach equilibrium by a dynamic process. A selection process that leads to a stable heterogenous equilibrium is not fully discussed in Frank's work. In addition, the model (as described) may not even have a stable static equilibrium. These problems can be corrected with modest changes in the model's assumptions. In particular, heterogeneity can make this class of model much more stable.

Frank applies his model to a number of organizations. His examples are intended to be persuasive, but require more structure to be convincing. My argument here takes two paths. First, while norms in organizations could be consistent with Frank's general framework (that is, ethical rules could be basically identical across people and biologically/genetically based), in fact they seem to be more varied, cultural, and subtle. Second, the striking behavioral facts that Frank describes could have other causes. We must look at other possible explanations for these facts, and be able to distinguish among the different explanations. That work still remains be done for most of Frank's applications.

Why Consider *Social* Values?

Economic theory has been based upon individual utility maximization. Individual utility is most commonly interpreted, in practice, as individual self-interest, and self-interest as more goods for oneself. That view of people is very narrow, since human societies have been built upon mutual commitments that are hard to explain in terms of pure self-interest. From the most common and fundamental commitment to have and raise children to the moral commitments to honesty and fairness toward others, these values are crucial to society. Such moral values help explain many episodes in history, even economic history.

However, as Frank has shown (in this volume and in earlier work [Frank 1987 and 1988]), there are numerous important social institutions based partly on ethical values such as a conscience. Adam Smith, in *The Theory of Moral Sentiments* ([1759] 1976), states a similar view. Alfred Marshall points out that ethical values can play a major role in economic choices (1920, 6–7 and chaps. 2 and 12). Smith and Marshall both emphasize the importance of education and social pressure in determining ethical values. But Frank brings out the underlying biological principles that could lead to the ethical value we call a conscience.[1] It seems fairly clear that societies cannot survive effectively without an accepted moral order—a point neglected by mainstream economists, but emphasized by sociologists and Austrian economists.[2] (Not everyone need agree with or obey that moral order, but a moral order gives people a framework of accepted rules to use as a starting point for action. Koford and Miller in this volume show how custom and norms play this role in society.) How a particular moral order is established, and how it affects the institutions of the economy, could then be crucial points for economists to examine. Frank emphasizes one form of moral order: how a biological propensity to follow a moral rule can have survival value and so influence the nature of organizations. And he shows that this propensity is fundamentally social: it is based on people's ability to trust others in social work situations.

Sources of Values

Non-self-interested values could have two sources. One is biological or genetic. Parental altruism is a convincing example.[3] Parents love and care for their children, but not because those specific children are uniquely delightful. They are *not* considered consumption goods like cars or ski trips. Parental love and caring are nearly universal, and so similar to parental care in species with less cultural endowment that they must be largely genetic.[4] Frank's previous work on the conscience and on relative status deals with other traits that may be largely genetic.[5] In this volume, Frank describes emotions that drive people to demand fair treatment and take revenge when treatment is unfair. Such emotions as love, hatred, and anger surely have a genetic base. Blushing when exposed as guilty is presumably genetic, as is the ability to internalize guilt. But it is socialization that induces guilt for particular beliefs. The combination of socialization and the genetic base are needed for the behavior.

The second source of values—social controls—can influence behavior independently from purely genetic effects. Social controls must also have

---

1. Other references on the biological source of the conscience are Badcock 1986; Brunner 1987; Pugh 1977; Trivers 1985.

2. See, e.g., Hayek 1960 and 1973; Parsons 1937; Weber 1968.

3. See Becker 1977; Hirshleifer 1977.

4. Some insect and fish species care for their offspring, but have no "culture" that could transmit such values; they care for *their* offspring, not just young in general.

5. The conscience is a quite complex puzzle from the standpoint of evolution, since others may be able to take advantage of it (see Badcock 1986; Trivers 1985). Male striving for status is found in a wide variety of species, and among most primates. The kinds of status hierarchies observed are fairly similar to those found among humans in both society and formal organizations (Sapolsky 1990).

genetic roots; genes need provide only a biological structure for socialization. Those specific values could be internalized by everyone in a society and, thus, become the social norms or rules of fairness that Frank examines.[6] Anthropologists and sociologists have emphasized how the system of social norms determines values (e.g., Shweder and Bourne 1984). If socialization varies across people within a society, there could be a variety of specific values. If socialization is highly uniform, values would be highly uniform. To examine the distribution of values, one must look at the motivations of socializers (religious leaders, educators, parents), not just the utilities of the people who receive the social values.[7]

However, recent research has emphasized that humans do not follow either pure genetic controls or pure cultural controls (Lumsden and Wilson 1981; Boyd and Richerson 1985).[8] Social controls tend to work with—or against—genetic controls. Social or cultural controls can change much more quickly than can genes, so that the two can become inconsistent. People then will be torn between different values—cultural values and genetic values. That makes it relatively unlikely for a single, well-defined ethical value to exist.

Thus, the type of values that Frank describes may be unusual—restricted to blushing or similar, largely genetic factors. However, even such nominally genetic factors have a cultural element: people in one society will blush for reasons different from those in other societies. Since people vary in how they internalize their society's culture, and in how they accept and reject their society's cultural values, some people in a society will blush in response to stimuli that do not cause others to blush. Thus, Frank's result could be caused by cultural factors as well as genetic factors.

This point can be considered using the blushing example. Blushing presumably increased in importance after language was developed, since it permits higher levels of cooperation and deception. Anthropologists believe that, for most of human prehistory, people lived in small groups and engaged in cooperative hunting and gathering. So blushing might have come to a purely genetic equilibrium in that social situation. However, a purely genetic equilibrium requires high selection, a stable environment, and many generations. If Homo sapiens has existed for less than 100,000 years, only 5,000 generations are available to come to equilibrium. The more recent development of

---

6. A test of the alternative hypotheses is to see if such rules are consistent across cultures. Ethnographic data on cultural patterns could be used to investigate this question.

7. There does not appear to be very clear evidence on the distribution of values in social populations. Generalizations that values are more consistent in Japan or Europe than in the United States might be true, but the emphasis in empirical work has been on differences in *average* values.

8. Hull (1988, chap. 12) describes these theories.

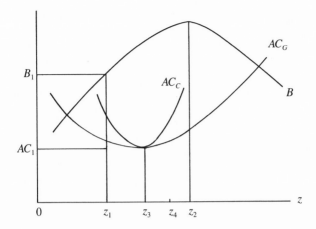

Fig. 1. Short-run and long-run equilibrium

agriculture and cities must imply major changes in optimal blushing, for they imply large increases in the number of people one would interact with and an increase in people's time horizon. But there have been only about 10,000 years—500 generations—to adjust to these changes, and mortality may have been low enough to retard selection pressures. It is unlikely that a static genetic equilibrium could be optimal for current conditions.

Given the slowness of genetic change, most sociobiologists believe that a combination of genetic and cultural change would be most probable. It could adjust quickly enough to changing conditions to reach equilibrium. Cultural evolution appears to adjust within a few generations, allowing for fairly rapid adjustment of cultural values. But the genetic foundation for cultural values can also change. If current genetic values are largely adjusted for the circumstances of a hunter-gatherer world, changes may be needed to fit an urban, industrial world. But is natural selection rapid enough today for significant genetic changes to occur?

This point is shown more formally in figure 1. The horizontal dimension, z, represents levels of a variable such as the degree of blushing when dishonest, from 0 on the left to high levels on the right. The vertical dimension represents average cost and benefits to a person associated with specific levels of the activity. So at a specific activity level, z_1, the cost per unit of carrying out the (blushing response) activity is AC_1, while the benefit per unit is B_1. The net gain to the agent with z_1 is $B_1 - AC_1$. The *average cost* of a level of an activity is defined in biological theory as the energy cost of the genes, physical structures, and the activity in a physical sense; in the sociobiology literature it is the "social energy" cost of maintaining a given level of activity.

The general concept of cost is that there is some energy or resource use required to maintain any specific structure or activity pattern. A *biological structure* could be a set of genes maintained in all cells of the body, while a *social structure* could be a cultural norm where the cost is that of education and acculturation to the specific norms.

Following Lumsden and Wilson (1981), the genetic component of behavior adjusts slowly and so provides a substratum for the cultural component. Its current level is represented by the AC_G curve. (It is analogous to the long-run average cost curve.) Evolutionary genetic theory finds that there are few fundamental genetic constraints on the AC_G curve; therefore, this curve would eventually locate so that it has minimum costs at the location where B has the highest z-level. The steepness of the AC_G function depends on the past variation of the optimal z over time. So, if the optimal level varies considerably, there will be a wider low-cost region.[9] In figure 1, the long-run *past* maximum average benefit must therefore have been at z_1. However, the *current* average benefit function, B, has its maximum at z_2, indicating that recent conditions have increased the average benefits of activity z. This activity is assumed to have a cultural as well as a genetic component. In figure 1, the increased cost of the cultural activity is added to the genetic cost.[10] The genetic function creates a general ability to establish a specific cultural rule, say blushing at specific dishonest behaviors that must be defined culturally. These cultural values can change much more quickly than can the genetic values of z. The cost of obtaining a specific cultural value of z is shown as the AC_C curve—which is analogous to the short-range AC curve in its relation to the long-range AC curve. The average cost of the activity including the specific cultural component, AC_C, is shown with cultural values changing from z_1, the old optimum, toward z_2, the new optimum, but the cultural value has moved only partway. Net long-run benefits—the difference between B and AC_G—will be maximized when the AC_C curve reaches z_4. However, since the adjustment process is evolutionary, the cultural curve will move toward z_4 in proportion to the gradient of net gains.

Figure 1 shows that an evolutionary process selects values by both a genetic and a cultural mechanism. The conclusion is that the process is very likely to be in disequilibrium—in a transition toward a long-run equilibrium.

---

9. Biological heterogeneity is known to be very high; it is maintained at a very high resource cost. It is believed that sex, which *doubles* reproductive cost, has its basic benefits in assuring heterogeneity. So genetic heterogeneity must have very substantial benefits—essentially the ability of species to respond to the unexpected (Trivers 1985).

10. This technique allows the curve to look like the short-run average cost curve. A more detailed model would develop the additional costs of the cultural component of values, and add them to the genetic cost curve.

Thus, theoretically modeling just the static equilibrium is insufficient.[11]

Formal evolutionary theory indicates that the cultural and genetic components are basically like short-run and long-run average cost functions, respectively. However, the genetic components change as well, although quite slowly. They might be similar to technological knowledge in Nelson and Winter's (1982) evolutionary theory of the firm. Then, if the average benefit function were to remain stable for a very long time, genetic evolution would bring the minimum of the AC_G curve to z_2.

This example contrasts with Frank's model on one strong predictive element, a genetic propensity toward a moral value (honesty) shown by an indicator. Thus, people can use an indicator of z to predict others' honesty, and Frank's model must be basically correct. But the model cannot show that society today has the "optimal" or "equilibrium" level of z. The model also cannot tie blushing to a specific form of honesty, such as telling the truth to the Internal Revenue Service. That tie must be cultural, and so can vary across cultures and individuals.

The precise nature of the tie between cultural and genetic values is not yet known. Evolutionary theory requires only that genetic values provide a range of possibilities that experience fills in. The question of the nature of language ability is an example. Humans have an innate, genetic ability to learn language; the degree to which specific grammar and sounds are constrained by genetics remains uncertain.[12] Primate species can give useful insights on this question. They have social relations, they are fairly closely related to us, and they have a wide variety of behaviors that can be used to do a comparative static analysis. In *Primate Societies* (Smuts et al. 1987), a large collaborative work, the authors attempt to find generalizations about primate values and cultures as a function of environmental and genetic differences. However, specific conclusions are premature. The primate researchers found that primate behavior is much more complex and varied than previous models had indicated, and it was more heterogeneous within species than expected.

Frank's analysis of fair division illustrates these problems. He proposes that a 50-50 split of gains or losses is a fair division, but that specific rule is artificial. People in different situations have different rights; only in a totally featureless world does the 50-50 split seem fair. Distribution of gains between

---

11. Oster and Wilson (1984) have admitted this, noting that only in populations with very stable environments for many generations can equilibrium models be fully appropriate.

12. Language seems to develop in an evolutionary manner, according to analysis of linguistic groups. But such other cultural patterns as religion, which also must have a genetic component, appear to develop discontinuously. When this occurs, the specific ethical properties of a rule like blushing will be hard to analyze. For instance, consider ethical values in Iran over the past two decades. What statements are false or improper, and when?

parents and children, landlords and sharecroppers, law partners and associates, or professors and graduate students are hardly 50-50, yet at least one side of the relationship would consider them fair. Thus, while fairness is probably a basic biological concept, the specifics are *not* the same for everyone or for every culture. Also, *within* any group views of fairness also vary. Some cultures, social classes, and ethnic groups believe strongly in fairness, while others do not, or accept "to the victors belong the spoils."

This section has questioned whether one can specify purely genetic moral values or whether one must specify combined genetic and cultural values. For many problems, a mechanism that combines both is required. Since cultural values vary widely in modern societies, such a mechanism implies heterogeneous values, which make it difficult to determine how people will behave.

These complex values are likely to vary over a continuum of values and on several dimensions. This makes a stable equilibrium more likely. The next section shows that the added dimensions and the continuum of values increase the strength of Frank's general argument, while modifying some details.

Dynamics and Stability of Equilibrium

> In the absence of stabilizing forces, host-parasite systems will have a tendency to oscillate; consequently, one may observe sustained oscillations of limit-cycle or more complicated type, or system collapse. (Levin 1983)

Frank's formal model is not described in detail in this volume, but is specified fully in several versions in Frank 1987 and 1988. The model's dynamic adjustment speed is proportional to the current gain from adjustment, as in standard adjustment models. Such models have become standard in evolutionary theory as well as in economics (e.g., Russell and Wilkinson 1979).

Such an adjustment process may not be stable, however. And it may be inappropriate for cultural/genetic systems. First, stability problems occur because ethical values are typically a matter of "right" and "wrong" with a discrete difference between them.[13] Equilibrium in such models has generic knife-edge instability problems. Second, the speed of adjustment of genetic "abilities to internalize values" seems very slow, while the speed of adjustment of cultural values is much faster and possibly erratic.

I begin with a discussion of Frank's model where agents are endowed with either a genetic tendency to blush when lying, or not. The problem of

---

13. Since most situations are shades of gray, ethical values may represent a need for simplicity in social interactions.

equilibrium occurs when there are two discrete "types" of agents with substantially different payoffs. Frank's figure 4 (in this volume) shows such payoffs for the two discrete types at every point.[14] *Globally stable* models have payoff curves that are continuous and cross each other once. This means that, at the equilibrium point, the payoffs to each group are exactly the same. Away from the equilibrium point, differences in the payoffs increase with distance from the equilibrium. The dynamic adjustment in this case is always in the direction of the equilibrium, and, as the equilibrium is approached, the speed of adjustment falls until it reaches zero at the equilibrium.

However, Frank's basic model, described by his figure 4, has a discrete payoff difference at every point away from the equilibrium and also *at* the equilibrium.[15] Suppose that the proportion of cooperators and defectors were at the equilibrium. In Frank's example, there are 75 percent cooperators and 25 percent defectors. But this is not a strict Nash equilibrium. For the discrete "jump" in the payoff function for defectors at this point makes it impossible for all agents to be equally well off. To see this, think about what creates the difference in payoffs away from the "equilibrium." With a low proportion of cooperators, cooperators incur the cost of scrutinizing to be sure to interact with another cooperator. In that region (in Frank's fig. 4, with less than 75 percent cooperators), cooperators have a higher payoff than defectors. With a proportion of cooperators of 75 percent or more, the cooperators have their highest payoff by not scrutinizing, and defectors then have a higher payoff. Since the payoffs to defectors and cooperators are not equal at 75 percent, that point is not an equilibrium. At 75 percent, the payoffs to defectors are higher, so the proportion of defectors should rise. In general, an agent would gain by "changing type" at *every* point, given the distribution of all others' types. (In this model, agents do not optimize intentionally; rather, they inherit values that depend probabilistically upon the payoffs to cooperators and defectors in previous generations.)

Another test of equilibrium is a trembling-hand test. Such a test is particularly appropriate if some natural selection process with a random component determines the distribution of types. Suppose that by chance—beginning at 75 percent cooperators—just a few of the defector types reproduce as cooperators, so that the proportion of cooperators rises to 77 percent.[16] The payoff to being a defector is now high. Think of the model as having distinct periods, such as years or generations—sufficient time for agents to reproduce and

---

14. In contrast, Frank 1987, fig. 5, shows payoffs for two discrete types that approach each other around the equilibrium value.

15. I am grateful to Jeff Miller for improving the analysis of this point.

16. Strictly, we should say that, in the replacement of old or dying defectors, the new ones do not replace them in the same proportion.

receive either biological or cultural endowments. Parents or socializing institutions would observe the relative payoffs of the two types and be more likely to socialize in proportion to the difference in payoffs. In the next period, perhaps 10 percent more of the agents will be socialized to be defectors. In the succeeding period, the payoff of being a cooperator will be higher, and so more agents will then be socialized to be cooperators. This process easily generates cycles, and there is no reason for the cycles to be dampened.[17]

Define cooperator = C, defector = D. In discrete time, the adjustment process might be described as a linear function

$$Pr(C_t) - Pr(C_{t-1}) = k[\text{Payoff } C_{t-1} - \text{Payoff } D_{t-1}]. \tag{A1}$$

Also, adjustment lags are very common in economic and cultural processes. It would be unusual for the change in $Pr(C)$ to change abruptly if the payoffs changed abruptly. (In biological processes, the connection should be closer.) If the adjustment depends on the past adjustment, it might be

$$Pr(C_t) - Pr(C_{t-1}) = f\{k[\text{Payoff } C_{t-1} - \text{Payoff } D_{t-1}],$$
$$h[Pr(C_{t-1}) - Pr(C_{t-2})]\}, \tag{A2}$$

which would assure some continuity as the function approached continuous time.

With the adjustment function, A1, if the adjustment process begins far from the equilibrium, it continues at a constant rate until it crosses the equilibrium. Then it reverses when 75 percent cooperators is exceeded.[18] With the adjustment function in A2, after crossing the 75 percent cooperators point, the function declines at a constant rate until it has reversed direction, and then continues to decline until it again crosses the 75 percent point. For the latter, cycling around 75 percent cooperators is likely, although the cycles are likely to be dampened.

The problem of determining sufficient conditions for a stable equilibrium is quite general. We think that, in the real world, there is probably a stable equilibrium to the cooperator-defector case: that there should be an equilibrium with a stable proportion of each. Our task is to find appropriate assumptions that "assure" the equilibrium. This problem has occurred in screening models (Spence 1973) and principal-agent shirking models (Shapiro

---

17. If the payoff functions were at all nonlinear, there would be a good chance of chaotic adjustment.

18. Given the payoffs described by Frank, the absolute value $|C - D|$ above 75 percent cooperators is twice that below 75 percent cooperators, so the rate of change would also be twice as high.

and Stiglitz 1984; Koford and Penno 1988). It is not a problem specific to Frank's model. (Either instability is generic, or there is something wrong about this class of models.) I suggest that the problem is that the real world has more heterogeneity, on many dimensions, than is allowed for in these models (Koford and Penno 1988). Frank (1987) described heterogeneity by a random variable that seems to represent local variations from the average payoff value. If payoffs come from something like random matching of people, individual locations will have proportions of cooperators different from the average, and so adjustment based on the local proportion will vary continuously with the proportion of cooperators.

Several questions arise with the "random matching" model. First, matches are not random, but are some combination of intentional and random. Reputation or "nearness" might be factors in intentional matches. This problem of local variations in matching and in types is difficult to analyze—at the extreme, there are several separate populations. Second, people's strategies are surely more complex than just to cooperate or defect. Revenge against defectors, for example, might be a good strategy, since defectors would avoid such a person.

Alternatively, there could be a continuum of intermediate ethical types between cooperators and defectors, or a range of other payoffs that agents receive for honesty. These have to be partially unobservable. This is consistent with Frank's approach: while people's ethical values are partly known and used by others, they are not perfect solutions to problems of cooperation. However, this alternative framework implies a different formal setup and modeling strategy.

Frank's model also would be more stable if each type had internal variation in its propensity to adjust. (Such variation may be implicit in Frank's theory.) Changes in culture fit this best: they are often discontinuous and seem to have large fixed costs. Suppose that, in a cultural model, adjustment costs for any given type have a uniform distribution, with the minimum at zero and the maximum at a level greater than the difference in utilities. This could represent the difficulty of changing cultural values, which surely varies from family to family. Then, in any time period, not every family will prefer to change values. In the neighborhood of the equilibrium, the rate of adjustment will be approximately proportional to the distance from the equilibrium, and the rate of adjustment declines to zero just at the equilibrium.

Adjustment speed could also depend on not just the difference in values but on the relative proportion of the two types. This can be done by adding a random error element, as in Frank 1987. In Frank's model in this volume, all agents of a given type reproduce their type according to the identical function when $Pr(C) > 75$ percent, and also when $Pr(C) < 75$ percent. That is, there is a single, given reproduction function (like A1 or A2) based upon the overall proportions of cooperators and defectors. In Frank 1987 and 1988, a random reproductive error is included. It could represent the randomness inherent in reproduction. This comment gives another rationale for such a random element.

In most environments, not all cooperators have the same local experience as the average experience; how could they experience the true average percentage, which is the best indicator of their optimal survival strategy? They learn it only from experience. For the biological model, it is clear that an individual's survival depends upon local experience. A cultural model of families gives similar local experience that will vary from person to person. But that local experience may not be an accurate guide to the experience that one's descendents will face in the larger environment.

Suppose, then, that when the difference between $Pr(C)$ and 0.75 is great enough, say, 10 percent, all individuals recognize that fact as in A1. But when the difference is less, there is a probability that the local and overall distributions will differ sufficiently that the locally estimated $Pr(C)$ will be on the other side of the critical 0.75 value. For example, the overall $Pr(C)$ could be 80 percent, which would imply that survival favors becoming a defector. But one individual might meet two cooperators and one defector, so that individual's estimated proportion of cooperators is only 67 percent. It would seem better to be a cooperator. Suppose that the probability of such an error rises linearly, until at 0.75, the probability of an error is 50 percent, as shown in figure 2.

With this data, Frank's figure 4 is modified as shown in my figure 3. The calculations of the defector payoffs are somewhat complex, so one example will illustrate. At $Pr(C) = 0.75$, the probability that a cooperator will decide it is worthwhile to detect defectors is 0.50. So half of the cooperators (37.5 percent of the total) will expend resources to determine who is a cooperator and succeed in pairing with other cooperators, while the other half will match randomly with the defectors (25.0 percent of the total). The expected payoff to a defector is now the average of the probability of meeting a cooperator times the payoff from meeting a cooperator and the probability of meeting another defector times the payoff from meeting another defector:

$$\left(\frac{.375}{.375 + .25} \cdot 6 \right) + \left(\frac{.25}{.375 + .25} \cdot 2 \right) = 4.4 \ .$$

Other values are also found numerically. The expected payoff to a cooperator is the weighted average of the expected payoff from detecting (which is always 3) and expected payoff from matching randomly, which is $Pr(C)$ times 4. This function does not change at $Pr(C) = 0.75$, since the two expected payoffs are both 3 at that point; elsewhere it takes a parabolic form showing

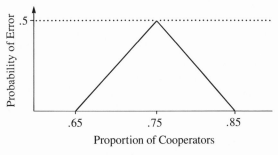

Fig. 2. Probablility of error function

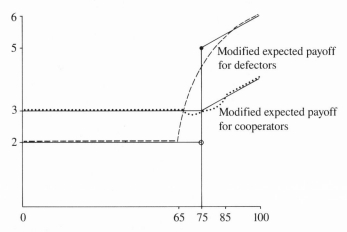

Fig. 3. Equilibrium when strategies are randomized. (Adapted from Frank, fig. 4, in this volume.)

the lower expected returns from errors in estimating the true $Pr(C)$. The new equilibrium is not at 0.75, but at $Pr(C) = 0.68$, as in figure 3.[19]

Does this modification reduce the dynamic nstability problem? It does assure continuity. But genuine stability also depends upon the specific nature of the experience. Experience of the proportion of cooperators comes from recent encounters with other people. If a small number of encounters—say five or ten—occurred, there would be a wide distribution of experiences, as the result of the binomial distribution. But it is hard to see how people could collect the information more precisely, so a wide distribution of estimates seems inevitable. In a genetic context, suppose that evidence of dishonesty led to varying numbers of duels between cheated cooperators and defectors. The

---

19. Frank (1987 and 1988) has described such a static equilibrium.

defectors would die more often in duels when a high local proportion of cooperators were willing to duel.

Cultures also pool information. That could greatly increase the accuracy of estimates. However, if the true ratio is changing, there should be increased uncertainty about the ratio and a wider range of views (following a Bayesian approach). So dynamics can widen the distribution of estimates. However estimates are made, the heterogeneity of estimates make a stable equilibrium much more likely.

Cultural rules often do not change smoothly, however. Fads, fashions, and new views of fairness occur often, though unpredictably. If the rules of honesty were taught by society, then, in terms of figure 1, they do not adjust gradually from z_1 toward z_2. Rather, they stay at z_1 for a time, and, when it becomes obvious that another rule would be better, there is a discontinuous leap to some new rule.[20] That could be at z_4, but it might well overshoot the optimum. The youthful cultural values from the 1960s, 1970s, and 1980s give reason to expect big shifts in specific cultural values from one generation to the next. In the same way, adjustment in the proportion of cooperators from one generation to the next could be quite dramatic. If, at present, defectors seem to have the advantage, perhaps everyone in the next generation will be a defector. With generational lags operating, current experience could lead to drastic changes in twenty years. The stability of such a dynamic system is quite unlikely.[21]

Cultural Evolution and Social Optimality

While values may be the result of an evolutionary process, can one say whether current values are "optimal," or, even "effective" for our current society? This is not an issue if our values are genetic and so fully determined. But it is of interest if most specifics of our values are culturally determined. From this point of view, current ethical standards might not be either desirable or an equilibrium.

Human cultures seem to be evolving to a different level and structure of cooperativeness. Earlier human culture, with small bands of related people who had to compete with other small bands, had quite different needs for ethical values. Currently, broader, more "objective" standards that apply to people one does not know may be more useful. Figure 1 shows this situation: values are evolving against the fixed genetic predisposition in the direction of

---

20. In practice, as Timur Kuran has argued, this depends upon the agreement of a society's elites.

21. These are the standard conditions needed for the "hog cycle," which has also appeared in young people's choice of professions such as law, medicine, and even, it is rumored, economics.

a higher-benefit, culturally defined rule. It seems accepted that cultural values can change in a period of hundreds to a few thousands of years, while genetic changes should take thousands of years.[22] Also, as cultures change, individual cultures compete. Any specific society is very unlikely to be at a static equilibrium given these various sources of disequilibrium.

Frank's analysis does not contradict these points, because he takes the structure and level of moral values as exogenous. But, in considering whether current values are desirable, we need to keep in mind that current values are almost surely a disequilibrium phenomenon, in transition from one set of values to another, and that, with cultural competition, such transitions are not usually linear.

Can the relative desirability of different values be evaluated? In the case of the cooperator and defector, could society's overall wealth be increased if more people felt ethically obliged to act as cooperators? This is a particularly important question in a heterogeneous society with several conflicting values. Some may be more productively efficient than others. Competition among these different value systems may be difficult to examine analytically (but see Samuelson 1988; also see Badcock 1986; Trivers 1985, chaps. 15–16). Such competition has been examined with Axelrod's (1984) computer simulation modeling of competition among strategies with random pairings. Frank's model may provide a framework for answering this question; it involves the alternatives of the cost of a less productive organization, and the cost of evaluating other agents' quality. Total social surplus could be determined for different types of social rules that might affect the proportions of cooperators and defectors.

There are some difficult social policy concerns if some cultures—gypsies come to mind—teach moral rules that are the equivalent of defection. On the one hand, there will be an equilibrium level of defection, given culture and technology; it seems logical that some group would play that equilibrium role. On the other hand, if cultural rules are partly exogenous and fewer people were taught to be defectors, the equilibrium would shift to less defection. Something like this has apparently been happening in some European societies, in Western business culture, and even in the U.S. Congress.

Concluding Comments

Economics has largely neglected ethical values. Frank shows that ethical values, and specifically *differences* in ethical values, will be naturally selected. We economists should no longer be surprised to see ethical actions in

---

22. Lumsden and Wilson (1981) claim that fifty generations—1,000 years—is sufficient to show significant genetic change, but this claim is controversial.

daily life. Rather, we should begin to incorporate this stylized fact into our theories, and begin to study it empirically.

Understanding social values gives us a major additional pathway of insight into human social behavior—one that other social scientists have long correctly accused economists of neglecting. As with most new pathways, more work needs to be done. One required theoretical advance seems to be developing assumptions that assure a stable equilibrium and that are founded on basic principles of genetics and/or culture. It may also be important to develop models of short-run disequilibrium and adjustment of social values. Empirical work needs to improve methodology; while Frank has found numerous examples of the use of conscience, it is hard to prove that these examples *must* represent conscience and not something else. Can the strength of conscience be measured quantitatively? Can indicators of honesty be determined by a formula that could be taught to MBA's and used in business? That requires much detailed work on methods, and some luck in finding fruitful ways of measuring and using the concepts. Such work would enable social economics to be a useful and powerful field of analysis.

REFERENCES

Axelrod, Robert. 1984. *The Evolution of Cooperation.* New York: Basic Books.
Badcock, C. R. 1986. *The Problem of Altruism.* Oxford: Blackwell.
Becker, Gary S. 1977. "Altruism, Egoism, and Genetic Fitness." *Journal of Economic Literature* 14(3):817–26.
Boyd, Robert, and Peter J. Richerson. 1985. *Culture and the Evolutionary Process.* Chicago: University of Chicago Press.
Brunner, Karl. 1987. "The Perception of Man and the Conception of Society: Two Approaches to Understanding Society." *Economic Inquiry* 25:367–88.
Frank, Robert H. 1987. "If *Homo Economicus* Could Choose His Own Utility Function, Would He Want One with a Conscience?" *American Economic Review* 77:593–604.
Frank, Robert H. 1988. *Passions within Reason: The Strategic Role of the Emotions.* New York: Norton.
Hayek, Friedrich A. 1960. *The Constitution of Liberty.* Chicago: University of Chicago Press.
Hayek, Friedrich A. 1973. *Law, Legislation and Liberty.* Vol. 1, *Rules and Order.* Chicago: University of Chicago Press.
Hirshleifer, Jack. 1977. "Economics from a Biological Viewpoint." *Journal of Law and Economics* 20:1–52.
Hull, David L. 1988. *Science as a Process: An Evolutionary Account of the Social and Conceptual Development of Science.* Chicago: University of Chicago Press.
Koford, Kenneth, and Mark Penno. 1988. "Markets and Organizations When Some Agents are Ethical." Presented at the annual meeting of the American Political Science Association, Washington, D.C. Revised May 1989.

Levin, Simon A. 1983. "Some Approaches to the Modeling of Coevolutionary Interactions." In *Coevolution,* ed. Matthew H. Niteckij. Berkeley: University of California Press.

Lumsden, Charles J., and Edward O. Wilson. 1981. *Genes, Mind, and Culture.* Cambridge, Mass.: Harvard University Press.

Marshall, Alfred. 1920. *Principles of Economics.* 8th ed. New York: Macmillan.

Nelson, Richard R., and Sidney G. Winter. 1982. *An Evolutionary Theory of Economic Change.* Cambridge, Mass.: Harvard University Press.

Oster, George F., and Edward O. Wilson. 1984. "A Critique of Optimization Theory in Evolutionary Biology." In *Conceptual Issues in Evolutionary Biology,* ed. Elliott Sober. Cambridge, Mass.: MIT Press.

Parsons, Talcott. 1937. *The Structure of Social Action.* New York: McGraw-Hill.

Pugh, George E. 1977. *The Biological Origin of Human Values.* New York: Basic Books.

Russell, R. Robert, and Maurice Wilkinson. 1979. *Microeconomics: A Synthesis of Modern and Neoclassical Theory.* New York: Wiley.

Samuelson, Larry. 1988. "Evolutionary Foundations of Game-Theoretic Solution Concepts." Presented at the University of Delaware, Newark, Del.

Sapolsky, Robert M. 1990. "Stress in the Wild." *Scientific American* 262 (January): 116–23.

Shapiro, Carl, and Joseph E. Stiglitz. 1984. "Equilibrium Unemployed as a Worker Discipline Device." *American Economic Review* 74 (June): 433–44.

Shweder, Richard A., and Edmund J. Bourne. 1984. "Does the Concept of the Person Vary Cross-Culturally?" In *Culture Theory: Essays on Mind, Self, and Emotion,* ed. R. A. Shweder and R. A. LeVine. Cambridge: Cambridge University Press.

Smith, Adam. [1759] 1976. *The Theory of Moral Sentiments.* Indianapolis: Liberty Press.

Smuts, Barbara B., et al., eds. 1987. *Primate Societies.* Chicago: University of Chicago Press.

Spence, A. Michael. 1973. "Job Market Signalling." *Quarterly Journal of Economics* 87:335–74.

Trivers, Robert. 1985. *Social Evolution.* Menlo Park, Calif.: Benjamin Cummings.

Weber, Max. 1968. *Economy and Society.* New York: Bedminster Press.

Part 5
Applying Norms in Organizations and Professions

The fruitfulness of a theory is shown, in large part, by its successful application. Part 5 contains essays that apply principles that are informed by social norms to important policy questions in business and the legal profession. These essays add content to the concepts of social norms in specific circumstances; they also show how social norms can be influenced by important external agents—statutes and courts.

In the first essay, "Corporate Crimes and Innovative Punishments," Peter A. French argues that current legal doctrines for corporate crime are poorly adapted to current technology and society. The world social climate has changed to one that imposes many additional requirements on corporations. For a firm to do the absolute legal minimum is not always morally acceptable.

One result of the increased expectations of corporations—in such areas as pollution, product safety, worker health and safety—is that it is not entirely clear to workers and management what is legal and what is not legal. In fact, the increased expectations have created many "gray areas" of the law that are only resolved by the courts when an issue arises.

Social norms enter into this question in an additional way. The growth of huge corporations has made it much more difficult to identify a problem with a single person's identifiable action. Rather, successes and failures are more accurately identified with a system that tends to a particular result. In fact, the result often occurs only with some probability (think of NASA's experience with the space shuttle). In these circumstances, it is often the *internal social norm* of the corporation that is the crucial element in the outcome.

French proposes that when corporations encounter these systemic types of legal problems, a novel legal doctrine should be used to deal with them. French is concerned with "corporate crime" that involves both gray areas of the law and systems elements, where internal corporate norms are relevant. He does not apply the doctrine to, say, a CEO who orders employees to dump toxic wastes into the local town's water supply in the middle of the night. French's new doctrine is the Principle of Responsive Adjustment (PRA).

Under PRA, the *first* criminal violation of a particular type by a corporation will not incur criminal sanctions. Rather, the corporation is on notice that it must develop an internal system that will assure that such violations do not occur in the future. Then, if a second violation occurs, the corporation will be criminally liable.

An example will show the close connection to social norms. Many large chemical firms come from a tradition in which they have long been strongly concerned about exposure of workers to toxic substances, but they had been less concerned about toxic wastes. The problem of exposure has been strongly internalized in social norms. Managers have long been regularly concerned about the number of accident-free days in their plants, and promotion has depended partly on the maintenance of a safe workplace. This is a social norm very different from that in some less-developed countries, where a macho attitude is taken, and concern for worker safety is considered by workers and managers as a sign of personal weakness. The norm of worker safety did *not* apply to toxic wastes until a decade ago, when several scandals and criminal suits made it clear that toxic wastes had become a major concern. Recently, large firms have faced the difficult challenge of changing their internal management structures and their social norms to assure that managers and workers will take proper action to assure that toxic wastes are disposed of legally and properly.

PRA thus deals with the need for corporations to develop new norms to assure that laws regarding corporate behavior are enforced. French also proposes an additional rule, Enforced Corporate Responsive Adjustment (ECRA), to assure that corporations would actually develop and inculcate new internal norms. Corporations found guilty of violating PRA would be required by the court, as part of their punishment, to carry out a policy of revising their internal procedures in such a way that the internal norms would change. Under PRA and ECRA, workers must internalize values and develop new procedures that assure that the law is carried out.

In "Appropriate Sanctions for Corporate Offenders," Mark A. Cohen considers some limitations upon the use of PRA and ECRA. Most corporate crime that is prosecuted actually involves small firms and criminal actions by the owner/manager, so that PRA would not apply. Also, French may be overly pessimistic about the use of fines to create appropriate incentives to obey the law. If fines are efficient, ECRA would not be needed.

In "Bargaining and Contract," Jules L. Coleman, Steven Maser, and Douglas Heckathorn develop a general theory of the enforcement of contract. The "problem" of contracts is that, as a general principle, they are highly incomplete. Thus, when unexpected circumstances arise, it is necessary to construe the contract to determine what it "should" mean regarding the unexpected situation. Ultimately, this amounts to what the courts will rule that the contract means. Coleman, Maser, and Heckathorn show how people writing contracts will write them differently, depending on their expectations of the courts; here they are applying the usual backward induction analysis of game theory to the law. Their analysis emphasizes the creation of common understandings among people who bargain and write contracts. If the courts can create a common understanding about how it will enforce and interpret contracts, that common understanding may become an internalized social norm among executives and legal advisors. In addition, there are specific social norms relating to contracts that Coleman, Maser, and Heckathorn consider valuable. These tend to discourage opportunistic behavior and encourage contracts that are self-enforcing and mutually advantageous. Thus, the overall goal of Coleman, Maser, and Heckathorn is the development of a social norm or custom of efficient contracting.

Corporate Crimes and Innovative Punishments

Peter A. French

In a January 1988 issue of the weekly *Corporate Crime Reporter*[1] the follow-ing stories were featured.

1. A felony involuntary manslaughter charge was filed in Los Angeles against a construction company, a soils engineer, and two company officials;
2. EPA knowing endangerment convictions were returned on fifteen charges against a Denver concrete additive manufacturer;
3. A national bank in Massachusetts was indicted on currency reporting violations;
4. New York commodities salesmen were convicted of conspiracy and mail fraud;
5. Companies in New Jersey and California were charged with bid rigging;
6. A mortgage company executive in Maryland was sentenced to twelve-and-one-half years in prison for fraud;
7. An eighteen-count federal grand jury indictment for racketeering and other violations was brought against four associates of the Wedtech Corporation; and,
8. Ivan F. Boesky was sentenced to three years imprisonment for SEC violations.

It was an ordinary week in the annals of corporate crime.

The impression conveyed by the *Reporter,* that the number of corporate crimes is escalating, probably is not totally fair to the facts. Some types of crimes, especially the newer types, do show dramatic increases, but it is hard to prove that we are living in a more corporate crime-ridden society than that of our grandfathers. Most sociological indicators suggest that corporate and white collar crime has increased since Sutherland's studies in the 1940s,[2] but,

---

1. *Corporate Crime Reporter* 2, no. 1, 11 January 1988.
2. Edwin Sutherland, *White-Collar Crime* (New York: Dryden, 1949).

as with many other kinds of crime, much of that rise may be attributable to better reporting and more concise definitions. In any event, crime in the boardroom, the executive suite, the stock exchange, and the lawyer's chambers is a daily fact of late twentieth-century American life and is clearly a major problem.

How is corporate crime to be controlled? The safest thing for a philosopher to do when confronted with such a question is to retreat to a careful examination of Plato's rehabilitation theory of punishment in *The Laws* followed by a brisk contrasting analysis of cost accountability punishment in Jeremy Bentham.[3] Such an exercise would surely be edifying but somewhat remote from the real concern. I will resist the temptation and push ahead into less comfortable philosophical territory.

First, it is necessary to reiterate a distinction between corporate and white-collar crime that is often ignored. By *corporate crime* I mean crime attributable to a corporate entity or any responsible person acting on its behalf. *White-collar crime,* in the strict sense, refers to offenses committed by persons from within their professional or corporate stations for personal reasons, and includes actions taken against the corporations that employ them.[4]

In this essay, the social control of corporate criminality is the central concern. Strategies for dealing with the white-collar criminal can, I believe, be based on the same moral foundation on which I build recommendations for enforcing social norms in the corporate world.

Brent Fisse and I, both jointly and separately, have challenged the orthodox view that corporate liability for crime depends on proof of corporate intentionality for the causally relevant acts at or before the time of the untoward event.[5] We have argued that corporate responsibility may best be assessed on the basis of the corporate defendant's response to the harm it has caused. Fisse has called this the concept of reactive fault, and I have developed the corresponding principle of responsive adjustment (PRA).

Reactive corporate fault, according to Fisse, is an unreasonable corporate failure to undertake appropriate preventative and/or corrective measures

---

3. Plato, *The Laws,* trans. Thomas Prangle (New York: Basic Books, 1980), books 9 and 10; Jeremy Bentham, *An Introduction to the Principles of Morals and Legislation* (London, 1789).

4. I developed this definition and defended it in Brent Fisse and Peter A. French, *Corrigible Corporations and Unruly Laws* (San Antonio: Trinity University Press, 1985), chap. 1. To commit a white-collar crime, one has to occupy a certain kind of position in the professional/business world (including government service). See Peter A. French, *Collective and Corporate Responsibility* (New York: Columbia University Press, 1984), chaps. 13 and 14.

5. Fisse and French, *Corrigible Corporations,* especially chap. 10; Brent Fisse, "Reconstructing Corporate Criminal Law: Deterrence, Retribution, Fault, and Sanctions," *Southern California Law Review* 56 (1983): 1183–1213; French, *Collective,* chap. 11.

in response to the corporate commission of an act that constitutes a violation of law.[6] The idea of reactive corporate fault reflects, as Fisse notes, two practical realities worthy of our attention:

1. communal attitudes of resentment toward corporations that fail to react diligently when they have caused harm, and
2. the common managerial practice, in accordance with the principle of management by exception, of treating compliance as a routine matter to be delegated to inferiors unless major problems, generally involving the reputation or image of the corporation, occur.[7]

PRA entails that the corporate intention that motivates a lack of responsive corrective action (or the continuation of the offending behavior) looks back to retrieve the actions that caused the offense, even though they were not clearly corporately intentional at the time of the offense.[8]

Commonly, when an untoward event occurs and the facts do not support an ascription of moral responsibility to the causally responsible party because the event was not intended, the perpetrator's subsequent behavior is observed to see if measures are taken to avoid similar events. If appropriate behavioral changes are not made, moral reevaluation of the earlier behavior may occur and the perpetrator held morally responsible for the untoward event regardless of the fact that, at the time of its occurrence, the perpetrator did not have the morally relevant intention. (Certain excuses, primarily those that claim continuing incapacity or diminished responsibility, defeat the moral reappraisal.)

Suppose, as in the landmark strict liability case of *Regina v. Prince*,[9] that a man, named Prince, contrary to law, took a girl who is under sixteen years of age "away" from her parents and suppose at the time he believed that she was older than sixteen and she gave him every reason to believe so and a reasonable person would have guessed that she was over sixteen. We stipulate that it was not Prince's intention to commit the act for which the law holds him strictly liable. On the basis of the traditional rule of accountability, Prince should not be held morally responsible for his illegal assignation. An intuitively appealing, behaviorally oriented, principle of accountability, PRA, will, however, under certain conditions, license a radical alteration of the finding.

Suppose that Prince, after serving his punishment, intentionally seeks out other young girls and makes no special attempt to discern their true ages

---

6. Fisse and French, *Corrigible Corporations*, 187.
7. Ibid.; see also Lester R. Bittel, *Management by Exception* (New York: McGraw, 1964).
8. French, *Collective*, chap. 11.
9. 13 Cox Criminal Case 138 (1875).

(remember he has a penchant for young teenage girls). In other words, imagine that Prince decides to take himself down to the local school and pursue another teenage girl to whom he has taken a fancy. Prince's intention with regard to his behavior with such girls is formed in a personal history including his conviction in *Regina v. Prince*. Prince is aware of his past; his past behavior and its subsequent punishment are a part of his current consciousness. The memory of those events is part of his mental history and that mental history constitutes, along with his concerns for his well-being in the future, his identity as a person. If, after committing the crime, Prince had taken precautions to ensure that he learned the ages of the girls he courted, etc., we would allow his ignorance of the age of the girl in the legal case as an excuse for moral purposes (although he must bear the punishment for the strict liability offense). But, in our extension of the story, Prince makes no responsive adjustments in his behavior that would assure that he would not repeat the offense. He embarks upon a course that could well lead to a similar violation. By the adjustment principle, we claim that Prince's subsequently manifested intention to continue his romantic pursuits of underage girls constitutes an affirmation of the strict liability violation behavior. Prince, then, may legitimately be held morally responsible for the earlier strict liability offense.

Intentionality has a significant role to play in PRA, but we must extend the time frame that generates the relevant corporate state of mind (mens rea), to attribute responsibility sometimes to the corporate offender when its policy, at the time of its causing harm, was ordinary, boilerplate compliance. The time frame will need to be expanded to include what the corporate offender does in response to its commission of the harmful act. We will need to focus on whether the corporate offender implements internal reforms to prevent repetitions. Refusal to do so would be an intentional act and may take forms from practiced indifference to blatant repetition. The intuition to which the principle appeals is that a person's past action, even if unintentional, can be taken into the scope of the intentions that motivate that person's present and future actions.

The PRA/reactive fault approach to corporate criminality need not claim that the offending action was intentional when it occurred. Perhaps it was not intentional, and no future intentional actions can make what was not intentional in the past intentional. But what was done in the past can be captured in a present intention.

PRA embodies the idea that, after an untoward event has happened, those who contributed to its occurrence are expected to adopt courses of future action that will have the effect of preventing repetitions. We have strong "moral expectations" regarding behavioral adjustments that correct character weaknesses, habits, etc., that have produced untoward events. PRA, however, is more than an expression of such expectations. It allows, when the expected adjustments in behavior are not made and in the absence of strong reasons for nonadjusting, those in question are to be held morally responsible for the earlier untoward event that provoked attention. PRA does *not* assume, however, that a failure to "mend one's ways" after being confronted with the harm one has caused is strong presumptive evidence that one had specifically intended that outcome. The matter of intentions at the original act is closed. PRA expresses the idea that a refusal to adjust practices that led to an untoward occurrence is to *associate* oneself, for moral purposes, with the earlier behavior.[10]

PRA does not suggest that some future intention can affect a past event, that a future intention manifested in a future act could make something intentional that was not intentional when it happened. There is no "backward causation" in the application of PRA. By intentionally doing something today, however, a person can change our understanding of something that happened yesterday, making it an act for which that person should bear moral responsibility. A person's past is included in the scope of that person's present and future intentions. That is what PRA insists on.

F. H. Bradley wrote, "In morality the past is real because it is present in the will."[11] PRA provides an expression of this elusive notion. The idea is that adjustments in one's behavior that rectify flaws or habits that have actually caused past evils (or routinizes behavior that has led to worthy results) are morally required. Put another way, the intention that motivates a lack of responsive corrective action or the continuation of offending behavior affirms the behavior that caused the evil. By the same token, failure to routinize behavior that has been productive of good results divorces that behavior from one's "moral life." Intentions certainly reach forward, but they also have a much neglected retrieval function by which they illuminate past behavior that was not, at the time of its occurrence, an action of the agent. A present intention to do something or to do it in a certain way can draw a previous event into its scope. Moral agents are not purely prospective, ahistorical, abstract centers of action. They have lives, pasts, out of which their intentions emerge. PRA captures, to some extent, the Aristotelian idea that we do not hold people morally responsible for unintentionally "slightly deviating from the course of goodness"[12] as long as they do not subsequently practice behavior that makes such deviations a matter of character.

The most radical element of PRA is that it provides for a retrieval of past unintentional behavior in a present intention to do something. A detailed technical account is surely required. Act descriptions have a well-known

10. French, *Collective*, especially chaps. 3, 4, and 12.

11. F. H. Bradley, *Ethical Crisis* (Oxford, 1876), 46.

12. Aristotle, *Nicomachean Ethics*, trans. M. Ostwald (Indianapolis: Bobbs, 1962), 51.

feature that Joel Feinberg called the "accordion effect."[13] Like the accordion, the description of a simple bodily movement can be expanded in different directions by causal linkages and other associations. For example, the act of pulling the trigger of a gun, through a series of redescriptions, may be expanded to encompass the description of "the killing of Sebastian." Accordions, of course, can be drawn apart in both directions. The description of a present act may be associated with past behavior by the ordinary relations "like yesterday," "as before," or "again." Descriptions such as "to pull the trigger again" clearly retrieve previous behavior, though they do not make that previous behavior intentional at the time it occurred.

Of course agents may plead that they never intend to do things under retrograde "accordioned" descriptions. They only intend to do what they are about to do and nothing else. Such a plea must be rejected if we are talking about something other than purely abstract agents, isolated in the present. The descriptions of events under which a person intends actions are formed within that person's mental or personal history. To ignore that fact is to reduce the actor to an unidentifiable entity trapped in the moment of action.

PRA insists that persons learn from their mistakes, that the pleas of mistake and of accident cannot be repeatedly used to excuse frequent performances of improper behavior. "It was an accident" will only work if it was not the result of behavior that is repeated after the offending event. "It was inadvertent or a mistake" will exculpate only if corrective measures are taken to insure nonrepetition. Such excuses can be, and often are, reevaluated after the individual's actions have been observed subsequent to the event for which the excuses were offered. It would, however, usually be wrong to say that, in such cases, we decide that the individual must have had the relevant intention in the first instance of the offending behavior. We may grant that no error was made at that time in describing the event, but the event takes on a new description in the light of subsequent action. It has always seemed to me a great puzzle that Western moralists are so committed to locking up the past and sealing it away. We constantly reevaluate the past, our pasts in ordinary life, claiming, divorcing, and then reclaiming episodes in our lives that come to take on different sorts of meaning as we live longer. Ordinary morality may be harsher than its philosophical cousin in this respect. It is certainly richer.

PRA says that a person may be held morally responsible for a previous event to which that person had unintentionally, even inadvertently, contributed, if he or she subsequently intentionally acts in ways that are likely to cause repetitions of the untoward outcome. A strict set of temporal closures need not apply to PRA. For example "moral enlightment," many decades

---

13. Joel Feinberg, *Doing and Deserving* (Princeton: Princeton University Press, 1970), 134.

after, may demand reevaluation of an event that was not originally thought to have been bad or harmful and PRA will require moral accountability of the perpetrator if, after enlightenment, no behavioral adjustments were made.

PRA has another important intuitively appealing aspect. Suppose that we think of all of those things for which a person can be held morally responsible as adding up to that person's moral life, which, as a complete moral biography, may itself be morally judged. PRA forces the incorporation of originally nonintentional pieces of behavior into a person's moral life because PRA does not let people desert their pasts. It demands that present and future actions respond to past deeds. It forces us to think of our moral lives as both retrospective and contemporaneous, as cumulative. It does not let us completely escape responsibility for our accidents, inadvertencies, unintended executive failures, failures to fully appreciate situations, bad habits, etc. The moral integrity of a person's life depends upon a moral consistency that is enforced by PRA.

A number of criticisms of PRA have been made, though most seem to be based on a persistent misreading that claims PRA rewrites history. Time's arrow continues its inevitable course from past to future, but the shotgun of moral evaluation scatters its pellets in many directions. There is a major difference between thinking that the past can be changed by actions in the present (backward causation) and thinking that we can, and ought to, change our moral evaluations of those who were the cause of harmful things happening. And, most important, it is in the present and into the future that PRA allows holding someone responsible for a past deed where a specific intention cannot be ascribed in isolation of subsequent behavior. PRA does not say that if we had access at the crucial time, we would have discovered the specific intention. It says that now we have the intentional reactive fault that includes within its scope the past action.

PRA, then, offers a promising way of avoiding contentious attribution of criminal intentionality to a corporation. It is rare that a company displays any criminal intention at or before the time of the commission of the offense. The typical legal solution, at present, is either to impose strict liability or to impose liability vicariously on the basis of the intent of a representative. The former approach avoids the issue by making intention irrelevant at the level of the attribution of liability (though intentionality may be relevant in relation to sentence). The latter approach (which is essentially a form of strict liability) is based on a representationalism that utterly ignores the fundamental criminal element of mens rea. To generate the relevant corporate intentionality that will displace strict or vicarious liability, focus must be on a corporate defendant's policy. That focus is achieved by a PRA-sanctioned extension of the time frame of judicial inquiry to encompass what a defendant has done *in response to* the commission of the *actus reus* of an offense. What matters, then, is not a corporation's stated general policies of compliance, but its specific implementation of a program of internal discipline, structural reform, and compensatory or restitutionary relief. This temporal reorientation flushes out blameworthy corporate intentionality more easily than is possible when the inquiry is confined to corporate policy at or before the time of the *actus reus*. Remember the Firestone 500 tire affair? It is impossible to show a palpable flaw in Firestone's general compliance policies, but easy to expose Firestone's intentional adoption of a reactive policy of not promptly implementing a recall program in response to the overwhelming evidence that the tire was defective.

The expansion of corporate criminal liability into a responsive time frame will produce several new ways to look at problems of handling corporate criminal liability. Here I focus on three: the role of interventionism, the due diligence plea, and the design of penal sanctions.

Philosophers and legal theorists have joined a slew of social commentators in developing a plethora of proposals for controlling corporate behavior through government intervention in the internal decision structures of corporate offenders. Christopher Stone's famous book, *Where the Law Ends: The Social Control of Corporate Behavior,*[14] led the parade. Stone, in those days, championed the view that judicial means should be used to intrude into a corporation's decision making.[15] And how would it intrude? By mandating decision procedures, new boxes in the flow chart to be occupied by watchdog directors, etc. Stone was reluctant to recommend application of interventionism across the board. He would limit its use to recidivism cases and to generically hazardous industries. Stone seems to believe that the interventionist strategy is too drastic in what must be the vast majority of cases. But what is to be done in such cases?

The American Bar Association proposed a continuing judicial oversight sanction.[16] But the ABA recommends that such a sentence should only be imposed when the criminal behavior is serious, repetitive, and the result of "inadequate internal accounting or monitoring controls"[17] or when a danger to public safety exists. The ABA proposal takes no account of the corporate offender's responsive compliance activities unless the case is extremely severe. The only sanction recommended in cases that are not serious or repetitive is a fine. We may suppose that in that category are misleading advertising cases, which tend to be paradigmatic of defective standard operating pro-

---

14. Christopher Stone, *Where the Law Ends: The Social Control of Corporate Behavior* (New York: Harper and Row, 1975).

15. His views have changed significantly of late. See Christopher Stone, "Corporate Regulation: The Place of Social Responsibility," in Fisse and French, *Corrigible Corporations,* chap. 2.

16. American Bar Association, *Standards for Criminal Justice,* vol. 3 (Boston: Little, Brown, 1980), sec. 18.

17. American Bar Association, *Standards,* sec. 18-28 (a)(V)(A).

cedures and so prone to repetition. Fines, even rather hefty ones, hardly have a record of producing the significant changes in corporate decision structures and standard operating procedures that would be desirable if they are to be brought into compliance. The Hopkins Report shows that effective changes in defective or deficient corporate operating procedures cannot be expected as a result of fines.[18] Hence, in the ABA proposal, one actually waits for repetitions before more effective sanctions are utilized.

If interventionism is too limited but also intrudes the government too deeply into corporate life, as does the ABA continuing oversight sanction, while fines are ineffective, is there a better way to guarantee an appropriate corporate response to its harm-causing behavior? I think there is. The assumption of the Stone and ABA approaches is that the courts can examine corporate responses to the commission of criminal offenses only by inserting themselves rather deeply in the corporate decision process. Success, they seem convinced, depends upon the depth of the government's intrusion into corporate life. That assumption, however, ignores the alternative of requiring convicted corporations to file compliance reports that detail their own internal responses to the offense. Judicial intervention could, and should, be held in abeyance, used only if the corporation's own reaction is judged unsatisfactory. I call this approach Enforced Corporate Responsive Adjustment (ECRA).

ECRA brings PRA to bear on the judicial handling of corporate offenses. It demands an adjustment in the legal framework for dealing with most such offenses. A two-stage judicial hearing procedure is required. In the initial stage, the issue before the court will be whether the action resulting in the offense was committed on behalf of (or by) the corporate defendant. That established to the satisfaction of the court, the defendant corporation will be required to prepare a compliance report that spells out what steps it will take by way of internal discipline, modification of existing compliance procedures, and, as appropriate, compensation to victims. The second stage of the judicial procedure will determine whether the corporate offender has satisfactorily responded to its harm-causing or risk-imposing actions (as established at the first trial stage). If adequate measures have been taken to adjust, the corporation will be acquitted of the offense. If not, the corporation will be convicted of the offense on the basis of PRA and be liable to a variety of further penal sanctions that could include even extreme forms of interventionism and judicial supervision. It is important that the use of such drastic violations of the integrity of the corporate internal decision structure should be contingent on the corporate defendant's own intentional failure to make a responsive adjustment to try to insure that there are no repetitions of its harm-causing behavior.

---

18. Andrew Hopkins, *The Impact of Prosecutions under the Trade Practices Act* (Canberra, Australia: Australian Institute of Criminology, 1978).

In short, ECRA preserves managerial freedom as long as the court is satisfied that effective responsive adjustment has been undertaken. In notable ways ECRA is a cousin of John Braithwaite's model of enforced self-regulation, in which corporations are required to formulate their own regulatory standards.[19] Intervention is restricted to the development and enforcement of overarching principles and social goals. ECRA is not so sweeping. It requires corporate offenders to formulate their own reactive programs in response to specific violations. ECRA has the virtue of minimizing state intervention, while not, as in the case of fines, excluding it altogether. It has the virtue of placing the onus of managerial alterations on shoulders both best trained and most likely to be effective in bearing it: the managers of the firm. Braithwaite, Fisse, and I have noted that, though there probably are some fundamental, minimal requirements for effective corporate compliance systems, the variables differ widely from corporation to corporation without necessarily affecting the compliance outcome. Also, ECRA will not be restricted to only the more serious and/or repeated offenses. Lesser offenses will be more effectively dealt with by ECRA than by purely monetary sanctions.

The application of ECRA will, undoubtedly, produce a hue and cry because it does acquit an offending corporation that "cleans up its act" in response to its harm causing. I am afraid that strong retributive sanctions may not be satisfied. But it would be, I think, a greater shortcoming if we forego the common law principle that criminal responsibility requires proof of mens rea. Doing so could have the undesirable effect of undermining our social "commitment to the moral force of the criminal law."[20] ECRA insures that a link to intentionality is preserved and thereby blocks the move to more and more strict liability offenses. The downside is that corporate offenders may be perceived to be allowed a free "first bite of the apple." It might be thought that a significant amount of harm will escape punishment. In the criminal sense, of course, that is strictly true, but ECRA is not recommended as a principle in tort law. Hence, existing grounds for suit in tort, including punitive damages, are available to victims. It is imaginable, though I do not make the case here, that ECRA could be put to good use as the regulator of punitive damages in tort. It would then affect some desirable tort reform. Certainly the so-called first bite does not go without producing a desired effect: a change in procedures and/or policies within a corporation that has committed a criminal offense. In any event, the appearance of unwarranted lenience will need to be addressed subsequently.

---

19. John Braithwaite, "Enforced Self-regulation: A New Strategy for Corporate Crime Control," *Michigan Law Review* 80 (1982): 1466–1507.

20. John Braithwaite, "Taking Responsibility Seriously: Corporate Compliance Systems," in Fisse and French, *Corrigible Corporations,* 57.

The adoption of the responsive adjustment time frame approach corrects some problems with the due diligence defense. Recall the first case cited from the *Corporate Crime Reporter.* A Los Angeles construction company (and a soils engineer and two company officials) was indicted for felony manslaughter. A worker died in a cave-in at the construction site. He was cleaning dirt out of trenches when an embankment collapsed, burying him. The indictment charged that the soils engineer's report was grossly inadequate because he did not recommend shoring for a vertical cut. It also charged that the excavation contractor had informed the general contractor about safety concerns. No shoring was installed. This is not a strict liability offense, and it might admit a defense of due diligence. The offense revolves around not taking due care to prevent the harm. What standard of due diligence would have been relevant in a proactive time frame? Would it really have been adequate to the situation?

Due diligence claims to use an objective standard of care that takes the prevailing standard of an industry as a benchmark. That objective standard may be adjusted to meet the needs of particular circumstances, but there are clear limits on the amount of alteration allowed, as the standard must still be applicable across the industry. In many industries, however, no generally accepted standard for a compliance system exists. Still, if there does exist a customary compliance system in the industry and the corporate defendant has adopted it, should that exculpate?

Suppose that the Los Angeles construction firm had met all of the safety standards normally upheld by construction firms in that area. It would likely be judged to have exercised due diligence and, on the traditional theory, acquitted of the manslaughter charges. If it did nothing to change its excavation methods after the first death, industry standards have not appreciably changed, and another death occurs, it could again plea due diligence and should again look forward to acquittal. But something surely is wrong. Due diligence, proactively understood, flies in the face of basic intuitions about justice. However, if the industry standard does not set the benchmark, then a corporate offender is not provided with clear prior notice of conduct subject to criminal liability. Furthermore, if a court should determine that the industry standard was set too low, then good faith compliance with the standard will not shield a corporation from criminal liability. What then happens to fundamental fairness? It is surely unjust to disallow a due diligence plea on the grounds that the corporation should have anticipated a failure in its procedures that only came to light in the industry after the harm causing occurred. Also, the advance specification of acceptable standards only invites the search for loopholes.[21]

The proactive due diligence defense cannot help but pull the standard

---

21. Discussions with Brent Fisse helped clarify for me these difficulties with due diligence.

down to a common denominator level that would put the force of the law behind older, traditional, compliance technology. No legal incentives are provided for corporations to find innovative solutions or to apply state of the art techniques to prevent harm. Law tied to a proactive time frame for offenses is stuck in a dangerous rut that deprives potential victims of adequate protection. It can extricate itself only by imposing higher standards that the defendant can rightly claim "descend from the blue."

Some of the legal/moral deficiencies with due diligence also arise because existing industry standards lack particularity. They also lend themselves to myriad interpretations in the hands of good company lawyers. In measuring the significance of these problems, account should be taken of various ways in which they are now minimized. First, standards tailored to individual corporations have been imposed under an injunction or consent order. This is common in the enforcement of antitrust laws, securities regulations, and corruption offenses.[22] Second, broad standards of due care for an industry have been made more precise by using injunctions to crystallize their meaning and application to particular situations.[23] Third, some innovation has been possible through the imaginative use of negotiation and bargaining in enforcement,[24] prospective standard setting in judicial decisions,[25] and administrative techniques for inducing technological change (e.g., forced technology through offsets against penalties).[26] These methods are valuable, but they do not provide rules of criminal liability that are particularistic rather than universalistic, focused rather than rife with loopholes, and dynamic rather than static or, at best, tortuously incremental.

Standard setting in conjunction with ECRA is dominated by a reactive time frame and overcomes the problems. Using the ECRA model, a corporate offender would be required to produce a compliance report in which it specifies the standards it will seek to meet in response to its harm causing. The standard setting is then reactive, not a matter of routine prevention or an excursion into possible worlds scenarios. The standards are not only tailored both to the particular corporation and its activities, but also to the particular case that exposed its decision-structure weaknesses. The old due diligence

---

22. See William Donovan and Breck McAllister, "Consent Decrees in the Enforcement of Federal Anti-Trust Law," *Harvard Law Review* 46 (1933): 885–932.

23. See Note, "Declaratory Relief in the Criminal Law," *Harvard Law Review* 80 (1967): 1490–1513; Note, "The Statutory Injunction as an Enforcement Weapon of Federal Agencies," *Yale Law Journal* 57 (1948): 1023–52.

24. See Keith Hawkins, *Environment and Enforcement* (Oxford: Clarendon Press, 1984).

25. See M. L. Friedland, "Prospective and Retrospective Judicial Lawmaking," *University of Toronto Law Journal* 24 (1974): 170–90.

26. See Richard Stewart, "Regulation, Innovation, and Administrative Law," *Yale Law Journal* 88 (1979): 1713–34.

defense would not succeed even if the company could not have foreseen the harm produced by its following the existing standards of the industry. In fact, due diligence and due care would have little or no role to play.

ECRA provides fair notice of criminal prohibitions, but loophole-prone rules are eliminated. The focus is shifted from industrywide standards that may, in fact, be too low (the harmful result is evidence that they, indeed, may be too low) to the adequacy of the corporate offender's response to the need to develop a higher standard of care. Proactive due diligence imposes static and often undemanding requirements of care. ECRA, unconfined to ex-ante due diligence, looks to the care that *should be* taken regardless of any existing industry standard, and so it is more dynamic and demanding, often perhaps requiring state-of-the-art technology to satisfy its demands. ECRA then works to reduce the tension between stability-inducing rules of law and the rapidly changing corporate, technological, and social world to which they are to be applied.

While I am citing advantages of the ECRA approach, it should not be forgotten that there is also a moral and social payoff. ECRA should bring exemplary corporate responsive adjustments to the attention of the general public and instill models of good corporate citizenship across an industry.[27]

Important for nonformal social control, as I have noted elsewhere,[28] ECRA is especially well suited to engender a shame-based morality within the corporate culture. The moral foundation of ECRA is laid, I think, less in guilt and more in shame, and that can be a positive device for producing desirable social outcomes. This leads, however, to the third new way of looking at problems with corporate criminal liability: innovative sanctions.

The proactive time frame commitment that has governed most thinking about corporate criminality produces a bias toward the adoption of the notion of vicarious liability that largely locks the judicial system into a very restricted number of applicable sanctions, dominated by fines. Fines have been used because, viewed from the proactive perspective, it is nearly always impossible to prove that a corporation committed an offense with the appropriate corporate mens rea. Boilerplate compliance policies are intended to prove the absence of the corporate criminal state of mind. With access to the corporate mens rea effectively blocked, many U.S. jurisdictions have adopted the vicarious liability approach for corporate cases. All that is required is demonstrable fault on the part of an employee acting on behalf of the corporation.

---

27. This is a matter in ethics that needs much more discussion. I have begun to work on it in "Spatial and Temporal Ethics," presented at the conference on "The Frontiers of American Philosophy," Texas A&M University, 1988.

28. Peter A. French, "Principles of Responsibility, Shame, and the Corporation," in *Shame, Responsibility, and the Corporation*, ed. Hugh Curtler (New York: Haven, 1986), 17–56.

The mens rea of a manager or employee, of course, is typically easier to expose than corporate intentionality. No published policy of compliance can serve as a shield.

Vicarious liability, as Fisse has argued, "projects a noninterventionist attitude toward corporate decision making."[29] It is no wonder it is championed by the staunchest defenders of corporate enterprise. The emphasis in vicarious liability is almost solely on the state of mind of a single representative, rather than on the corporate internal decision structure. Avoidance of interventionism, conjoined with the historical relationship between vicarious liability and vicarious tortious liability, generates the bias in favor of monetary remedies of damages and the offending corporation's identification of fines with enterprise costs.

Fines, however, have serious limitations and can be passed on to undeserving populations in the form of higher prices, layoffs, etc. Despite the 1973 report of the Task Force on Corrections of the National Advisory Commission on Criminal Justice Standards and Goals that found the fine "far less costly to the public, and perhaps more effective than imprisonment or community service,"[30] fines against most corporations have proven to have little deterrent capacity. The problem of affordability is exacerbated by the fact that many corporations can go a long way toward recouping fines by raising prices or reducing production costs. Oliver Wendell Holmes, Jr., and H. L. A. Hart both have noted that though there is a difference—or should be—between a fine and a tax, in many cases the line is blurred to indistinction.[31] It seems evident to me that in most corporate criminal cases drawing the line may be, in practice, extremely difficult. Taxes are often imposed to discourage activities that have not been made criminal. "Conversely fines payable for some criminal offenses . . . become so small [e.g., in relation to the offender's income] that they are cheerfully paid and offenses are frequent. They are then felt to be mere taxes because the sense is lost that the rule is meant to be taken seriously as a standard of behavior."[32]

Interventionist sanctions, such as punitive injunctions, are not so easily assimilated. But some noninterventionist sanctions should prove almost equally successful in producing the desired alteration in corporate procedures

---

29. Fisse and French, *Corrigible Corporations,* 204.

30. See Sally T. Hillsman, Barry Mahoney, George F. Cole, and Bernard Auchter, "Fines as Criminal Sanctions," *Research in Brief* (Washington, D.C.: National Institute of Justice, September 1987), 1.

31. See Oliver Wendell Holmes, *The Common Law* (Boston: Little, Brown, 1881), 300; *The Pollock-Holmes Correspondence* (Cambridge, Mass.: Harvard University Press, 1953), 1:21, 119, 177, and 2:55, 200–234; H. L. S. Hart, *Punishment and Responsibility* (New York: Oxford University Press, 1968), 6–7.

32. Hart, *Punishment,* 7 n. 8.

and policies, and at least one of those is also directly derivable from the previously mentioned shame base in morality related to ECRA: court ordered and directed adverse publicity, or what I have elsewhere called the Hester Prynne Sanction.[33]

If the proactive time frame approach is in force, and we are blocked from adequate information about the "corporateness" of the intention to commit the offense, the implementation of an adverse publicity sanction may appear to be too severe and, thereby, unwarranted. Fines seem the only justifiable option. However, by shifting to the ECRA approach, corporate policies and procedures are no longer shielded, and so willful, deliberate noncompliance by the corporate offender may be exposed, and the offending corporation appropriately targeted for Hester Prynne or other innovative sanctions.

I agree with some of my most fervent critics, particularly John Ladd, who see Hester Prynne as a drastic punishment, an ideal of ignominy and disgrace, an assault on image, even identity.[34] That is why it is so devastating and, hence, effective in the corporate world. It attacks the heart of business: reputation. Therefore it should only be used when there is no doubt about the corporate offender's criminality. ECRA insures that condition is met.

This is not the place to champion Hester Prynne over other types of sanctions in corporate criminal cases. I argue here only that the innovative noninterventionist sanctions that a number of legal theorists have proposed as alternatives to fines, because they promise to be more effective in producing compliance, will be supported by far more reliable sentencing data if ECRA replaces the proactive perspective in our corporate criminality theory.

The great danger in the fines approach is that corporate offenders may totally escape the gravity of noncompliance, though they have in place procedures that do not work toward the maintenance of the conditions necessary for social welfare. Monetary sanctions are, at best, only oblique ways of changing defective corporate practices, though with some corporations and some crimes a monetary penalty may be sufficient. There is, however, no need to settle on only one type of sanction. An incremental escalation strategy or a mix of sanctions should prove both efficient and effective. Stone's interventionism is, of course, among the more severe options. Perhaps it comes in just short of revocation of business permits and corporate charters. Insofar as protection of the integrity of the corporate enterprise ought to be a major commitment of our society, it should only be used in extremely serious

---

33. Peter A. French, "The Hester Prynne Sanction," *Business and Professional Ethics Journal* 4, no. 2 (Winter 1985): 19–32.

34. See John Ladd, "Persons and Responsibility: Ethical Concepts and Impertinent Analyses," in Curtler, *Shame*, 77–98.

cases—where the sentencing data unequivocally demonstrate violation of PRA. Still, even in such cases, Fisse seems to favor punitive injunctions requiring recalcitrant corporate offenders to install state-of-the-art technology at accelerated speed, instead of interventions of the *Where the Law Ends* variety.[35] Stone has moved further away from his early position to what he now calls a volunteerist approach intended to foster "a measure of mutual trust and respect" in corporate/social relations.[36]

Another advantage of the ECRA approach to corporate criminal liability is that it generates very reliable sentencing facts. The focus of the crucial second phase of the ECRA trial is not on the criminal act but on whether the company had failed to appropriately respond to the crime. That issue will be the subject of detailed evidence.

Furthermore, PRA helps to expose the need for sanctions capable of effecting a smooth transition between less and more drastic means of regulation. Suppose that a corporate offender has been subjected to a civil injunctive order stipulating that effective pollution control devices are to be installed in its plant. Efforts at compliance were made but then abandoned as a result of competing cost pressures. The company is held liable on the basis of PRA. Something needs to be done to ensure compliance. Imposing a fine is only an oblique method of making the company comply. And, given the defendant's recalcitrance, issuing a further civil injunction would fail to capture the gravity of the reactive noncompliance. Fisse argues that the ideal sanction for both of these concerns is a punitive injunction requiring the defendant corporation not only to install the necessary device, but also to do so in some punitively demanding and constructive way (e.g., at accelerated speed or by going beyond state-of-the-art technology).[37]

I will close by briefly commenting on what I suspect will be the two major objections to ECRA: that it is prone to be too lenient and that it will be inefficient. The first objection is the "first free bite of the apple." As Clinard and Yeager have demonstrated, negotiated settlements dominate other methods of applying sanctions in cases of corporate criminality today.[38] Considerable chunks of the apple are regularly being devoured without even fines being assessed. More important, however, it would be a complete misunderstanding were one to think that ECRA allows a free first bite. For any corporate offense, it requires a responsive adjustment from the corporation, some-

---

35. Fisse and French, *Corrigible Corporations,* 207. See also Richard Stewart, "Regulation, Innovation, and Administrative Law: A Conceptual Framework," *California Law Review* 69 (1981): 1256–1377.

36. Stone, "Corporate Regulation," 34.

37. Richard Stewart, "Regulation," 1979.

38. Marshall Clinard and Peter Yeager, *Corporate Crime* (New York: Free Press, 1980), 87.

thing that may be very costly and, in the absence of a satisfactory response, injunctions, adverse publicity orders, and other measures are recommended as a first resort. The pressure and costs brought to bear on the convicted corporate offender could well exceed any simple monetary penalty.

The second objection is more interesting. It claims that ECRA suffers from inefficiency because it will impose significant burdens of investigation, supervision, and management on the justice system. Admittedly these kinds of cost factors will increase under ECRA, and surely they will be more costly than the application of totally noninterventionist monetary sanctions. How can they be justified as alternatives to fines?

The simple answer is that:

The level of fines required to satisfy the economic calculus for the deterrence of serious corporate offenses is so high as to be beyond the resources of most corporate offenders, and hence we need to resort to alternative means of social control that, although regrettably more costly in terms of enforcement resources, is more likely to achieve effective prevention of unwanted harms.[39]

A more complex answer challenges the basic assumptions of the Posner-led economic analysis of law. In effect, it challenges the application of the economic calculus to the problem in the first place. Applying the calculus requires one to make probability predictions with respect to the occurrence of harm, the extent and gravity of that harm, and the chances of detection and conviction. John Byrne and Steven Hoffman have persuasively argued that, in corporate cases, such calculations are impossible at the level of exactitude required.[40] Furthermore, the calculus method assumes "a unified managerial rationality" that is a figment of the economist's imagination. Scepticism about the results of these economic analyses would seem to be in order. Even if we admit the probabilistic calculation method as our guide to the development of an efficient general criminal liability system, two rules of thumb emerge when it is impossible, as in the corporate cases, to adequately assess the required probabilities. Fisse and I have framed those two rules in something like the following way:

1. develop proscriptions based on considered assessments of the nature of unwanted harms in society; and

---

39. Brent Fisse and Peter A. French, "Corporate Responses to Errant Behavior," in Fisse and French, *Corrigible Corporations,* 209.

40. John Byrne and Steven Hoffman, "Efficient Corporate Harm: A Chicago Metaphysic," in Fisse and French, *Corrigible Corporations,* chap. 6.

2. use fault-concepts and sanctions geared at impelling responsive corporate reactions to violations of those proscriptions.[41]

I leave it to other moral and social philosophers to tell us what should fall under the first rule. Doing so is to tell us what the social world ought to look like and how it ought to function. With respect to corporate offenders, ECRA meets the demands of the first part of the second rule, while an innovative mix of sanctions including Hester Prynne and punitive injunctions should respond to its second part.

---

41. Fisse and French, "Corporate Responses," 210.

Appropriate Sanctions for Corporate Offenders: Comment on French's "Principle of Responsive Adjustment"

Mark A. Cohen

In this comment I discuss the appropriateness of French's "principle of responsive adjustment" from the perspective of economic theory. I am also concerned that French's essay could leave some readers with a few misconceptions about the nature of corporate crime. Thus, my purpose is to describe what is currently known about corporate crime, as well as to offer some comments on the practical implications and value of French's proposals.

Although French admits that part of the "rise" in corporate crime might be attributable to better reporting, he leaves the reader with the impression that there is good evidence that corporate crime has increased since the 1940s.[1] In fact, there is simply no empirical evidence on the magnitude of corporate crime that would allow us to conclude that corporate crime is either on the rise or decline. One of the main problems with measuring corporate crime is that only those who are "caught" are counted. For most street crimes, researchers have been able to rely on victim surveys to estimate the number of rapes, robberies, burglaries, etc. Even if we do not identify or catch all criminals, we can count victims. However, with corporate crime (as with many victimless crimes such as prostitution and illegal gambling), it is nearly impossible to measure the extent of criminal activity.

Nevertheless, the topic of French's essay—the proper punishment for corporate criminals—could not be more timely. There is no doubt that corporate crime is in the news these days. Casual evidence suggests that criminal enforcement efforts have increased substantially during the past few years (examples include EPA's new criminal enforcement authority and the stepped up effort of the SEC at enforcing insider trading laws). I recently compared

---

1. Although French states that "most sociological indicators suggest that corporate and white collar crime has increased since Sutherland's studies in the 1940s," he offers no empirical evidence and cites no references other than Sutherland.

the "white-collar crime" sections of the 1981 and 1988 *Wall Street Journal Index*, and found that the number of articles about white-collar and corporate crime has increased more than threefold in the past seven years. This increased prosecution and news coverage might help explain why many people perceive that corporate crime has increased.

Most important from the standpoint of corporate punishment, the U.S. Sentencing Commission has recently been struggling with the problem of designing appropriate sentencing guidelines for corporations.[2] The Commission acknowledged that there was a lack of agreement among the staff and commissioners on the correct approach to corporate sentencing.[3] Thus, the question of designing appropriate corporate sanctions is both timely and controversial.

Before commenting on French's proposal directly, it is important to note that his "principle of responsive adjustment" only applies to a very small proportion of corporate offenders indicted and convicted by the federal government. A recent study of all 1,283 federal corporate convictions from 1984–87 found that "only 10% crossed the threshold of $1 million in sales and 50 employees; less than 3% had traded stock."[4] Thus, most firms convicted of criminal activity appear to be closely held, with management and owners essentially being the same individuals. This suggests that, in most cases of corporate crime, the corporation is merely a conduit for individual criminal behavior. Thus, French's analysis of moral accountability of corporate entities seems to have little relevance to the vast majority of cases.

Of course, this does not mean that French is wrong in pursuing his topic. Indeed, the few cases where his concerns would apply are likely to be the most visible crimes—those that make the nightly news and national newspapers, such as the recent cases against Drexel Burnham Lambert (insider trading), Chrysler (odometer tampering), Ashland Oil (oil spill), Beechnut

---

2. As of this writing, the last formal Commission proposal was titled "Preliminary Draft Sentencing Guidelines for Organizational Defendants" (1 November 1989). However, after considerable public debate and controversy, this draft was never submitted to Congress.

3. Indeed, prior to the November 1989 draft, the Commission had already circulated several alternative proposals—both formal and informal. See U.S. Sentencing Commission, "Discussion Draft of Sentencing Guidelines and Policy Statements for Organizations," *Whittier Law Review* 10, no. 1 (1988): 7–75; John C. Coffee, Jr., Richard Gruner, and Christopher D. Stone, "Standards for Organizational Probation: A Proposal to the United States Sentencing Commission," *Whittier Law Review* 10, no. 1 (1988): 77–102. Other unpublished proposals were made by (1) the Justice Department, (2) a Commission sponsored working group of defense attorneys, and (3) a staff proposal for policy statements instead of guidelines.

4. Mark A. Cohen, Chih-Chin Ho, Edward D. Jones III, and Laura M. Schleich, "Organizations as Defendants in Federal Court: A Preliminary Analysis of Prosecutions, Convictions, and Sanctions," *Whittier Law Review* 10, no. 1 (1988): 112.

(substitution of ingredients in apple juice), and Rockwell (defense contract fraud).

Having placed his proposal in its proper context, let me briefly recap the major points of French's essay. First, he would have the courts base criminal liability on a determination of the organization's response to its learning that the crime has been committed. "What matters, then, is not a corporation's general policies of compliance, but its implementation of a program of internal discipline, structural reform, and compensatory or restitutionary relief." Second, once criminal liability is established, he would have the courts determine punishment on the basis of "innovative" nonmonetary sanctions, such as stepped up compliance policies, court-ordered adverse publicity, and other forms of "punitive injunctions." It is the latter part of the essay–appropriate corporate sanctions—that the rest of this comment will focus on.

French argues rather forcefully against corporate fines as the primary means of punishment. First, he notes that fines "can be passed on to undeserving populations in the form of higher prices, layoffs, etc." Second, "fines against most corporations have proven to have little deterrent capacity." Unfortunately, the first argument could just as easily be made against French's nonmonetary sanctions (and may actually apply to his proposed sanctions more than to fines), and the second argument is simply unfounded.

The fact that fines against corporations may ultimately hurt workers and consumers has been noted in the literature before.[5] However, it is not clear that a lump sum fine will have this effect on either prices or employment. Unless the fine is so large that it virtually bankrupts the firm, a lump sum fine will have no effect on profit-maximizing prices or output. This is because price and output decisions are made on the basis of marginal costs. Even if a firm decides to try to recoup some of its losses by raising prices, this effect is likely to be rather short lived. If the corporate criminal is forced to raise prices, consumers will switch brands. If workers are laid off due to slack demand, other firms will hire those workers to satisfy their newly increased demand.

In fact, not only could French's first argument against fines be applied equally to the nonmonetary sanctions he endorses, but the latter remedies are *more* likely to hurt consumers and workers than a lump sum fine. That is because his proposals are likely to raise *marginal* costs, not just total costs. For example, one of his proposals is for government-mandated adverse publicity. Suppose the court orders the firm to spend an amount equal to 10 percent of its annual advertising revenue to inform consumers of past mis-

---

5. See, e.g., John C. Coffee, Jr., "Corporate Crime and Punishment: A Non-Chicago View of the Economics of Criminal Sanctions," *American Criminal Law Review* 17 (1980): 419–76.

deeds. This raises the cost of marketing the product—a cost that will likely be passed on to consumers. Similarly, suppose the corporate violation was failure to install pollution control equipment. His proposed remedy might be to require installation of environmental controls that go "beyond state-of-the-art technology." Once again, this might raise marginal costs and, hence, raise prices.

In addition, it should be noted that French's proposal for "punitive injunctions" is primarily designed to impose costs on the firm above the normal compliance costs they avoided through the commission of the crime. Although I agree that punitive sanctions are needed to deter firms from committing crimes, French's proposal would generally cost *society* more than an equivalent monetary sanction. For example, suppose the court requires the firm to install environmental controls that are beyond the state of the art. In all likelihood, the firm will be installing controls that would not pass a social cost-benefit test. Hence, from society's standpoint, this is an inefficient use of resources. Alternatively, if the court ordered an equivalent monetary fine, that money could (presumably) be put to more productive uses.[6]

Although I believe punitive nonmonetary sanctions are generally inferior to equivalent monetary sanctions, there are some instances where French's proposal might be socially beneficial.[7] For example, suppose the court orders the firm to adopt an advanced technology not yet tested in the field. Without imposing this extra cost on the offending firm, the government will have little experience with this new technology. Thus, the sanction might provide government regulators and engineers with valuable information about the viability and cost effectiveness of the new technology. "Technology-forcing" punitive sanctions must be used sparingly, however, to avoid the imposition of expensive, unjustified technologies.

A second example of a nonmonetary sanction that might be beneficial is the case of imposing a new technology designed to reduce government monitoring costs and/or increase the ability of the enforcement agency to detect future violations. This type of sanction might be justified for a corporation that has continually demonstrated its unwillingness to be a "good corporate citizen" through repeated noncompliance. Of course, before we can rationalize these increased monitoring devices, we must first dismiss the option of

---

6. This argument in favor of fines instead of equivalent nonmonetary sanctions has been made by many other authors. See Gary Becker, "Crime and Punishment: An Economic Approach," *Journal of Political Economy* 78 (1968): 169–217, for a discussion of the desirability of substituting fines for jail sentences when an equivalent monetary fine can be imposed. Becker applies this theory to the case of corporate punishment in "Make the Punishment Fit the Corporate Crime," *Business Week* (13 March 1989): 22.

7. I am grateful to Ken Koford for raising this possibility as well as the subsequent examples.

simply increasing the monetary penalty for repeat offenders. One such rationalization might be for a firm that is both a repeat offender and that has a high
likelihood of bankruptcy if faced with a large monetary penalty. In that case,
increasing monetary penalties will have little deterrent effect; hence, some
form of enhanced monitoring program might be reasonable.

French's second argument against fines is that they have little deterrent
value. This statement presupposes that we have been able to measure the
frequency of corporate crime over time (which is simply not true, as noted
earlier). Indeed, it is nearly tautological to note that the expected level of fines
did not deter a known corporate criminal. This is no more an indictment of
current fine levels than it is to note that imposing the death penalty on all
murderers will not deter all people from that crime. The question is not
whether the sanction deterred the known criminal, but whether it deterred
potential criminals.

Few would dispute the claim that current monetary sanctions imposed
against corporate criminals are too low, by themselves, to deter an adequate
number of potential violators. Indeed, according to a recent study of corporate
offenders sentenced in the federal system from 1984–87, the average fine was
about $48,000.[8] If we include restitution or other voluntary or court-ordered
criminal sanctions, the average monetary penalty is slightly over $140,000.
These monetary sanctions (including restitution) represent an average "multiple" of criminal sanctions to monetary harm that is probably close to one (if
not less).

Obviously, if criminal fines were the only sanctions imposed on corporate offenders, a multiple of one would only be "optimal" from an economics
standpoint if the probability of detection was equal to one—an unlikely
event.[9] However, monetary sanctions are only a small part of the total punitive sanctions corporate criminals are subject to.

Civil penalties and other civil remedies are commonly used in conjunction with criminal sanctions—and are often significantly more punitive than
the criminal sanctions. For example, antitrust violators are subject to treble
damages plus attorney's fees from private plaintiffs who were harmed. Any
regulatory violation resulting in actual injury (or exposure to long-term risk of
injury) is subject to potential tort action—usually dwarfing any criminally
imposed sanction. Debarment from future government contracts is a penalty
frequently imposed on corporations convicted of fraud against the government. In addition, depending on the nature of the violation, corporations stand

---

8. See Mark A. Cohen, "Corporate Crime and Punishment: A Study of Social Harm and
Sentencing Practice in the Federal Courts, 1984–1987," *American Criminal Law Review* 26
(1989): 605–60.

9. See Becker, "Crime and Punishment."

to lose a considerable portion of their reputation from the publicity surrounding the offense.[10]

Although the evidence is sparse, there is some indication that the total penalty from corporate crime does have a significant deterrent effect. For example, Block, Nold, and Sidak examined the role of private and public enforcement of antitrust price fixing laws.[11] The authors found their "empirical results revealed that increasing DOJ's enforcement capacity or filing a DOJ price-fixing complaint had the deterrent effect of reducing markups in the bread industry." Despite the fact that "government-imposed price-fixing penalties were trivial . . . [they] found support for the proposition that the effective deterrent to price fixing was the credible threat of large damage awards to private class actions that followed DOJ's case against the same conspiracy."[12]

Finally, I should note that before one makes serious policy recommendations to increase the punitiveness of corporate criminal sanctions, we should examine collateral penalties against individual offenders charged along with the corporation. The U.S. Sentencing Commission's recent guidelines for sentencing individual offenders imposed dramatic increases in the frequency of imprisonment for white-collar offenders. For example, "the proportion of fraud sentences involving some confinement would rise under guideline sentencing from 41 percent to 76 percent."[13] For antitrust offenders, the new guidelines will impose a prison term for virtually all offenders, compared to an imprisonment rate of 39 percent before the guidelines.[14] Until we have had a chance to examine the deterrent effect of these increases in white-collar sanctions, it would be premature, at best, to recommend increasing the punitiveness of corporate sanctions.

---

10. There is some limited empirical evidence on lost reputation. See, e.g., Sam Peltzman, "The Effect of FTC Advertising Regulation," *Journal of Law and Economics* 24 (December 1981): 403–48; James L. Strachan, David B. Smith, and William L. Beedles, "The Price Reaction to (Alleged) Corporate Crime," *Financial Review* 18 (May 1983): 121–32.

11. Michael Kent Block, Frederick Carl Nold, and Joseph Gregory Sidak, "The Deterrent Effect of Antitrust Enforcement," *Journal of Political Economy* 89 (1981): 429–44.

12. Block, Nold, and Sidak, "Deterrent Effect," 444.

13. Michael K. Block, "Emerging Problems in the Sentencing Commission's Approach to Guideline Amendments," *Federal Sentencing Reporter* 1 (May 1989): 451.

14. U.S. Sentencing Commission, *Guidelines Manual* §2R (November 1990).

Bargaining and Contract

Jules L. Coleman, Steven Maser, and Douglas Heckathorn

Legal rules facilitate as well as constrain human freedom. H. L. A. Hart captures the difference between these two functions of law by distinguishing between primary and secondary rules.[1] Primary rules impose obligations and thereby constrain behavior; secondary rules empower individuals to create relations that confer rights and impose duties.[2] Thus, the criminal law constrains individual liberty; the law of contracts enhances it.

Within this framework, the foundation of contracting is mutual agreement. Contractual duties are self-imposed. They are consequences of individuals authoritatively exercising their autonomy under private, enabling rules. Coercive civil authority is justifiably employed to enforce contractual obligations because the parties have agreed to so constrain themselves. Of course, even if the parties to a contract agree to bind themselves to one another, it does not follow that they have agreed, thereby, to have their obligations to one another enforced by the state (or by any other third party).

On the assumption that contracting parties are narrowly rational and fully informed, a contract between them that foresees and responds to all possible contingencies—a fully specified contract—would be efficient, or Pareto optimal. That is the definition of a fully specified contract. Because a fully specified contract is efficient, it puts the parties to it in a position where neither can improve his or her lot except at the other's expense. A fully specified contract is also an equilibrium, that is, it is self-enforcing in the sense that no party has an incentive to defect from its terms unilaterally.

While imagining problems in contract design and execution and devising

---

This is a shortened version of "A Bargaining Theory Approach to Default Provisions and Disclosure Rules in Contract Law." *Harvard Journal of Law and Policy* 12, no. 3 (1989): 639–709."

1. H. L. A. Hart, *Concept of Law* (Oxford: Clarendon Press, 1961).

2. Hart is not always consistent in drawing the distinction. He characterizes secondary rules as power conferring. Some confer power on private individuals, others authorize officials. Unfortunately, the rule of recognition, which for Hart is the signature of a legal system, is a secondary rule, but it confers power on no one.

adequate safeguards against all possible sources of contract failure is a logical possibility, it remains (for everyone but the gods) a practical impossibility. Even were it practically possible, fully specifying a contract might be irrational in that the expected costs of a more complete specification may exceed the expected gains from nailing down a particular solution to an imaginable, but unlikely, possibility.

Unlikely events are not impossible, however. Contingencies arise with which the contractors have not explicitly dealt. Such is the stuff of contracts casebooks. When contingencies arise for which no adequate provisions have been made ex ante, the parties may disagree about their respective rights and duties ex post. Sometimes they are able to resolve the conflict privately. If they are unable to resolve the conflict privately, however, the parties may find themselves in court.

The Rational Contract

We begin by looking at how two parties engage in a contractual transaction, how they secure a rational bargain, *without law.* Our analysis benefits from recent formal literature on bargaining under both complete and imperfect information, part of the theory of cooperative games. It looks at how people resolve disputes involving elements of both conflict and cooperation. We depict contracting as a divisible Prisoner's Dilemma game. Here, the parties secure no contract unless they agree on a way of enforcing their agreement and of distributing any potential gains. The conditions under which they invoke third-party participation, including judicial or legislative intervention, and the form of that participation, depend on the costs of consummating the deal. Those costs derive from the inherent risks associated with imperfect information concerning their transaction and the resources they devote to minimizing those risks.

A bargaining-theoretic approach to contract law has features that recommend it over competing approaches. First, the bargaining approach admits reward triggering norms as a basis for social control. Typically, economic and sociological theories, especially those based solely on the Prisoner's Dilemma logic, depend on negative reinforcements to induce compliance with norms.[3] But according to bargaining theory, while one might sanction someone for failing to offer concessions or for violating an agreed upon division, the idea is to reward and to encourage concession making to secure cooperation. We can ask whether legal doctrines do that and, if so, in what ways.

Second, it takes explicit account of fairness as a part of contractual

---

3. Robert Ellickson, "Of Coase and Cattle: Dispute Resolution among Neighbors in Shasta County," *Stanford Law Review* 38 (1986): 623–87.

exchange. If people worry about fairness and, if in every theory of rational contracting, the parties ineluctably confront fairness concerns, then when and how do the courts take account of it? In fact and in theory, fairness matters. Because division is a concern for rational contractors, under what conditions will that concern require courts to act—and in what capacities?

Our approach shares the importance of efficiency with law and economics. It differs from many forms of economic analysis by virtue of bargaining theory's emphasis upon the division or fairness problem. Our approach shares the importance of context with the law and society tradition. Rational decision making is necessarily sensitive to the context of the decision. The status quo is relevant; contracting always occurs within a preexisting web of continuing, contractual relationships. The resources parties bring into bargaining are relevant. And the uncertainties peculiar to different contexts are relevant.

Our approach shares the importance of fairness and justice to the legitimacy of civil authority with moral theories. However, unlike other theories, it appeals to criteria of fairness or justice endogenous to transaction relationships. It does not view contracting as necessarily constrained by external standards of fairness; rather, it views the process of rational contracting as, in part, specifying the relevant conception of fairness.

Three Problems in Contracting

The terms of an agreement to cooperate among two or more people, their *contract,* stipulates (1) specific actions by each to be carried out at some time in the future, and (2) rewards and penalties to be meted out following compliance or defection. These terms constitute safeguards crafted to minimize and allocate risk. In doing so they create risks of their own. What are the conditions under which rational actors will agree to cooperate if explicitly charged with designing a policy to cope with risk and uncertainty in their environment?

The decision-making calculus that rational actors use in crafting a contract requires resolving three distinct but intertwined problems: (1) cooperation, (2) division, and (3) defection. These problems are captured in a game called the *Divisible Prisoner's Dilemma.*

The divisible prisoner's dilemma involves three principles of rationality: (1) rational cooperation, (2) rational division, and (3) rational compliance. Failure to satisfy any one of the three demands of rationality leads to contract failure; satisfying all three is necessary and sufficient for agreement and performance on a contract.

An example of the Divisible Prisoner's Dilemma is depicted in normal form in figure 1. For the moment, assume that each player knows both payoffs

Player B

Performance

		Contract 1	Contract 2	Nonperformance
		Contract$_1$	Status quo	B free rides
	Contract 1	19, 7	9, 2	3, 11
		C$_1$	D	NP$_b$
Player A	Contract 2	Status quo	Contract$_2$	B free rides
		9, 2	16, 10	3, 11
		D	C$_2$	NP$_b$
	Nonperformance	A free rides	A free rides	Status quo
		22, 1	22, 1	9, 2
		NP$_a$	NP$_a$	D

Fig. 1. Divisible Prisoner's Dilemma

in all of the cells. Player A (row) and player B (column) each make a three-dimensional choice. Each must decide whether to contract or not; and if the choice is to contract, whether to seek contract 1 or contract 2. In making this decision, each of three problems of rational contracting emerges.

The *cooperation problem* is resolved by whether or not the parties share a common interest in contracting over acting individually. If they both prefer to contract, then they solve their cooperation problem. If either or both of them prefer to act individually, no contract between them is possible. This particular failure to contract results from an inability to solve the cooperation problem. In our example, the two contracts represented by cells 1 and 5 represent higher payoffs for both parties than do the noncontract alternatives. Thus, we would expect the players to solve their cooperation problem. Doing so is not sufficient for contracting, however. Two problems remain. A *division problem* arises if player A prefers contract 1 to contract 2, whereas player B has the opposite preference. Consequently, opposed preferences regarding how to contract complicate the common preference for a contract over no contract. Third, a *defection problem* arises if a player gains from unilaterally defecting from a contract, once agreement is secured.

The defection problem is illustrated powerfully in the nondivisible, or standard, Prisoner's Dilemma in which the dominant strategy for each player is to defect from whatever agreements he or she has made. In our example, A gains by defecting to cell 7 or 8, and B gains by defecting to cell 3 or 6.

Phases in Contracting

Each problem in the contractual relationship corresponds to a distinct phase of the contracting process and involves a distinct principle of rationality. First, in the *prephase,* the decision whether to cooperate, that is, whether to seek a contract, is made. If the parties are rational, each predicates an affirmative decision on expectations that joint gains will be attainable under the contract. Second, in the *negotiation phase,* the decision of how to contract is made. That is, the parties agree upon the terms of the contract, specifying the manner in which the gains resulting from the contract and the burdens of enforcing it are to be allocated. Finally, in the *postphase,* each party makes the decision to fulfill or to violate the contract and monitors the compliance of others.

Each phase contains a potential pitfall. That is, individuals may fail to contract because: (1) one or more of the essential parties prefers to act independently rather than to seek a contract; (2) the parties fail to agree upon the terms of the contract; or (3) the contract collapses owing to a violation of its terms. Each phase is distinct not only in the sense of carrying its own pitfalls to contracting; to succeed at each phase, a contract must meet the demands of distinct but ultimately related rationality conditions. The phases of contracting and their respective rationality conditions are developed below.

Prephase: Joint Rationality
No one can expect another person to engage in contracting unless each perceives an opportunity for *mutual* gain. We can put this fact in an analytically precise way. A necessary condition for agreeing to a contract is that its expected outcome satisfies what may be called the *joint rationality* condition. Define U_i as the utility individual i expects to secure in contracting; D_i as i's utility from disagreement (i.e., the status quo); $U = (U_a, U_b)$ is a given agreement's utility vector; and $U' = (U_a', U_b')$ is any other feasible agreement's utility vector. Then U is jointly rational if, for each feasible outcome U',

$$U_a \geq U_a' \quad \text{or} \quad U_b \geq U_b' \tag{1}$$

The joint rationality condition is shown in figure 2.

C_1, C_2 represents the contract curve, the set of Pareto-optimal outcomes to the northeast of D. D, in turn, represents the disagreement point, the outcome of contracting that results if the parties fail to reach agreement. NP_a and NP_b are the nonperformance outcomes. NP_a results when A and B reach agreement with which B complies and A defects. NP_b represents the outcome that results when A complies and B defects. These are the free rider outcomes. Both are Pareto optimal in the sense that no points lie to their northeast

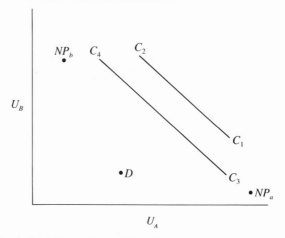

Fig. 2. Divisible Prisoner's Dilemma in utility space

in the utility-space representation of the game. Though Pareto efficient, they are not Pareto superior to D, and, thus, they do not lie on the contract curve C_1, C_2. NP_a, NP_b, and all the points on the contract curve, C_1, C_2 are jointly rational or Pareto optimal. Only points on the contract curve, however, are Pareto optimal *and* Pareto superior to D.

If information is imperfect or incomplete, each party has an incentive to expend resources to inquire whether a bargain with someone else promises to be advantageous. These resources are *transaction resources*. At the cooperation or prephase, parties may expend transaction resources to identify and secure D at the outset. Everyone wants a referent from which they can evaluate feasible outcomes. Contracting will break down and may not even begin without it (as is the case in labor-management negotiations with newly certified unions whose legitimacy is uncertain). Similarly, individuals cannot take for granted the existence of the contract curve, even though opportunities for more efficient cooperation tend to exist in every relationship. If people must expend resources to determine the location of the disagreement point or the contract curve, some or all of the gains from contracting are consumed, that is, in terms of figure 2, C_1, C_2 moves toward C_3, C_4.

The magnitude of the cooperation problem, which can be described in terms of the distance between the contract curve and the disagreement point, measures the social gains foregone by failing to cooperate. It is a measure of the players' joint stake in the game. The greater the attainable gains from contracting, the more resources people are willing to expend to achieve them. However, as they do that, the contract curve lengthens, exacerbating their potential defection and division problems.

Contracting to secure mutual gains consumes transaction resources that are scarce and costly. In the old law and economics tradition, transaction costs are assumed to be low in contracting situations, so that parties are able to gather all pertinent information and to assign all relevant risks.[4] Because it assumes individuals have perfect information, are completely rational, and face no impediments to entering transactions, "It would be surprising if such superhumans were *not able* to manage their own affairs without the intervention of government."[5] As it happens, however, sometimes they are not.

The newer, law and economics tradition emphasizes transaction costs even in contract (as opposed to tort or "stranger") situations. Because it assumes that individuals have imperfect information, limited rationality, and encounter substantial impediments in contracting, it would be surprising if such patently imperfect individuals were *able* to manage their affairs without the intervention of government. As it happens, in some cases, they do.

This discontinuity between "prohibitive" and "nonprohibitive" transaction costs is, of course, an analytic artifice begging for elaboration. The private and governmental controls that people craft depend on the relative size of the transaction costs involved. Because each of the three decision-making problems in any relationship involve unique hazards from imperfect information, the undifferentiated, generic treatment of transaction costs is analytically untenable as well.

The Negotiation Phase: Concession Rationality
Recognizing that contracting would increase efficiency, that it would generate benefits in excess of costs, is not a sufficient condition for contracting to occur.[6] Contracting requires that parties to the negotiations resolve the division problem, either directly (by agreeing upon allocations of benefits and costs) or indirectly (by agreeing upon a set of procedures by which these allocations are to be determined). The problem is not just the cost of establishing a set of feasible and acceptable outcomes. Even if that cost is nil, the *strategic* nature of the choice may induce a noncooperative outcome.[7] Strategy may require players to disguise their true intentions in pursuit of an agreement, moderating or exaggerating their demands based on their view of

---

4. Just think of the Coase theorem and the long line of Chicago-style law and economics that sees itself as driven by Coase's insight that where transaction costs are low, individuals contract around inefficiencies. Thus, the identification of contract with low transaction costs. Coase himself did not commit the mistake of identifying contracting with low transaction costs.

5. Daniel Farber, "Contract Law and Modern Economic Theory," *Northwestern University Law Review* 78 (1983): 303–39.

6. Gary McClelland and John Rohrbaugh, "Who Accepts the Pareto Axiom? The Role of Utility and Equity in Arbitration Decisions," *Behavioral Science* 23 (1978): 446–56.

7. Robert Cooter, "The Cost of Coase," *Journal of Legal Studies* 9 (1982): 1–33; Jules Coleman, "Market Contractarianism and the Unanimity Rule," *Social Philosophy and Policy* 2 (1984): 69–114.

how each will respond to the other. Thus, failure to resolve the division problem can complicate the process of contracting even to the point of defeating it.

Returning to figure 2, the division problem arises because the players have opposite preferences regarding where agreement should occur along the contract curve.[8] In bargaining-theoretic terms, C_1, contract 1, is player A's *best hope outcome* because it is the outcome that is: (1) most preferred by A, (2) no worse than disagreement for B, (3) feasible, and (4) enforceable. Similarly, C_2, contract 2, represents B's best hope. The players' best hopes correspond to opposite endpoints of the contract curve. When a *concession* is defined as agreeing to an outcome less preferred than one's own best hope, it is obvious that agreement requires concessions. Either one player makes all the concessions required for agreement by assenting to the other's best hope outcome, or both players make concessions resulting in agreement at an intermediate point on the contract curve. If bargaining over the allocation of concessions fails, so too does contracting.

Intuitively, we recognize the problem of settling on a division of cooperative gains as endemic in human behavior and know that people resolve it when the conditions are right. Empirical studies confirm that standards of "fair division" sometimes guide rational agreement even in the absence of third-party enforcement. In particular, Kahneman, Knetsch, and Thaler have shown that when unanticipated events induce unanticipated divisions, they do not necessarily threaten the economic viability of an arrangement.[9] In other words, individuals sometimes appeal to a sense of fairness to solve division problems when failure to reach agreement in division may jeopardize an opportunity for mutual gain. Laboratory experiments testing the Coase theorem also demonstrate that parties are able to secure jointly maximizing outcomes, though different methods of assigning property entitlements influence the division of the gains.[10] Other studies confirm (1) the importance of the status quo in choices over division rules, and (2) the heavier weight ascribed to losses than equivalent gains in evaluating outcomes.[11] In short, empirical studies suggest that players are often able to solve their division

---

8. Whereas mixtures between contracts 1 and 2 are assumed to be feasible in this game (hence, the C_1, C_2 line), mixtures between other outcomes of this game are assumed not to be feasible. We adopt this convention to simplify the analysis.

9. Daniel Kahneman, Jack Knetsch, and Richard Thaler, "Fairness and the Assumptions of Economics," *Journal of Business* 59 (1986): 5285–5300.

10. Elizabeth Hoffman and Matthew Spitzer, "Entitlements, Rights, and Fairness: An Experimental Examination of Subjects' Concepts of Distributive Justice," *Journal of Legal Studies* 14 (1985): 259–97.

11. Daniel Kahneman, Jack Knetsch, and Richard Thaler, "Fairness as a Constraint on Profit Seeking: Entitlements in the Market," *American Economic Review* 76 (1986): 728–41; Norman Frohlich, Joe Oppenheimer, and Cheryl Eavy, "Choices of Principles of Distributive Justice in Experimental Groups," *American Journal of Political Science* 31 (1987): 606–36.

problem and point to some of the relevant factors in settling on particular divisions: namely, the allocation of initial entitlements, a sense of fairness, the relative disparity in weighting equivalent gains and losses, and so on.

Under a broad range of conditions, then, contracting parties settle on distributions of the gains from trade, which simply means that they allocate concessions. They also have in mind which points, among those available on the contract curve, they intend to safeguard by the terms of any contract. Put analytically, a necessary condition for agreeing to a contract is that its expected outcomes satisfy what may be called the principle of *concession rationality*.[12]

The problem with many bargaining theories is that, while they take account of the parties relative bargaining strength, they assume away many of the other problems that lead to bargaining failure, for example, uncertainty. Thus, they typically yield the result that (1) bargainers will secure a cooperative division of the gains, that (2) reflects their initial relative bargaining strengths. This outcome is not surprising, but because of all the evidence of noncooperation (wars, strikes, etc.), these models are neither predictive nor descriptive.[13] Again, though all bargaining models view the relative costliness of conflict as affecting relative bargaining power, many do not take into account the best hopes of the parties, or aspiration levels, which influence the bargainers' willingness to incur costs in reaching agreement. That is inconsistent with a sizable body of experimental evidence indicating that aspiration level is positively related to bargaining power.[14]

In contrast, what we call *resistance theory* renders an explicit account of the conditions under which negotiations break down, treats aspirations as part of the decision-making calculus, and describes the information rational contractors require to reach agreement. Thereby, it illuminates the conditions under which people will expend resources to contract.[15] As conceived in resistance theory, bargainers assess the relative strengths of their strategic positions based on the utility structure of the game, for example, based on the location of the disagreement point, on the location and shape of the contract

12. Formal, theoretic accounts of bargaining have been proposed by economists, game theorists, social psychologists, and strategic analysts. See Oran Young, *Bargaining: Formal Theories of Negotiation* (Urbana: University of Illinois Press, 1975); John Harsanyi, *Rational Behavior and Bargaining Equilibrium in Games and Social Situations* (New York: Cambridge University Press, 1977); Alvin Roth, *Game-Theoretic Models of Bargaining* (New York: Cambridge University Press, 1985); Ken Binmore, Ariel Rubinstein, and Asher Wolinsky, "The Nash Bargaining Solution in Economic Modeling," *Rand Journal of Economics* 17 (1986): 176–88.

13. Cooter, "The Cost of Coase."

14. Samuel Bacharach and Edward Lawler, *Bargaining Power, Tactics, and Outcomes* (San Francisco: Jossey-Bass, 1981).

15. Heckathorn, "Unified Model," and "A Formal Theory of Social Exchange: Process and Outcome," in *Current Perspectives in Social Theory,* vol. 5, ed. Scott McNall (Greenwich, Ct.; JAI Press, 1984).

curve, and on their risk and time preferences. The strength with which a bargainer strives to avoid concessions, termed his or her *resistance*, depends on (1) the costliness to the individual of the concessions required by the agreement: the greater the concession cost, the greater will be the resistance to the agreement; (2) the costliness of conflict: an increase in conflict's cost increases the willingness to make concessions and diminishes resistance; and (3) the aspiration level: higher aspirations enhance resistance. The very existence of opposing proposals reveals conflicting aspirations. They establish concession limits and distributional expectations based on those assessments. Only outcomes where those limits and expectations overlap satisfy concession rationality.

Formally, where D_i is any bargainer i's utility from disagreement (conflict); B_i is i's aspiration level or best hope—the enforceable outcome on the contract curve that he or she most prefers, or equivalently, the outcome he or she most prefers which is enforceable, feasible, and no worse than conflict for any other bargainer; and U_i is i's utility from a given outcome U, i's resistance to outcome U, $R_i(U)$ is defined as

$$R_i = (B_i - U_i)/(B_i - D_i). \tag{2}$$

During negotiations, each bargainer assesses his or her own resistance against that of others. Under conditions of complete information, each will agree to an outcome only if the concessions he or she requires are at least matched by the relative concessions of others. On the assumption of equal rationality, each party will make equal relative concessions.[16] It is not rational to be exploited. Expressed in terms of resistances, this means that the bargainer will agree to an outcome if his or her own resistance to it would equal or fall below the resistances of others. Formally, where $R_i(U)$ is any bargainer i's resistance to outcome U and $R_j(U)$ is another bargainer's resistance to outcome U, that outcome lies in the agreement set of i, A_i, if

$$R_i(U) \le R_j(U). \tag{3}$$

Concession rationality requires that an actor's concession behavior fulfills this requirement. Resistance theory posits that, in the presence of complete information, people exhibit concession rationality. Under conditions of complete information, rational individuals make equal relative concessions. When information is incomplete, a bargainer will agree to an outcome if he or she judges it to be rational in that sense, that is, if his or her own resistance is matched or exceeded by the expected resistance of everyone else.

---

16. This is also David Gauthier's view; see Gauthier, *Morals*.

That is, where i's resistance to U is $R_i(U)$ and i's expectation concerning j's resistance to U is $E_i[R_j(U)]$, the set of outcomes to which i would agree, his or her agreement set A_i, includes outcomes fulfilling the requirement

$$R_i(U) \le E_i[R_j(U)]. \tag{4}$$

Of course, for an outcome to be agreed upon, it must lie in the agreement sets of each individual with the ability to block an agreement. For example, in a system of bargainers A and B, it must lie in the intersection of sets A_a and A_b.

The implications of concession rationality for the outcome of bargaining can be illustrated graphically (fig. 3). The outcomes where players' resistances are equal lie on the line connecting the disagreement point D (9,2), where each resistance equals one, to the *ideal point I* (19,10), a nonfeasible outcome where players simultaneously attain their best hope payoffs and resistances are consequently equal to zero. If person A exhibits concession rationality as defined in equation 3, his or her agreement set lies on or to the right of the line ID; and if person B is similarly rational, his or her agreement lies on or above the line ID. Hence, if both exhibit concession rationality and they possess complete information, their point of agreement must lie on the line ID.

Resistance theory is one way of specifying the content of concession

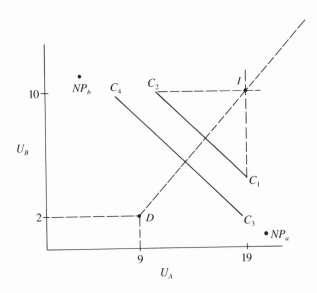

Fig. 3. Equal resistance line

rationality. Concession rationality, in turn, expresses a condition of rational cooperation or rational contracting. It specifies a requirement of rational bargaining. Its domain is the division of the gains from cooperation or the parties' joint stakes in contracting.

The division problem can be more or less troublesome. The magnitude of the division problem in a particular case is a function of the discrepancy between the players' best hopes or, equivalently, of the length of the contract curve. If the individuals' best hopes exactly coincide, as in the nondivisible Prisoners' Dilemma game, the contract curve shrinks to a point and agreement requires no concessions. As the contract curve lengthens, the required concessions increase. That, in turn, makes divisional bargaining an enterprise with higher stakes. Consequently, expending resources to enhance the strength of one's bargaining position becomes more rational, as do any measures to minimize one's own concessions and to maximize those secured from others.

Postphase: Individual Rationality
We have noted that, in the nondivisible Prisoner's Dilemma, there is no bargaining over the gains from cooperation. The parties' best hopes coincide and no concessions are required. That is why the Prisoner's Dilemma is best thought of as illustrating the problem of rational defection, not the problem of rational agreement. The payoffs from cooperation are set and no concessions are required. Once agreement is secured, however, the question remains whether it is in the interest of either or both parties to comply with it.

The defection problem reflects the problematic nature of mutual trust, owing to the presence of burdensome provisions and potential loopholes in most contracts. Frequently, an individual can gain by defaulting on a contract, often at the expense of those who perform according to its terms. A prerequisite for contracting, then, is a system of enforcement with which to preclude or deter noncompliance or to compensate parties injured by others' noncompliance. Not surprisingly, debating whether negotiations are undertaken in "good faith" and carefully scrutinizing contracts for hidden loopholes are prominent features of virtually all contracting.

The compliance or defection problem can be expressed in terms of a third condition of rationality. A necessary condition for rational agreement to a contract is that its expected outcome satisfies *individual rationality*. Neither player will permit himself or herself to be left worse off than the status quo, or disagreement point. That is, where U_i is individual i's expected utility from participating in a contract, and D_i is i's utility from disagreement, i is individually rational if

$$U_i \geq D_i. \tag{5}$$

With reference to figure 3, player A prefers defection if point NP_a is to the right of the point on the contract curve at which agreement occurs, and player B prefers defection if NP_b is above the contract point. Player A would not agree to an outcome lying to the left of point D, such as point NP_b in which B free rides, even though NP_b is jointly rational. Such an agreement would make A worse off than he or she would be were no agreement made, thus violating the individual rationality condition. Nor would player B accept any outcome below point D, such as NP_a, for analogous reasons. Hence, if both players are individually rational, neither will tolerate the other's free riding. The outcomes of figure 3's game that satisfy each player's requirement of individual rationality include the status quo point, D, and all of the points on the contract curve C_1, C_2. Rational parties will not agree to contracts that they expect to make them worse off; thus, they must find a way to eliminate or to minimize the risk of defection. This is no easy task.

Individual rationality, then, requires that an agreement be *enforceable,* not just that an individual be protected against an outcome worse than the status quo.[17] To be an enforceable agreement, the parties must expect that each estimates a cost of violation exceeding the gain from unilaterally defecting. That is, no agreement on C_1, C_2 is enforceable without penalties sufficient to deter defection, called the *force of agreement.*[18]

Viewed graphically, an enforcement system that penalizes defection displaces the defection points NP_a and NP_b toward the origin, making compliance more rewarding relative to defection. In figure 3, for example, if each player faces a violation cost that makes him or her indifferent between defecting and the best hope outcome, then no points on the contract curve will be enforceable. But if each faces a violation cost that makes him or her indifferent between defecting and the other party's best hope outcome, then the entire contract curve constitutes a domain of enforceable agreements.

The resistance solution to a bargaining game of complete information can be described in terms of rationality conditions. Individual and joint rationality, which together comprise the classical notion of economic rationality,[19] together suffice to motivate contracting but not agreement on any unique contract. With reference to figure 3, they restrict the outcomes of agreement to a portion of the contract curve, C_1, C_2. This contains, of course, many

---

17. At least in the case of cooperating to produce a public good, which can be studied as a Prisoner's Dilemma game, experimental evidence reveals cooperation rates significantly better when people expect an agreement to be enforceable as compared to when they receive money-back guarantees that will be no worse off than when they started if the group effort fails. See Robin Dawes, John Orbell, Randy Simmons, and Alphonse van de Kragt, "Organizing Groups for Collective Action," *American Political Science Review* 80 (1986): 1171–85.

18. Heckathorn, "Theory of Social Exchange."

19. Harsanyi, *Rational Behavior.*

feasible outcomes. In classical economic theory, no choice among them can be said to be more or less rational than any other. The choice among them cannot be a matter of rationality. Thus, in the usual forms of economic analysis, the choice among Pareto-optimal (collectively or jointly rational) outcomes is said to be a matter of distributive fairness or equity, not a matter of economics (or rationality).

The additional requirement of concession rationality, the bargaining theory approach we adopt, restricts that outcome to a point on the equal resistance line, ID in figure 3, so the cumulative effect of these requirements is to specify the intersection of the contract curve and the equal resistance line. For bargainers A and B with complete information, the outcome of the bargaining U satisfies the expression

$$\min[R_a(U) = R_b(U)]. \tag{6}$$

Agreement and performance on a contract occur, then, if and only if it satisfies all three requirements for each party to the transaction. Taken together, then, these conditions are necessary and sufficient; they define a party's interests in a contractual relationship.

Safeguarding the Rational Contract

In this model bargaining takes place sequentially (in logical time). First, individuals search for potentially advantageous cooperative opportunities, then they seek agreement on the gains, and finally they monitor compliance with the contract's terms. Each phase leaves room for contract failure. Thus, guarding against failure is rational—up to a point. That is, one does not want to spend more on preventing failure than failure costs in terms of forgone benefit. The important analytic point is that at least some expenditure of resources to guard against contract failure is rational for all players. We call this process of expending resources to prevent contract failure *rational safeguarding*.

The order in which actors safeguard their interests in contracting reverses the order in which they contract (again in logical time). Both parties have incentives to defect from unprotected agreements. If it is rational for player A to defect from an agreement, then it cannot be rational for player B to bargain with player A over the gains from trade, and vice versa. Bargaining without compliance is a waste of resources and is therefore irrational. If bargaining over the gains from trade is to be rational, the parties must be reasonably confident of one another's subsequent compliance. Thus, the defection problem must be resolved prior to pursuing a division of contract gains.[20] Similar

---

20. Jody Kraus and Jules Coleman, "Morality and the Theory of Rational Choice," *Ethics* (1987): 715–49.

considerations apply regarding the other phases of bargaining. Crafting safe-guards to satisfy joint rationality is pointless unless the parties expect both the division and defection problems to be soluble. Early phase decisions are dependent upon expectations regarding decisions at a later stage; anticipating breakdown at a later phase may block affirmative decisions at a prior one. Each party would prefer that the other bear the full costs of safeguarding. This preference cannot, in general, be successfully insisted upon. Concessions are rational and an agreement about distributing the costs of safeguarding can be secured. This "contract," that is, the contract over safeguards, has all the same conditions and pitfalls of bargaining over the gains from trade. So, in the complete rational contract, the parties bargain both over the costs of safeguarding and over the gains from trade.

Negotiations over safeguards in a contract comprise a series of nested subgames, corresponding to a type of sequential decision making termed *backward induction*.[21] Here, the outcome of one game effects the potential payoffs of the next, and issues are analyzed in the reverse of their ultimate behavioral order. Treating the divisible Prisoners' Dilemma in this way trans-forms it from a single game in which the defection incentive dominates, so contracting never gets underway, into two cooperative games.

The two cooperative games are analyzed as follows. The first game involves negotiating over enforcement costs. In this game, we once again assume that the players command resources adequate to enforce an agree-ment, so that they need not call upon third-party enforcement mechanisms. (This assumption is crucial; otherwise we generate an infinite regress of nonenforceable contracts.) The only question at this stage—in this game—is, who shall bear which costs in solving the defection problem? If *this* bargain-ing problem is solved, then the second cooperative game is played. The players' mutual interest is to bargain over points on the contract curve only. The enforceable solutions to the second game, therefore, lie on the contract curve. Thus, the second bargaining game is over points on the curve.

The first, or enforcement, game is connected to the second, or division of the gains, game in three ways. First, solving the enforcement game is a necessary condition for playing the division game; second, any particular solution to the enforcement game will affect solutions to the division game. How much one is willing to concede in bargaining over the gains from trade may well depend on how much one has had to expend in creating safeguards against defection. Third, because they are both bargaining games, the theory of rational bargaining developed here applies to both. In principle, there should be equilibria solutions to the conjunction of these two games that satisfy the rationality conditions.

21. Martin Shubick, *Game Theory in the Social Sciences: Concepts and Solutions* (Cam-bridge, Mass.: MIT Press, 1982); see also Thomas Schelling, *The Strategy of Conflict* (New York: Oxford University Press, 1963); Heckathorn, "Theory of Social Exchange."

In general, party A will create a safeguard so long as the potential burden imposed on B to overcome it exceeds the cost to A of creating it; party A expects B to have a comparable incentive.

Safeguarding against Uncertainty

Problems in contract arise when information is not complete, when, instead, actors are required to behave under conditions of uncertainty. Almost every contract dispute that winds up in litigation turns on a point about an incomplete contract; the traditional reasons for incomplete contracts are matters of information cost: (1) some contingency may be unforeseeable, (2) planning for every foreseeable contingency can be expensive, and (3) some contingencies may involve private information. Indeed, because a complete contract must specify a suitable mechanism for transmitting information to deal with contingencies, it can be particularly costly to devise and, therefore, incomplete and subject to renegotiation.[22]

One consequence of this analysis is that the main reason for expending resources in contracting is to overcome some sort of uncertainty, uncertainty that threatens the equilibrium solution to which rational actors would otherwise agree. Because the possible sources of uncertainty differ in each phase of contracting, the logical character of the costs rational bargainers are willing to incur to reduce uncertainty differ as well.

People incur *search costs* because they are uncertain about the feasibility of alternative outcomes. Each bargainer wants information about the group's prospects. In that sense, information about group gains, or the opportunity to secure a Pareto improvement, helps to motivate contracting that satisfies the *joint* rationality condition.

People incur *bargaining and decision costs* because they are uncertain about the acceptability of alternative divisions. Each bargainer wants information about the agreement set. Securing adequate information about one another's resistances is necessary to create an agreement that satisfies the *concession* rationality condition.

People incur *monitoring costs* because they are uncertain about the enforceability of alternative outcomes. Each bargainer wants information about the consequences of the other party's defecting. In that sense, information about the force of the agreement is relevant to creating an enforceable contract that satisfies the *individual* rationality condition.

If an individual need only estimate his or her expected utility for the outcomes possible under a proposed contract against that of the status quo to ensure that its terms are no worse than not contracting, then the information

---

22. Jean Tirole, "Procurement and Renegotiation," *Journal of Political Economy* 92 (1986): 235–59.

required to judge outcomes by this test is the least stringent of all. But because each party needs to estimate the defection incentive and the force of agreement, then, in addition to the information needed to estimate joint and concession rationality, each must estimate NP_a and NP_b.

Significantly, each phase of contracting entails greater risks than the preceding one because, as an inspection of equations 1 through 6 reveals, more terms come into play at each step, so more information is required by succeeding calculations. That means more potential sources of uncertainty exist, and more estimates must be made, each with a risk of error. In other words, the mathematics suggest that gathering information sufficient to fashion safeguards against defection is more difficult than securing information sufficient to safeguard against exploitive divisions, and so on. The more general point is that, by incurring search, bargaining, and decision costs, individual contractors are able to mitigate ex-ante risks; by incurring monitoring costs they hope to mitigate ex-post risks. Thus, one can understand the object of contracting as the joint attempt to minimize the sum of the costs of uncertainty and of its avoidance, where uncertainty afflicts all three dimensions of rationality.

Factors Affecting Uncertainty

Just how much information is necessary to craft safeguards to optimal contracting depends upon the degree of uncertainty that exists in particular contract environments. Several different but often related contextual features influence the ability of decision makers to estimate the terms comprising the calculus of contracting; that is, they affect the amount and accuracy of the information that must be acquired, verified, communicated, or processed during the course of contracting.

First, as the number of principal parties to the potential contract increases, the number of lines of communication and the amount of information that must be processed during negotiation increases. Opportunities for joint gain can be obscured simply by the noise. Group size affects the defection problem because an individual's defection tends to be less noticeable in larger groups, weakening incentives for individuals to participate in sanctioning defectors.[23] Monitoring compliance in a large group is generally more difficult and more demanding of given resources than in a smaller group. Hence, contracting is riskier.

Second, as heterogeneity among the principal parties increases, the bargaining range—if one exists—and defection incentives increase. To be sure, differences of preference are required to provide a basis for exchange and

---

23. Mancur Olson, *The Logic of Collective Action* (Cambridge, Mass.: Harvard University Press, 1965).

contract, but the less interchangeable the actors, the more difficult the transaction. For example, the commonality among workers at particular job sites facilitates collective bargaining with management. Only minor adjustments are required to adjust for individual differences in seniority, skill level, and work classification. In contrast, when each party to a contract possesses a wholly unique set of attributes and relations to each other participant, bargaining may prove impossible even in a quite small group. Any bargain ultimately struck will inevitably leave more people disgruntled and, therefore, will create higher, more disparate defection incentives than would an agreement among a more homogeneous assembly.

Third, as the spatial dispersion of the group increases, communication costs increase. Bargaining and enforcement systems both require communication. In geographically concentrated groups, oral communication and incidental observations of behavior may suffice, but linking a dispersed group with equally adequate communication between each pair of individuals is technically more difficult. Conversely, improvements in the technology of communication, holding dispersion constant, reduce communication costs, so transaction resources go further.

Fourth, as the temporal distribution of the costs or benefits at issue in the transaction increases, they become more difficult to detect and control. For example, delayed defection costs impede monitoring because the adverse consequences become apparent only long after the fact. Similarly, delayed benefits hamper divisional bargaining because bargaining to allocate anticipated gains may appear to be an exercise in wishful thinking.

Fifth, and closely related, as the level of acceptable risk decreases, monitoring problems increase. If people engaged in contracting for the sheer thrill of it, then even expending resources in search of opportunities for gain might appear counterproductive. But in classical economics and game theory, the expected utility of a prospect is the product of its probability and utility. An actor who is rational (in that sense) is indifferent, for example, between the certainty of losing $10, a one-in-ten chance of losing $100, and a one-in-a-hundred chance of losing $1000. Yet such outcomes are not equivalent in their implications for contracting. In contrast to defection that imposes a certain cost, a defection that merely creates a risk of damage can remain undetected unless actual harm occurs. Monitoring is especially difficult when defection results in a very small risk of grave damage (analogous to the one-in-a-hundred chance of losing $1000), since only a tiny portion of defections actually impose damage. Just as the absence of damage does not imply that no defection occurred, the presence of a damage does not necessarily prove defection. Risk is simply endemic. That is why so much contract litigation involves assigning liability in the case of an unforeseen contingency that affects the ability of one party to perform.

Sixth, as the nontransferability of costs and benefits increases, negotiating becomes more intractable. Bargaining determines how costs and benefits will be allocated, so it requires that at least some costs or benefits be transferable. The problems of quantifying and intersubjectively verifying nontransferable costs and benefits underlie the distinction between fungible and unique goods that has been used, for example, to justify the choice between damages and specific performance in contract disputes.

Seventh, as instability increases within a relationship, more transaction resources are required to secure rational outcomes. The best way of understanding how instability increases costs is to understand how stability reduces them. Because decisions themselves convey information about the risks of interacting, frequent and consistent decisions reduce the incentives to expend transaction resources on searching and bargaining over acceptable divisions. Moreover, stability facilitates developing internal systems of enforcement with which to deter defection. For egoists in repeated plays of the same Prisoners' Dilemma game, cooperation rather than defection can become optimal because defection would disrupt a mutually rewarding pattern of cooperation.[24] If the short-term gains from defection are consistently offset by larger long-term losses, a stable pattern of cooperation emerges.

The Rational Expenditure of Transaction Resources

This is a good time to recap the analysis to this point.

1. Rational contractors seek to create mutually advantageous, enforceable agreements.
2. Doing so requires that they satisfy three independent rationality conditions: joint, concession, and individual rationality.
3. These rationality conditions correspond to three phases in the contract process and enable the parties to solve three problems of rational choice: (*a*) the prephase cooperation problem (joint rationality); (*b*) the negotiation phase division problem (concession rationality); and (*c*) the postphase compliance problem (individual rationality).
4. A process of rational bargaining can satisfy these conditions but still fail to reach fruition by virtue of uncertainty deriving either from incomplete or imperfect information or from potential defection.
5. Consequently, it will be rational for the parties to create safeguards against contract failure.
6. Creating safeguards requires parties to incur three distinct kinds of

---

24. Robert Axelrod, *The Evolution of Cooperation* (New York: Basic Books, 1984).

cost corresponding to the phases in contracting: (*a*) search costs (prephase); (*b*) decision costs (negotiation phase); and (*c*) monitoring costs (postphase).

7. The magnitude of these costs will depend on contextual factors shaping the extent of uncertainty under particular circumstances.

8. In general, the magnitude of uncertainty is greatest in guarding against defection, less great in securing a division, and least pressing in safeguarding against cooperation failure.

9. Rationality requires that crafting safeguards proceed in the opposite temporal direction from contracting corresponding to the general magnitude of risk of failure. Because the risk of defection dominates in the nondivisible Prisoner's Dilemma, uncertainty about compliance is greatest and, consequently, crafting safeguards against defection is most pressing.

10. The process of creating safeguards can itself be modeled as a rational bargain over the costs of safeguards. The costs of safeguarding depletes transaction resources.

The capacity of the contractors to employ their own resources to reduce uncertainty and create safeguards can be represented graphically. Figure 4 describes the types of interactions to which contractual arrangements may be matched in the form of a *transaction-space diagram*. The vertical axis represents the magnitude of the defection problem. The horizontal axis represents the magnitude of the division problem. And the axis perpendicular to both axes represents the magnitude of the cooperation problem.

When a transaction lies near the origin in figure 4, so that the problems are quite minor, the burden placed upon transaction resources is minimal. At the origin, for example, the parties easily recognize opportunities for gain and transactions correspond, when described in game-theoretic terms, to pure coordination. In transactions at increasing distances from the origin, indicating that the problems of identifying prospects, of bargaining, or of defection are more major, the availability of transaction resources becomes more problematic. The farther any transaction lies from the origin, the greater the transaction costs required for contracting.

In contexts where the seven factors affecting uncertainty are favorable to contracting, only modest resources are required to make contracting possible. For example, small residential groups such as nuclear families possess sufficient endogenous transaction resources with which to develop exceedingly complex systems of mutual understandings. Similarly, conditions in the most hospitable region of transaction space (i.e., the area close to the origin) correspond rather well to those identified in any introductory economics text as conducive to private exchange in perfect or near perfect markets. Even in the (otherwise) most inhospitable regions of transaction space (i.e., far up-

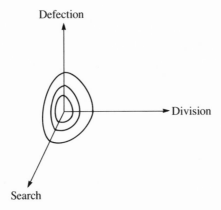

Fig. 4. Transaction resource frontier

ward and to the right of the origin, but still within the frontier), ingenious safeguards evolve, such as "exchanging hostages" and giving collateral,[25] where people arrive at and enforce contracts independently.

In contexts where the factors affecting uncertainty are unfavorable to contracting, the parties' transaction resources quickly become exhausted. The worst case arises when members of a large, geographically dispersed group with diverse interests consider negotiating an arrangement where the benefits and costs are delayed, nontransferable, and laden with risk. Locating a national nuclear waste storage facility is an example. Here, the transaction resource frontier will lie close to the origin, indicating that even slight concern over the feasibility of the alternatives or modest division or defection problems exceed the group's ability to contract independently.

Third-Party Intervention

The Preference for Endogenous Transaction Resources

We need not presume that a forum external to the original contract—notably, authoritative experts like judges operating under the auspices of the state—will be more efficacious than private ordering in resolving disputes. This presumption, called *legal centralism,* informs much of the theory of the law and economics tradition.[26] That courts or other jurisdictional bodies are nec-

25. Anthony Kronman, "Contract Law and the State of Nature," *Journal of Law, Economics, and Organization* 1 (1985): 5–32.

26. Karl Llewellyn, "What Price Contract? An Essay in Perspective," *Yale Law Journal* 40 (1931): 704–51; Marc Galanter, "Justice in Many Rooms: Courts, Private Ordering, and Indigenous Law," *Journal of Legal Pluralism* 19 (1981): 1–47; Oliver Williamson, *The Economic Institutions of Capitalism* (New York: Free Press, 1985).

essary to the very idea of contract and are thereby presupposed by the concept itself may simply be unwarranted. It surely does not follow from anything presented in our analysis to this point. To be sure, by assuming that courts exist and stand prepared to enforce whatever agreements private parties make, such a view isolates the problem of breach from those of cooperation and division. In doing so, however, it misleads. For there are surely tradeoffs among all three problems in contracting. Moreover, judges attempting to make decisions in accord with the theory are denied insights about the constraints rational actors would want on them as third party interveners. Private parties—including social scientists—may find judicial decisions less coherent. Indeed, the resource efficiency of decisions motivated by the paradigm is put in doubt. On grounds of theory, prediction, and policy, the presumption should be struck down in favor of a more realistic one.

Third-party intervention must be explained, not assumed. And it is more plausibly assumed if we start out presuming that people are never without some endogenous transaction resources with which to contract. That means they do not always rely upon, or even want, a third party to secure agreements.

Endogenous resources, however, are finite. The points in transaction space at which private parties exhaust them define what we call the *transaction resource frontier*. The frontier is simply a way of visualizing the limits to private settlement and the reasons for involving a third party. Attainable gains are lost when contextual features place transactions beyond the frontier and block contracting. That provides an incentive for parties to the transaction to seek third-party intervention. When transactions lie outside the transaction resources frontier, principal parties tend to seek third-party support.

A third party can facilitate contracting in any of three analytically distinct ways. First, it can help to resolve the cooperation problem by providing *exogenous transaction resources* to augment the endogenous transaction resources already present in the relationship. If, for example, communication channels are poor, owing to the large number of parties or their geographic dispersion, the centralized channels and information processing services provided by a mediating third party may well prove more efficient. Sometimes a mediator recognizes opportunities for mutual gain or audits the status quo more effectively than the principals. Described graphically, this type of intervention expands the transaction resources frontier to encompass a larger area of transaction space. Thus, it increases the region within which contracting among the principal parties becomes possible. It need not entail granting discretion to the mediator to allocate the gains by defining the terms of an agreement or to enforce one by punishing a breach.

Second, third parties can help to resolve the division problem by providing *division services*, for example, a coalition-building or arbitrating third party may be granted discretion to allocate the gains under the contract, or merely to narrow the range of divisions possible under the contract. Described graphically, this moves the transaction leftward in transaction space, closer to the origin where conditions for contracting are more favorable. It need not entail granting discretion to the arbiter to enforce an agreement, but arbiters, like mediators, need to be a central agent in processing information.

Third, third parties can help to resolve the defection problem by providing *enforcement services,* for example, a policing third party may be granted discretion to punish defectors, increasing the force of contractual agreements. Described graphically, this moves the transaction downward in transaction space, again closer to the origin. It may not entail granting the enforcer discretion to design the terms of an agreement, but to monitor behavior an enforcer needs centralized communication channels like a mediator, and, in applying the force of agreement across disputants, the enforcer's judgments may well involve arbiterlike divisions of responsibility.

The existence of finite resources and the occasional need to expend more than what the parties have available to them creates an incentive for both parties to seek outside help in making and securing contracts. Intervention by a third party, however, may be as problematic as it is promising. First, intervention by a third party complicates the transaction by creating a new contracting problem between it and the principal parties. An n-person game becomes an $(n + 1)$-person game. The more extensive the intervention, the more powerful the third party can become vis-à-vis the principals.

The third party creates a new cooperation problem. The process of searching for a suitable third party and negotiating the terms of its performance is costly. Improperly crafted third-party services may prove redundant or unnecessarily intrusive. The greater the intervenor's role in processing information and forging communication channels, the greater becomes the potential asymmetry between it and the principals. That can impede the principals' efforts to monitor it as well as each other. In short, cooperating with a third party may not be worth it, even when it is a prerequisite to contracting.

Intervention is likely to create a new division problem. How are the residual gains from intervention to be allocated among the principal and third parties? Again, the answer depends on their relative bargaining power. The power of the principals depends on how well they can effect divisions to begin with. But the more extensive the intervenor's role in determining how contractual gains will be divided, the greater its potential to either seize a larger than anticipated share or to become embroiled in partisan disputes among principals and empower some at the expense of others.

Intervention also creates a new defection problem. The outside party may fear that the principal parties will default on payments after services have been rendered. Alternatively, the more extensive the intervenor's role in establishing enforcement, the greater its potential to punish exploitatively. Indeed, a third party's special access to and control over information makes more difficult the principal parties' problem of preventing its defection by fraud or misrepresentation.

For these reasons, third-party intervention will always strike the principal parties as potentially more threatening than relying on equivalent endogenous resources. The implication is that people will prefer using endogenous resources because they tend to be less costly, more accessible spatially and temporally, and more readily mobilized than functionally equivalent resources that might be provided by a third party. Moreover, having maximum involvement in shaping the contract helps insure that it takes efficient account of their preferences and so strengthens their incentives to honor its terms. Studies of arbitration, for example, show that bargainers who succeed in reaching agreement are more likely to honor it than are those who fail and have one imposed by an arbitrator. Finally, even under the simplest conditions, contracting with a third party is asymmetric because the original parties, being more numerous, must bargain among themselves first.

Many of the problems of third-party intervention can be mitigated by competition among providers of the service. Competition gives principals an alternative and, thereby, a safeguard. Thus, it can reduce their bargaining problem and their fear of exploitive mistreatment. This is an important point, because it gives analytic plausibility to suggestions that, under conditions where it is otherwise particularly difficult to constrain a third party, competition among mediators, arbiters, and enforcers may be preferable to a state monopoly on power.[27]

Still, establishing and maintaining a mechanism for third-party intervention is no mere technical exercise by which deficiencies in endogenous transaction resources are corrected. Rather, it can be at least as conflictive and politically charged as private contracting. It, too, can fail. Thus, parties have incentives to avoid third-party orderings, such as courts provide, and instead to devise private ordering.[28]

When Only Intervention Will Do

The existence of uncertainty sufficient to threaten contract failure does not provide a sufficient reason for the parties to call upon third-party intervention. Only when endogenous transaction resources are depleted do the parties have sufficient reason to pursue outside intervention. As we have demonstrated,

27. Barnett, "Pursuing Justice in a Free Society: Part One—Power vs. Liberty," *Criminal Justice Ethics* 4 (1985): 50–72.

28. Galanter, "Justice."

third-party intervention can create costs in excess of gains. Only if the endogenous resources of the parties are inadequate *and* the expected costs of third-party intervention do not exceed expected gains, would it be rational for contractors to require third-party intervention.

Figure 4 depicts the range of cases in which safeguarding against contract failure requires the parties to consume transaction resources.[29] Type 1 cases fall within the frontier where between them the parties possess adequate resources to resolve whatever problems they face. Moving outward along each axis, endogenous resources prove to be increasingly inadequate. In type 2 cases, the parties possess internal resources sufficient to solve division and defection problems, but lack resources to identify opportunities for cooperation. In type 3 cases, the parties possess internal resources adequate to identify feasible contracts and to solve the division problem, but are unable to solve the defection problem through the use of their own resources. In type 4 cases, the parties possess internal resources sufficient to solve their defection problem, but are incapable of identifying or solving the division issues on their own. Off the axes, we find a universe of other cases in which the principals in varying degrees lack the resources to resolve combinations of these problems.

This model suggests that we should find that several different types of institutional arrangements emerge in contracting. First, there will exist cases in which private parties are able to solve their problems without recourse to the intervention of third parties. In fact, we find such institutions. The best example is the competitive market. In the market, parties are engaged in bilateral agreements, discrete in time and place. A governmental enforcement mechanism is not necessarily a precondition for exchange; self-enforcing conventions—sometimes called customary business practices—can work just as well. Markets provide ready sources of alternative exchange opportunities that can be sufficient to safeguard against one party's defecting *before* either performs on an agreement. Without resorting to violence or invoking third-party intervention, private parties can depend on reputational effects and devices like hostage giving to safeguard against the risks of defection *after* one party acts in reliance on a promised performance.

Transactions along the search axis beyond the transaction resource fron-

---

29. The axes and frontier correspond, in part, to a classification system described in Robert Ellickson, "A Critique of Economic and Sociological Theories of Social Control," *Journal of Legal Studies* 16 (1987): 67–99. Ellickson sees administering positive and negative sanctions as involving rules that divide human behavior into three categories: (1) good behavior triggers rewards; this can have something to do with doctrines encouraging concession making as well as trust; (2) bad behavior triggers punishment; his concern here is clearly with doctrines discouraging defection; and (3) ordinary behavior that warrants no judicial response; this corresponds to our type 1 situation where parties have sufficient endogenous resources. As he put it, "The prevalence

tier pose a risk of joint failure sufficient to exhaust the parties' resources for identifying opportunities for mutual gain; that discourages exchange. The simplest conventions, like drivers slowing down on approaching an intersection and stopping to wave a crossing vehicle through, break down. More densely settled areas and a more heterogeneous population of drivers will strain the convention, pushing the risks of motorized travel to the point where people begin to forgo its benefits or endure increasing costs. Someone can reduce the strain simply by setting a rule, almost any rule: when two vehicles approach an intersection simultaneously, the vehicle on the *right* proceeds first; where traffic density makes simultaneity increasingly expensive and variable to judge, install a traffic signal.

Contract law has, for example, the mailbox rule: an offeree has the power to accept and close a contract by mailing a letter of acceptance, properly stamped and addressed.[30] Little economic justification can be found to support dating the contract from the mailing of the acceptance rather than from its receipt. Its economic justification can be found in the market-expanding properties of having a rule.[31] Like trade associations in various industries that develop consensus standards for product attributes to expand the total market for their products, the court expands the resource frontier so that private parties will engage in more transactions.

Beyond the frontier along the division axis, the participants primarily lack resources with which to solve the division problem. The parties would not get to the division problem without having identified an opportunity for productive exchange. Solving the defection problem is less significant, either because of ample internal enforcement resources or because incentives to defect are comparatively weak.

Some scholars have noticed the significance of the division problem in contract doctrine. But almost all of these scholars have confused the rational division problem as a matter of private law with a social or public theory of "fair distribution." For example, Farber suggests that contract law has a mandatory risk-sharing system, a social safety net, and it is difficult for parties to bargain around it.[32] Thus, while freedom of contract means the power of

---

of tripartite systems is a clue that rulemakers are attuned to an overarching goal of minimizing costs, including administrative costs" (71).

30. Arthur Corbin, *Corbin on Contracts* (St. Paul: West Publishing Co., 1952), 124.

31. "One of the parties must carry the risk of loss and inconvenience. We need a definite rule; but we must choose one. We can put the risk on either party; but we must not leave it in doubt. The party not carrying the risk can then act promptly and with confidence in reliance on the contract; the party carrying the risk can insure against it if he so desires. The business community could no doubt adjust itself to either rule; but the rule throwing the risk on the offeror has the merit of closing the deal more quickly and enabling the performance more promptly." (Corbin, *Contracts,* 124)

32. Farber, "Contract Law."

parties to allocate risks between themselves, some contract rules reveal a countermanding principle of loss spreading, for example, rules against penalty clauses and warranty disclosure for personal injury to prevent catastrophic losses to one party. Similarly, Dalton has claimed that doctrines such as quasi-contract, duress, and unconscionability police the limits of acceptable bargains by private parties in the name of social (public) norms of fairness.[33] And Cohen claims that court adjudication supplements an original contract as a means of distributing gains and losses from unanticipated events. In this view, contract law consists of rules by which the courts accomplish this according to the equities of such cases. That follows not from the agreement between individuals but is a way of enforcing some kind of distributive justice within the legal system.[34]

These characterizations of the distributive dimensions of contract law may go too far. Our model implies that, when courts impose distributive schemes on the parties, their doing so is compatible with the interests of the parties in the contract. No appeal to a global concern for distributive fairness, therefore, is necessary to understand or to justify a court's willingness to impose a distribution of risk among the parties. The legitimate exercise of that authority is restricted to the domain of outcomes the parties would have bargained within, and not to the set of outcomes that would be preferable from the point of view of a principle of social justice or social insurance. However, to the extent that the court, acting as an arbiter, seeks to implement a doctrine likely to resolve a wide range of division disputes efficiently, it may turn to widely accepted principles of social justice for guidance on the grounds that those principles themselves represent an evolved, rational, or efficient solution to a wide range of division problems.

Transactions beyond the frontier along the defection axis indicate the defection problem is intractable internally but the cooperation and division problems are soluble. Parties here have relatively abundant internal bargaining resources but deficient internal enforcement resources. Intervention, therefore, takes the form of an externally applied enforcement system that moves the transactions downward, inside the frontier. Within the constraints of that system, individuals retain control over the terms of the contracts they enter.

The features that make a market such an attractive governance system—anonymity and disaggregated decisions adaptive to local circumstances—exacerbate the endemic risks of defection. At least since Adam Smith, classical economists have foreseen a productive role for a centralized enforcing

---

33. Clare Dalton, "An Essay in the Deconstruction of Contract Doctrine," *Yale Law Journal* 94 (1985): 997–1114.

34. Morris Cohen, *Law and the Social Order* (New York: Archon Books, 1967).

agent. If third-party intervention diminishes ex-post risks, people are freer to expend resources ex ante on searching for and reaching agreements that satisfy joint and concession rationality. Hence, common law, judicially crafted safeguards that penalize contract breach are widely regarded as promoting economic efficiency.

Even third-party safeguards designed primarily to reduce the probability of defection can influence the concession rationality of private decisions. That is because the remedies available under contract cannot escape dividing the residual risks of social intercourse and imposing different burdens of proof on the affected parties when one defaults.[35]

In areas of transaction space away from an axis and outside the frontier, the internal deficit of transaction resources is more profound. Here, assistance is required in solving a combination of problems that afflict contractual relationships. Indeed, even if in absolute terms a relationship is richly endowed with transaction resources, it is virtually assured of falling farthest from the three axes when all of the contextual features we identified impose large obstacles to contracting. Consequently, the degree of third-party intervention is greater because regulators must not only enforce contracts but also specify their terms and bring contractors to the bargaining table.

Implications for Contract Law

Our theory implies the following:

1. Not every effort to contract in the absence of law will succeed.
2. Contract failure can result from a failure to solve problems of either (a) cooperation, (b) division, or (c) defection (breach).
3. These problems are in principle solvable by rational parties negotiating with complete information.
4. Contract failure is, therefore, best thought of as owing to some or other forms of uncertainty.
5. Parties to an agreement seek to reduce uncertainty by expending transaction resources.
6. Contract failure in the absence of law results when these efforts at safeguarding are inadequate.
7. Law as a means of safeguarding cannot, therefore, be assumed by a theory of contract, but must be explained instead.
8. The best explanation of it is that law is rational for contractors only if (a) it provides transaction resources that are necessary to insure a

---

35. See the essays in Anthony Kronman and Richard Posner, *The Economics of Contract Law* (Boston: Little, Brown, 1979).

successful contract, and (*b*) the benefits of appealing to law to enable contracting exceed its costs.

9. Once law is in place, however, it is less costly for individuals to appeal to it to help resolve their contractual disputes than it would have been for them to *create* law for these purposes.

10. In reviewing cases in contract to understand or to criticize developing legal rules, we should inquire into whether uncertainty in cooperation, division, or compliance is the source of contract failure. We want to know whether the parties are in court because they lack sufficient search, negotiation or monitoring transaction resources. Then we can determine what kind of legal role the court is being asked to play: mediation, arbitration, policing, or all three. A full rational choice theory of contract law will demonstrate how different cases can be analyzed as falling into all three categories and the conditions under which rational default rules will, themselves, call for intervention by courts.

11. The rationality of legal rules, from the point of view of this theory, will not depend on their abstract rationality or efficiency, but on their rationality in the given *context* in which they are to apply.

12. The most relevant aspect of any context is the availability of endogenous transaction resources.

Contributors

Timothy J. Brennan is an Associate Professor of Policy Sciences at the University of Maryland Baltimore County. His research in economic methodology includes articles on voluntary transactions, utility theory, and explanation. Other publications cover principal/agent models, regulation, antitrust, and communications policy.

Mark A. Cohen is an Assistant Professor of Management at the Owen Graduate School of Management of Vanderbilt University. He is a former research economist and consultant to the U.S. Sentencing Commission. His research is in law, economics, and corporate crime. His articles have appeared in such journals as *Journal of Law and Economics, Law and Society Review, Criminology,* and *American Criminal Law Review.*

Jules L. Coleman is John A. Garver Professor of Jurisprudence and Philosophy Law at Yale Law School. He has published widely in law, philosophy, economics, and political science. His most recent book is *Markets, Morals and the Law,* and he is working on *Risks and Wrongs.*

Robyn M. Dawes is Professor of Psychology and Social and Decision Sciences at Carnegie-Mellon University. Since 1979 he and John Orbell have collaborated on a series of laboratory studies of social dilemma behavior. Dawes and Orbell are continuing their collaboration.

Robert H. Frank is Professor of Economics at Cornell University. He has published extensively in the areas of consumption externalities and nonegoistic behavior. He recently published *Passions within Reason: The Strategic Role of the Emotions.*

Peter A. French is Lennox Distinguished Professor of the Humanities and Professor of Philosophy at Trinity University. He is author of fourteen books including *Collective and Corporate Responsibility* and *The Spectrum of Responsibility.* He is a senior editor of *Midwest Studies in Philosophy* and the editor of the *Journal of Social Philosophy.*

Robert S. Goldfarb is Professor of Economics at George Washington University. His published research has been primarily in labor economics. Recent economic methodology papers explore the process of assumption change in economics (in collaboration with Griffith), and the claim that economists do not severely test their theories.

William B. Griffith is Professor of Philosophy at George Washington University. His primary research interests lie in the intersection of ethics and economic policy and the ethics of business and the professions. In collaboration with Goldfarb he has also explored methodological issues in economics.

Douglas Heckathorn is an Associate Professor of Sociology at the University of Connecticut. He is now completing a book on the interplay of normative and organizational controls.

Robert P. Inman is Professor of Finance, Economics, and Law at the University of Pennsylvania. His present research is on the political economy of fiscal policy at the federal, state, and local levels.

Kenneth J. Koford is Associate Professor of Economics and Political Science at the University of Delaware and Resident Scholar at the Jerome Levy Economics Institute. He has contributed to the analysis of legislatures using economic theory and to the analysis of how developing new markets can stabilize the macroeconomy.

Steven Maser is a Professor of Public Management and Public Policy at the George Atkinson School of Management, Willamette University. His recent publications apply bargaining theory and transaction cost economics to public policy, government regulation, and constitutional choice.

Jeffrey B. Miller is Associate Professor of Economics at the University of Delaware. He has written in both macroeconomics and comparative economic systems. His published papers include the analysis of managerial incentives in organizations, especially dynamic systems.

Dennis C. Mueller is Professor of Economics at the University of Maryland. He has served as President of the Public Choice Society and the Southern Economic association. He has made major contributions to the theory of public choice, especially equilibrium in legislatures and elections. Other contributions include empirical analysis of profitability in R&D and analysis of the managerial theory of the firm.

John M. Orbell is a Professor of Political Science at the University of Oregon. He is also associated with the Institute of Cognitive and Decision Sciences at the University of Oregon. Since 1979 he has collaborated with Robyn Dawes on a series of laboratory studies of social dilemma behavior. He continues his collaboration with Dawes.

Alphons J. van de Kragt was a sociologist at the Institute for Cognitive and Decision Sciences at the University of Oregon. He collaborated with Robyn M. Dawes and John M. Orbell on numerous papers. He died in October 1989.

Richard M. Weiss is an Associate Professor of Business Administration at the University of Delaware. He is the author of *Managerial Ideology and the Social Control of Deviance in Organizations,* and his work has appeared in various journals in sociology, psychology, and management.